Like Froth Floating on the Sea

To the memory of my parents
Arthur A. Antony, Sr.
and
Evelyn Dazet Antony

CHINA RESEARCH MONOGRAPH 56

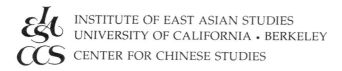

INSTITUTE OF EAST ASIAN STUDIES
UNIVERSITY OF CALIFORNIA · BERKELEY
CENTER FOR CHINESE STUDIES

Like Froth Floating on the Sea

The World of Pirates and Seafarers in Late Imperial South China

Robert J. Antony

A publication of the Institute of East Asian Studies, University of California, Berkeley. Although the Institute of East Asian Studies is responsible for the selection and acceptance of manuscripts in this series, responsibility for the opinions expressed and for the accuracy of statements rests with their authors.

Correspondence and manuscripts may be sent to:
Ms. Joanne Sandstrom, Managing Editor
Institute of East Asian Studies
University of California
Berkeley, California 94720-2318
E-mail: easia@uclink.berkeley.edu

The China Research Monograph series is one of several publications series sponsored by the Institute of East Asian Studies in conjunction with its constituent units. The others include the Korea Research Monograph series, the Japan Research Monograph series, and the Research Papers and Policy Studies series. A list of recent publications appears at the back of the book.

Library of Congress Cataloging-in-Publication Data

Antony, Robert J.
    Like froth floating on the sea : the world of pirates and seafarers in late imperial south China / Robert J. Antony.
        p.   cm. — (China research monograph)
    Includes bibliographical references and index.
    ISBN 1-55729-078-4 (alk. paper)
        1. Pirates—China, Southeast. 2. China, Southeast—Social conditions. 3. China—History—Ming dynasty, 1368–1655. 4. China—History—Qing dynasty, 1644–1912.
    I. Title. II. China research monographs ; no. 56.

DS753.2 .A57 2003
910'.9164'72—dc21

2002192209

Contents

Tables and Figures

Acknowledgments

The genesis of this book was in the stories my father told to me as a child about the sea and Chinese pirates. My father worked in the merchant marine for most of his life, and he visited at one time or another nearly every major port in the world. In the 1930s, during one of his early voyages, he had shipped out to the Orient as an ordinary seaman aboard an old freighter. I remember one story he told me about Shanghai. The waters around the port were teeming with pirate craft, fishing boats, and myriad other Chinese junks, all indistinguishable from one another. At night pirates would sneak up alongside their prey and, using long bamboo poles with hooks on their ends, would shimmy up the side of the ship to steal cargo and anything else that was not secured. The situation got so bad that every night the captain of my father's ship distributed weapons and assigned crewmen to stand watch. But no matter what precautions were taken, when day broke there would always be something missing. One night the pirates even pilfered a large motor bolted down to the aft deck. No one knew how they could have unhinged and removed this huge machine without making a noise or ever being spotted by the sailors on guard.

Although the Chinese pirates that I have encountered are of an earlier age, they were no less wily. And while I never came face to face with any of them, as had my father, the ocean bandits that I have discovered in the dusty archives are just as real. For Qing scholar-officials, such as Li Guangpo, pirates were nothing more than "froth floating on the sea." He was not the first to describe pirates in this manner, and, in fact, traditionally China's landed elite often referred pejoratively to pirates and seafarers as "froth" or "flotsam," a vile scum and hence debased group of people. This book is an attempt to recover and rewrite their history on their own terms.

The actual research for this book began some twenty years ago when I presented a paper on early-nineteenth-century pirates in the Canton delta to Professor Harry Lamley's seminar in Modern Chinese History at the University of Hawai'i. With his encouragement I expanded the paper, and the topic, into a doctoral dissertation. Throughout the long process of writing the dissertation and later this book, Professor Lamley has read and commented on every revision, and I have continued over the years to benefit from his advice. While owing my greatest scholarly debt to Professor Lamley, I have accumulated many other debts over the years. It would be impossible to acknowledge all my obligations to the many fellow researchers, colleagues, and former schoolmates over the past twenty years whose conversations have contributed to my understanding of the subject. Nevertheless, I would like to mention a few. I am especially grateful to Professors Jane Leonard and Robert Marks for their careful readings and discerning suggestions on several versions of the manuscript. Jack Wills, Chi-Kong Lai, K. C. Liu, and Nancy Park have read parts of the manuscript, and I thank them for their useful comments. Although we differ on several important points, I am indebted to Dian Murray for her insights and suggestions. In general I have condensed my discussions of topics that she has focused on in her studies and instead have paid more attention to other topics that interest me.

While a student at the University of Hawai'i, I benefited from the wisdom and generosity of Professors Brian McKnight, Robert Sakai, Alvin So, John Stephan, and T. Y. Tao. At Western Kentucky University I wish to thank my colleagues James Baker and Robert Haynes for taking time out of their busy schedules to read and comment on the manuscript and my students in the fall 2000 honors seminar "Piracy in World History" for getting me to think in larger terms and to ask the big questions. I have also benefited, as the numerous citations will attest, from my readings of two important books on Western seafarers and pirates: Marcus Rediker's *Between the Devil and the Deep Blue Sea: Merchant Seamen, Pirates, and the Anglo-American Maritime World, 1700–1750*, and Pablo Pérez-Mallaína's *Spain's Men of the Sea: Daily Life on the Indies Fleets in the Sixteenth Century*.

I am particularly grateful during my visits to Beijing to Wei Qingyuan and Qin Baoqi at People's University, Ju Deyuan and Zhu Shuyuan at the First Historical Archives, and Mei Xueqin at Beijing Normal University, as well as to Ye Xianen, Deng Kaisong, and Huang Qichen in Guangdong, and Huang Guosheng, Yang Guozhen, and Chen Zhiping in Fujian. In Hong Kong special thanks go to Tan Dihua and Betty Wei. In Taiwan Chuang Chi-fa at the National Palace Museum, Chang Wejen, Lin Man-houng, Hsiung Ping-chen, Paul Katz, Ch'en Ch'iu-k'un, Angela Leung, Ch'en Kuo-tung, and Tang Shi-yeoung at Academia Sinica were always generous with their time and suggestions. The staffs at the First Historical Archives, Beijing Library, National Palace Museum Library, and the libraries at Academia Sinica were unfailingly courteous and helpful to me. I was also fortunate to have met and shared discussions with many visiting scholars in China and Taiwan, particularly Akira Matsuura, Beatrice Bartlett, Lynn Struve, R. Bin Wong, Hamashima Takeshi, Tom Buoye, David Faure, Mark Elliot, Jim Hevia, Peter Perdue, Melissa Macauley, Blane Gaustad, James Millward, and Yasuhiko Karasawa. My debt of gratitude to them all is immeasurable.

Financial support from the Committee on Scholarly Communications with China, the Fulbright program, and Western Kentucky University allowed me to carry out the research for this book. A sabbatical leave and several summer trips spent in Taiwan as a visiting researcher at Academia Sinica's Institute of Modern History and the Sun Yat-sen Institute for Social Sciences and Philosophy permitted me the time and congenial environment to prepare much of this manuscript.

I also want to thank Joanne Sandstrom for her expert editing and the anonymous reviewers for recommending the manuscript for publication. Last but not least I wish to thank Lanshin for her unbending patience and enthusiasm over the many long years in writing this book.

Conventions and Equivalencies

With only a few exceptions, all Chinese names and terms are transliterated in pinyin romanization. I have retained the better-known English renderings for Canton, Hong Kong, Macao, and Amoy, and also have parenthesized several words when other names are in common use, such as Dan (Tanka), Huangpu (Whampao), Jinmen (Quemoy), Pingzhou (Peng Chau), Giang Binh (Jiangping), and so forth.

Throughout the book a person's age is calculated according to the Chinese system of reckoning in *sui*. The *sui* age is the age a person will attain in the current year, not the actual number of months that have elapsed since birth. For example, someone who was born in November will become one *sui* at the Chinese New Year, although by Western calculations he or she is only two or three months old. Thus, in general, a person who is thirty *sui* is actually only twenty-nine years old by Western reckoning.

In the footnotes dates to archival materials are given according to the Chinese lunar calendar as follows: QL 59.3.27, indicating the twenty-seventh day of the third month in the fifty-ninth year of the Qianlong reign, and JQ 6.r7.2, indicating the second day of the seventh intercalary month in the sixth year of the Jiaqing reign (the "r" indicates an intercalary month). In citing sources in the footnotes I use the following conventions: when given, publication dates are followed by a colon and then the page number (e.g., Chang 1983:68–69) or the volume number, which is followed by a slash and then page number (e.g., Morse 1926:3/117); if no publication date is given, then the source is followed simply by the page number (e.g., *XMZ* 43) or volume number followed by a slash and page number (e.g., *DGXZ* 33/25b). Full citations of abbreviations used in the footnotes are given in the Bibliography. Unless otherwise noted, all translations are my own.

Where indicated in the text, measurements are given in the Chinese style of calculating. Because of fluctuations in money the equivalencies given below are only approximate. References to dollars in the text refer to Spanish silver dollars.

Measures and Weights

1 *li*	=	1,890 feet
1 *jin* (catty)	=	1.3 pounds
1 *shi* (picul)	=	120 jin = 0.07 tons

Volume (for Rice)

1 *shi*	=	138.75 *jin*
1 *dou* (peck)	=	316 cubic inches (approx. 10 *jin*
	=	or 13.3 pounds)

Currencies

1 *wen* (cash)	=	approx. 0.00125 tael
1 *liang* (tael)	=	approx. 1.33 dollars
1 *yuan* (dollar)	=	approx. 700 to 1,100 cash

Sources: Ng Chin-keong 1983:xiv; and Lin Man-houng 1989: xvi, 239.

ONE

Prelude: The Empress of Heaven Saves Dianbai

It was late September 1801, the sixth year of the Jiaqing emperor's reign and the time of the Mid-Autumn Festival. The townspeople of Dianbai city, a county seat on the southwestern coast of Guangdong province, were busy preparing moon cakes and planning family outings to the hills beyond the city walls. Outside the south gate, at the market in Longchuan harbor, fishermen and sailors crowded the Empress of Heaven Temple to beseech the goddess for fair winds and good catches. Sea merchants and shopkeepers who worshipped alongside them at the temple prayed for wealth and protection from those who would deprive them of it. Further to the south, beyond the entrance to the harbor, lurking among the islands that dotted the coast, pirate junks were gathering like froth floating on the sea.

Dianbai was a strategically important but poor county. Nearly nine thousand *li* from Beijing and eight hundred *li* from Canton, Dianbai was still a remote frontier in the early nineteenth century. Its interior was hemmed with rugged mountains and infested with bandits and uncivilized aborigines, making overland passage to and from the county both difficult and hazardous. Water routes provided the chief access to the outside world; the sea was the lifeblood of the region. Rivers linked the walled farming villages of the hinterland to the market towns and fishing ports that lined the seacoast. Along the narrow coastline, where population was dense and arable land scarce, people "regarded the sea as fields" (*yihai weitian*). Most of the people earned their livings as fishermen or laborers working in the salt fields. By the late eighteenth century Dianbai had become an important supplier of marine products and salt for the entire province. Situated as it was along a major coasting route, merchant junks from Canton, Chaozhou, Hainan, and Fujian paid regular calls to Dianbai ports, and hundreds of salt junks plied back and forth each year between its salt fields and Canton. Figure 1 presents a panoramic view of the Dianbai coast looking southward out to sea, that dominating presence in the lives of the people of the county.

On the eve of the Mid-Autumn Festival as many as a hundred pirate junks, under the commands of Zheng Qi, Mo Guanfu, Wushi Er, and others, lay at anchor outside Dianbai harbor readying for what would be their most daring venture to date. Lately these ocean bandits had become quite bold in their attacks. Less than a week earlier they had raided Shuidong, a major port about seventy *li* to the west, where they sacked the customs office and plundered eighteen salt junks and several fishing boats. They then looted and burned down Baimiao landing and a few other small fishing villages, only desisting after hearing the sounds of gongs summoning local militiamen to the scene. But now the pirates were preparing to attack the county seat, the walled city of Dianbai. The last time that pirates had threatened the city was over a century and a half earlier, during the turmoil preceding the collapse of the Ming dynasty. At that time local officials had averted disaster by quickly fortifying the city walls.[1]

The pirates in 1801 prepared themselves well for this raid. They had already dispatched several of their men, disguised as merchants and peddlers, into the city to gather information.[2] From their spies they knew that Dianbai was vulnerable. Several hundred feet of the city wall were in disrepair, having previously collapsed in a typhoon that hit the city in 1774. The several forts and blockhouses around the harbor, as depicted in Figure 1, were mostly outdated and understaffed. There were fewer than a dozen war junks defending the entire county and only about a hundred soldiers billeted in the city. What is more, the county's chief official, Hang Yuyi, had just recently assumed his post as acting magistrate and therefore could not have been fully acquainted with the situation under his jurisdiction. Not coincidentally, too, the pirates planned to launch their attack on the day of the festival, expecting to catch the city off guard.[3]

That evening before battle, aboard their vessels, pirates lit incense and prayed to Mazu (Venerable Mother), the familiar

---

[1] GZD (6211) JQ 6.9.23; SYD, JQ 6.10.18; and *DBXZ* 20/7b.

[2] SYD, JQ 6.10.18; also see GZD (6211 *fupian*) JQ 6.9.23, and (6793) JQ 6.11.28.

[3] SYD, JQ 6.10.18; GZD (7209) JQ 7.1.19; *DBXZ* 1/8b, 7/3a–5b, 8/2a, 13/15b–17a; and Jiang Weitan 1990:317.

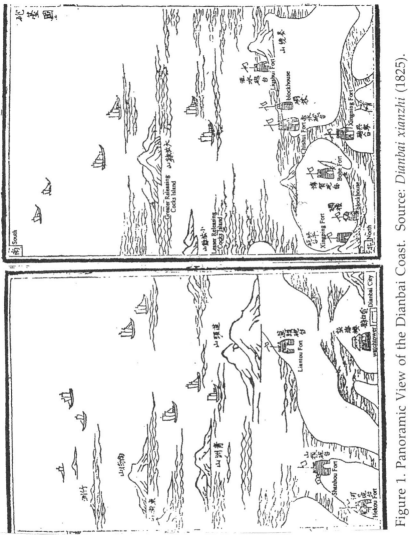

Figure 1. Panoramic View of the Dianbai Coast. Source: *Dianbai xianzhi* (1825).

name that seafarers gave to the Empress of Heaven (Tianhou), for victory in the morning. A nearly full moon promised fair weather. But that night as they slept, heavy black clouds suddenly appeared, and without warning, twisting winds, torrential rains, and waves as high as mountains battered their tiny ships, crashing them against the rocks between the Lesser and Greater Releasing Cocks Islands.[4] The destructive force of a powerful storm could be awesome, as the scene in Figure 2 vividly illustrates.

By daybreak scores of pirate junks had been sunk and countless lives lost in the tempest. Over the next few days villagers and soldiers apprehended hundreds of bewildered pirates and seized three boats, several cannon, weapons, and banners that had been washed ashore. Among these prizes was also a bronze seal of rank, which a Vietnamese ruler had presented to one of the pirate chieftains. While their captors had killed a few of the pirates on the spot, most of them were handed over to Magistrate Hang, who, after extracting confessions, forwarded the prisoners to the provincial capital at Canton for formal trial and punishment. Thirty-nine pirates were summarily executed, two by death-by-slicing and the rest by decapitation, and their severed heads were transported back to Dianbai to rot in public. Another forty-eight prisoners were tattooed and banished to Manchuria as military slaves, and the remaining twenty-one were each flogged and sentenced to three years of penal servitude.[5]

Townspeople and officials quickly attributed the unforeseen appearance of the typhoon and the destruction of the pirate fleet to the wondrous powers of the Empress of Heaven. It was even rumored that the emperor in far away Beijing on that same night had dreamed about the divine intervention that saved the city. In any case, after receiving a report from Governor-General Jiqing, to show his royal gratitude the emperor ordered Ma Shuxin, the intendant of the Gaolian circuit, to offer incense to the Empress of Heaven at her temple in Dianbai. To commemorate the event, local gentry and merchants erected a memorial tablet at the temple's door to record for posterity the emperor's blessing and to make known far and wide the efficacy of Tianhou.[6] Following the incident, Jiqing petitioned for construction of a new fort, the

---

[4] *DBXZ* 13/16b–17a; and Jiang Weitan 1990:317.
[5] GZD (6211) JQ 6.9.23.
[6] Ibid.; *DBXZ* 20/7b; and Jiang Weitan 1990:317–318.

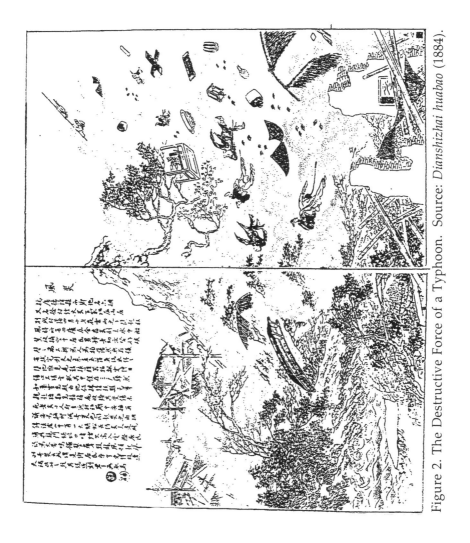

Figure 2. The Destructive Force of a Typhoon. Source: *Dianshizhai huabao* (1884).

Xingning battery, at the harbor's western entrance, and a year later repairs on the city's walls were finally begun.[7]

The pirates had not been destroyed, and after regrouping they continued for the next several months to plunder shipping along the coast all the way north to Huizhou prefecture. Even though several of the most notorious pirate leaders would be dead within a year, the pirate disturbances continued to grow over the next eight years. The late eighteenth and early nineteenth centuries were, indeed, a time of great piratical activities all along the southern coast, from Zhejiang to Vietnam, where tens of thousands of men, women, and children became involved in piracy. Pirates organized themselves into several formidable fleets, disrupting trade and effectively challenging Qing authority in the region until 1810.

The episode in Dianbai was a microcosm of the larger world of piracy, and of the tensions and contradictions in South China's maritime society from which it arose. Pirates, and seafarers in general, lived in a world that was less romantic than it was brutal and base.[8] The violence and destruction of both man and nature were real, everyday occurrences that shaped the lives and minds of the men and women who went to sea and who lived along its shores. In their cosmos little separated the natural from the super-natural realms. Everyone prayed to the same gods, though the gods meant different things to different people. The story that unfolds in the following chapters offers us a glimpse into that peculiar time, place, and mentalité that was South China in the middle years of the Qing dynasty (1644–1911).

In Dianbai, as elsewhere along the Guangdong and Fujian coasts, society seemed to have turned in on itself. Piracy was but one of the many social upheavals in China at the end of the eighteenth century. It was a time of profound change and transition driven by commercial expansion and population explosion. While some Chinese believed that they lived in the best of all possible worlds, others took note of several disturbing trends: the weakening of traditional values, the growth of massive unemployment and underemployment, and the development of a huge float-

---

[7] *Gaozhou fuzhi* 1889:17/17b, and 49/40b.

[8] Throughout this book I use the terms "seafarers" and "mariners" in a narrow sense to refer to common sailors and fishermen, but not to sea merchants, ship owners, and ship captains and officers.

ing population of itinerant laborers, seafarers, peddlers, and vagabonds.[9] As society became increasingly competitive and pugna-
cious, several major uprisings erupted: the Lin Shuangwen Rebellion on Taiwan (1787–1788), the Miao revolt in the mountains
bordering Guizhou, Hubei, and Sichuan (1795), the White Lotus
Rebellion in central China (1795–1804), and the Triad uprising
near Canton (1802–1803). Also below the Chinese border in Vietnam, when Tâyson rebels overthrew the lethargic Lê dynasty in
the 1780s, the Qing court sent Chinese armies to crush the rebellion, and fighting spilled over into the South China Sea. In the
wake of these disturbances there was throughout China, but especially in the southern coastal provinces, a concomitant upsurge in
piracy, banditry, smuggling, feuding, and secret-society activities.[10]

Guangdong and Fujian were ideally situated for both seafaring
and piracy (Figure 3). Physically separated by mountains from
much of the interior, coastal dwellers had always been oriented
toward the sea. The southern littoral was densely populated and
highly commercialized. Taken together the two provinces had the
longest coastline in China, stretching for many thousands of *li*,
and more than a third of the population, numbering in the several
hundreds of thousands, were sailors and fishermen. Others too, as
merchants, artisans, and farmers, depended on the sea for their
livelihoods. Fujian was bounded in the north by the tiny island of
Taishan, a no-man's-land on the border with Zhejiang, and in the
far southwest Guangdong was bounded by the Vietnamese black-
market town of Giang Binh (Jiangping). Situated on or near the
coast were the major entrepôts of Canton, Chaozhou, and Amoy.
In addition to these port cities, the jagged shores of Guangdong
and Fujian provided numerous channels and small harbors and
were dotted with a fringe of countless islands and sandy shoals.
During the eighteenth century the island frontier of Taiwan, which
was a part of Fujian province until 1886 (when it became a
separate province), also became increasingly important as the chief
supplier of rice for Fujian and as a safety valve for the excess
populations of both Fujian and Guangdong. Hainan Island,
buffering the waters between China and Vietnam, had long been a

---

[9] Important studies on the social and economic changes in China during the first
half of the Qing dynasty include those by Suzuki 1952; Ho 1959; Rawski 1985;
M. Lin 1989; and Kuhn 1990.

[10] See Lamley 1977; Antony 1988; and Ownby 1996.

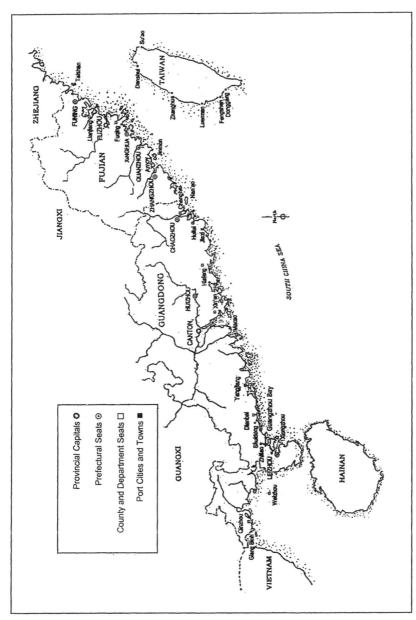

Figure 3. Map of Coastal Guangdong and Fujian, ca. 1800.

haven for smugglers and pirates. While the larger ports served as major hubs in the overseas junk trade, the smaller bays and harbors provided anchorages for fishing boats and coastal merchant junks, as well as for smuggling and pirate vessels.

South China's maritime world, however, stretched far beyond the provincial boundaries of Guangdong and Fujian. Here was a much wider area, reaching northward to Manchuria, Japan, and the Ryukyu Islands and southward to Southeast Asia, or what the Chinese called the "Southern Ocean" (Nanyang). This larger maritime zone included the Chinese emporiums of Tianjin, Shanghai, and Ningbo, as well as the port towns of the Philippines, Vietnam, Cambodia, Siam, Burma, Sumatra, Java, and Borneo.[11] While the South China Sea supported substantial deep-sea fishing, Chinese trading junks and Western merchantmen dominated the region's economy. The flourishing trade during the mid-Qing era provided the opportunity for an even more flourishing piracy.

This too was a region teeming with people. The southern coast of China had not only a high population density but also an eclectic demography. Among the Han Chinese were several subethnic groups with disparate traditions and their own distinct dialects. Among the coastal inhabitants the Hokkien (Hoklo) and Dan (Tanka) boat people stood out. The great majority of Fujian's mariners were Hokkien, though not all Hokkien went to sea. They hailed from southern Fujian, chiefly from Zhangzhou and Quanzhou prefectures, whence they migrated to the shores of Chaozhou and elsewhere in Guangdong, Taiwan, and Southeast Asia. Their merchants, ship owners, sailors, and fishermen dominated the maritime society and economy of Fujian and Taiwan, and indeed much of China as a whole. Hokkien fishermen sailed in junks notable for the huge eyes painted on the bows. Dan boat people, who spoke a Cantonese dialect, engaged in fishing, ferrying, and shipping along the coast and on rivers. Treated like outcasts by those on land, they lived their entire lives on the water. By the late eighteenth century they were concentrated in the Canton delta and around Chaozhou, though they were also found on the Fujian coast. So dense were their anchorages that land dwellers described them as "floating villages" (Figure 4). The Hokkien and Dan, as well as other people who made their livings as common sailors and fishermen, were generally all lumped

---

[11] For detailed descriptions of this maritime world see Wills 1979:206–210; and Murray 1987:6–12.

Figure 4. A Floating Village near Canton. Source: A. Colquhoun, *Across Cryse* (1883).

together, quite derogatorily, as "water people" (*shuishangren*) by the rest of society. Discernable by their shared poverty and discrimination, and despised by their neighbors on land, seafarers occupied a marginal existence on the fringes of respectable society. It was not uncommon for water people to fluctuate between legitimate pursuits and piracy.[12]

In writing this book my purpose is to explore the world of pirates and seafarers and the integral role that they played in shaping maritime society in Fujian and Guangdong during the late eighteenth and early nineteenth centuries. I am primarily interested in understanding piracy for what it can tell us about the nature of socioeconomic change in maritime South China during the late imperial age. My approach, what has been called "history from the bottom up," seeks to look at ordinary seafarers and pirates on their own terms and to reconstruct their daily lives and aspirations.[13] By reclaiming their social, economic, and cultural

---

[12] See Chen Xujing 1946; Blake 1981; and Ouyang Zongshu 1998.
[13] Several important studies that focus on the lives of ordinary seafarers in the

history, I hope not only to further our understanding of maritime society as a whole, but also to demonstrate how dynamic economic growth, commercial change, and population explosion promoted dislocation, conflict, and violence on China's southern coast.

A central argument I make in this book is that the contradictions inherent in maritime society in the mid-Qing period fostered conflict, violence, and predation in the form of large-scale piracy characterized by a preponderance of poor seafarers engaging in crime as a means of survival. Paradoxically, the height of the "prosperous age" between 1780 and 1810 was also the high tide of massive pirate disturbances.[14] Maritime society, though interdependent, was divided economically, socially, and culturally. Rising commercialization was offset by the more than doubling of the population during the first half of the Qing era, producing a society of great opportunities and even greater anxieties. By the end of the eighteenth century, on the South China coast, a lumbering subsistence economy clashed head on with a vibrant commercial economy. Although the maritime world boasted great wealth, it was unevenly distributed. As the gap between merchants, shopkeepers, and gentry on shore and fishermen and sailors at sea widened, quiescent frustrations, mistrusts, and apprehensions increasingly flared up into violent confrontations. Piracy was one of the chief weapons in the arsenal of poor and marginalized seafarers who waged a war on trade not to wreck it, but to gain a fair share in it. What they wanted was the opportunity for a decent living and an evenhanded access to the things denied to them by privation and prejudice.

Another key argument, which on the surface may seem elementary, is that pirates and seafarers shared a common sociocultural world that was quite different from that of their contemporaries living inland in cities, towns, and villages. I do not deny that mariners participated in the dominant culture or that there were important parochial and ethnic linguistic and cultural variations between seamen who came from different provinces or even different counties.[15] Instead, what interests me here is that

---

West are by Jesse Lemisch (1968a and 1968b); Marcus Rediker (1987); and Pablo Pérez-Mallaína (1998).

[14] On the "prosperous age" see Kuhn 1990:30–48.

[15] Borrowing concepts from G. William Skinner, Dian Murray (1987:2) has argued that, as on land, maritime China was divided into several separate economic, administrative, and cultural "water worlds." While this is undoubtedly true, we should not overlook the equally important sociocultural similarities that were

ordinary seafarers were able to share in a collective culture of their own making.[16] Scholars who have studied seafaring communities in other parts of the world have argued persuasively that seamen of different countries shared in common more cultural and social attributes with one another than they did with landsmen of their own countries.[17] The same was true for Guangdong and Fujian mariners in the late imperial age.

The unique experiences, poverty, and hardships of life at sea helped to shape the habits and customs of seafaring people. For the most part, seamen who became involved in piracy thought and behaved in similar ways. They all participated freely in a nebulous underworld culture of violence, vice, and crime, a culture that provided an alternative lifestyle that coexisted uneasily on the fringes of respectable society. The culture of pirates and seafarers had its own cant, amusements, sexual mores, and morals. In essence it was a culture of resistance and disconnection. It did not share the dominant Confucian values of honesty, frugality, self-restraint, and hard work; rather, it espoused deception, ambition, hedonism, recklessness, and getting ahead by any means. In a society that was becoming increasingly polarized, restless, and contentious, it is not hard to understand why the values of indigent seafarers did not always conform to those of their more affluent neighbors on shore. In the rough and violent world of seafaring, mariners could not afford to always abide by the niceties of the law or proper etiquette. To survive they had to devise their own lifestyles, habits, and standards of behavior, most of which stood in contradiction and opposition to that of dominant society. Many seamen, therefore, viewed piracy as a normal, rational, and even legitimate means of maintaining the minimal standards of living, and perhaps as a way out of impoverishment.

At the same time I also argue that the common culture shared by seafarers and pirates did not preclude predatory violence against one another. In fact, violence and crime, like typhoons, taxes, and official squeeze, were undeniable parts of the seaman's daily life. Most pirates were fishermen and sailors, and fishermen and sailors were the most frequent victims of pirates. Sociologists have long understood that areas with high population density,

---

shared among seafarers and that differentiated them from most people living on land.

[16] In this book I use the term "culture" in a broad anthropological sense as shared social customs, mores, and lifestyles.

[17] See, for instance, Weibust 1969; Fricke 1973; Ritchie 1986; and Scammell 1992.

high degrees of transience, and pronounced poverty generate opportunities for crime and also influence the breakdown of social controls that act as barriers against crime. Such areas, too, generally have greater degrees of tolerance for violent offenses.[18]

Piracy was an integral part of seafaring society. Although many individuals became permanent, professional pirates, many more mariners engaged in piracy as temporary undertakings, chiefly as a means of supplementing irregular work and low wages. Fishermen and sailors joined pirate gangs during slack seasons when legitimate jobs were hard to come by or when the costs of food rose beyond their means. Other seafarers and coastal dwellers relied on the money they earned from supplying pirates and fronting their booty. Because tens of thousands of people on both land and water came to depend on piracy, either directly or indirectly, for their livings, it quickly became a self-sustaining enterprise and, in fact, a significant and even intrinsic feature of South China's seafaring world.

Piracy too had important economic consequences. While it did detract from legitimate trade and profits, nonetheless it contributed to commercial expansion along the southern coast. Pirates were vital to the circulation of goods and people throughout the mid-Qing period. They stimulated trade and opened up new markets. Although the scale of illicit trade is impossible to measure, it certainly pumped large amounts of goods and money into local economies, particularly in those areas outside the normal or legitimate trading system. Significantly, piracy allowed marginalized fishermen, sailors, and petty entrepreneurs, who had otherwise been excluded, to participate in the wider commercial economy.

Although in recent years there have been a number of excellent studies on China's maritime history, they have focused almost exclusively on foreign relations, overseas trade, merchants, nautical technology, and the Chinese diaspora.[19] As yet there is no social and cultural history of ordinary seafarers, including pirates, nor have there been any meaningful discussions on how piracy

---

[18] See Stark 1987.

[19] For example, important new research on China's maritime history can be found in the ongoing series *Zhongguo haiyang fazhan shi lunwen ji* [Essays in Chinese maritime history] (1984–2002). Although dated, useful reviews of the literature on Chinese maritime history are in Gardella 1985; Pin-tsun Chang 1992; and Lai 1995; for an overview of the literature on maritime Asia, see Wills 1993.

helped to shape South China's maritime society. The ground-breaking studies by Jennifer Cushman, Ng Chin-keong, and Jane Leonard, for instance, have added significantly to our understanding about the importance of maritime trade to the Qing economy and to the overall well-being of the realm.[20] But by focusing on the positive achievements of merchants and officials in building the economy, these studies have overlooked the equally important, but negative, social consequences of economic development and change on ordinary seafarers.

Those scholars who have written about pirates, for their part, have likewise failed to incorporate them into the larger context of maritime history. The neglect of detailed discussions of the daily lives and travails of ordinary seamen and pirates has obscured important features of maritime history. Several studies have depicted pirates as swashbuckling heroes, as champions of the poor and avengers against injustice, and as primitive rebels in the vanguard of the revolution that toppled the Qing dynasty in 1911.[21] Other studies on Guangdong pirates by Dian Murray and on Fujian pirates by Thomas Chang have detailed the rise and fall of large-scale piracy between 1790 and 1810. Both authors argue that the upsurge in piracy had more to do with the outside support of Vietnamese rebels and the pirates' own internal leadership than, as I argue, with changing economic, demographic, and ecological circumstances.[22] Their emphasis is on the confrontation between the pirates and the Qing state; my emphasis is on the sociocultural world of pirates and their broader connections with seafaring life. While building on these earlier studies, this book diverges from them to examine in detail the underside of South China's maritime society and culture.

It is no easy task for historians to recover the lives of inarticulate and illiterate fishermen and sailors. Compounding the problem of reconstructing their lives is the fact that we must rely on documents written by elites on land. This study is based primarily on Qing imperial archives and officially sanctioned gazetteers. The former documents consist chiefly of criminal cases of piracy found among the thousands of extant, and mostly unpublished, palace memorials (*zouzhe*), routine memorials (*tiben*),

---

[20] Cushman 1993; Ng Chin-keong 1973, 1983, 1990; and Leonard 1984, 1988.

[21] For example, see Hu Jieyu 1959; Ye Zhiru 1988, 1989; Zheng Guangnan 1998; and Chen Zaizheng 1999. Ye Linfeng 1970 traces the legends surrounding the pirate Zhang Bao.

[22] Murray 1987; and T. Chang 1983.

imperial edicts (*shangyu*), and official record books (*dangce*), now housed in Beijing at the First Historical Archives and in Taibei at the National Palace Museum and Academia Sinica.[23] Since piracy was a capital crime, and one of grave concern to the throne, many of these case records are scrupulously detailed, particularly for the years between 1796 and 1804. As for the gazetteers, they were usually written by officials and gentry to highlight the main historic, geographic, economic, and cultural features of a particular county, prefecture, or province. They were mainly compiled for a highly literate audience like themselves. Needless to say, neither the archival documents nor the gazetteers looked sympathetically at ordinary seafarers, considering them instead as criminals or outcasts. To say the least, the main sources used in this study are biased.

Nonetheless, when used with care these documents are quite valuable, and as David Ownby has shown in his study of secret societies, the archival sources "can be used in ways Qing officials did not anticipate."[24] These sources, especially the palace and routine memorials, shed important new light on conditions in coastal society and on the daily lives of ordinary people. In particular, much of the information about the poor and marginalized segments of Chinese society cannot be gained elsewhere. In criminal cases, for example, the depositions of suspects and witnesses contain not only detailed descriptions of the actual crimes but also of the individuals and circumstances involved: the names of junk owners, skippers, and crews, the ship's provenance and ports of call, and type and value of cargo, as well as the names, places of birth and residence, and occupations, and occasionally the age and marital status of those arrested as pirates. The gazetteers likewise provide much useful information on local customs and orthodox religious cults, weather and climate, export commodities and markets, shipping routes, and fishing conditions. Such ethnographic information is invaluable to the social historian.

This book is organized topically in eight chapters. Following this brief introduction, chapter 2 sets the stage by surveying the

---

[23] The main body of evidence I use in this study is derived from 547 palace memorials, 172 routine memorials, 144 imperial edicts, and 86 record books of palace memorials, covering the years from 1780 to 1810. For relevant discussions on the usefulness of the Qing archives in doing social history see Antony 1988:15–22; Ownby 1996:22–24; and Sommer 2000:17–29.

[24] Ownby 1996:23.

three great pirate epochs of the late imperial era: the *wokou* of the mid-Ming (1522–1574), the *haikou* of the Ming–Qing transition (1620–1684), and the *yangdao* of the mid-Qing (1780–1810). By the late eighteenth century, in response to economic and demographic shifts, the nature of piracy had changed significantly from earlier epochs. Before the late eighteenth century, when sea bans (*haijin*) severely restricted legitimate trade, Chinese merchants and foreign adventurers dominated piracy in the South China Sea. But after the opening of ports to foreign trade in the 1680s, most merchants disengaged themselves from active roles in piracy. A century later, as population pressure increasingly worked its havoc on the laboring poor, large numbers of marginally employed fishermen and sailors took to piracy for survival. The great merchant-pirates, such as Hong Dizhen and Zheng Zhilong, who had dominated piracy in the earlier epochs, had been replaced by the end of the eighteenth century by commoner seafarer-pirates, such as Zhang Bao and Cai Qian.

Chapter 3 examines the dynamic relationships and contradictions between prosperity and poverty in South China's seafaring society in the eighteenth and early nineteenth centuries. The commercialization of the maritime economy did create fabulous wealth, but the fruits of that wealth were enjoyed chiefly by merchants, ship owners, and gentry investors. For ordinary seafarers the rewards of life at sea were few and the hardships many. For most of them life was little more than a "scramble for existence in an uncertain society."[25] Although economic growth and prosperity had created new job opportunities, by the end of the eighteenth century many of the working-class gains were offset by the population boom, which put great strain on the labor market. Irregular work and low wages forced many seafarers into debt and chronic poverty. Under those circumstances maintaining a decent and honest livelihood became increasingly difficult.

Not surprisingly, the vast majority of pirates came from this underclass of poor, marginalized, and disgruntled fishermen and sailors. Chapter 4 carefully examines the social composition of pirate gangs in Guangdong and Fujian between 1780 and 1810. My conclusions challenge generally held assumptions about pirates. Among fishermen and sailors, I argue, occasional piracy was a regular part of their overall livelihoods and was always more important than professional piracy in South China's mari-

---

[25] Kuhn 1990:36.

time world, even during its heyday between 1795 and 1810. There was no clear or sharp shift, as Dian Murray and others have suggested, from petty, occasional piracy to large-scale, professional piracy in the first decade of the nineteenth century. I further show that pirate gangs contained not only various mixes of occasional and professional pirates, but also significant numbers of reluctant pirates, captives who had been forced to serve the pirates under duress. Indeed, I argue that captives, who during the height of the large-scale pirate disturbances greatly outnumbered actual pirates, were indispensable to the rise and longevity of piracy in the mid-Qing era.

Piracy was a violent predatory activity that involved a variety of crimes on both sea and land. Pirates robbed, kidnapped, and murdered; they tortured and sexually abused victims; and they extorted fishermen, merchants, gentry, and even officials. Through the systematic use of terror, kidnapping, and extortion, piracy became a pervasive force on the South China coast. Pirates used terror and brutality to exercise power and authority over the weak and helpless, and they successfully imposed their dominion over merchant shipping and fishing as well as over coastal villages, markets, and towns through well-organized protection rackets. As a result pirates came to constitute a level of control over seafaring society that transcended that of the state and local elites. Chapter 5 explores their use of violence and extortion to gain hegemony in seafaring society.

As seafarers, pirates relied on people on shore for their very existence. I examine the relationship between various elements of maritime society and pirates in chapter 6. Contrary to conventional wisdom, I show that pirates set up bases and rendezvous not only in remote places, but, more important, in core areas along major trade routes and even close to centers of state power. In fact, a veritable cross section of seafaring society aided pirates, including other seafarers as well as local gentry, merchants, soldiers, and officials. The redistribution of goods and services, I further argue, helped to incorporate many of the poorer, isolated coastal communities into the larger commercial economy, thereby stimulating trade and local economies.

Chapter 7 probes into the cultural world of seafarers and pirates, contrasting theirs to mainstream culture on land. Seamen lived in a relatively self-contained world that bonded them together in a collective culture that was defiant and resolute. It was a culture shaped by segregation, hardship, and poverty; it shared in common distinct speech, habits, and religious practices. The oppressive working and living conditions aboard most Chinese junks and in port towns created an atmosphere conducive to violence and vice. The favorite pastimes of seamen were drinking, brawling, whoring, and gambling. Because many mariners were too poor to afford brides, same-sex unions were common. Their rough-and-tumble lifestyles were also reflected in their religious beliefs and practices, which emphasized fatalism and pragmatism. Pirates, however, took things to extremes with magicoreligious rites of human sacrifice.

The conclusion, in chapter 8, returns to a more general discussion of maritime history from the bottom up, summarizing how pirates and seafarers played important roles in shaping South China's maritime society, culture, and economy in the late imperial age. Here I also place my study in the larger historical context by making comparisons between Chinese and Western pirates, not simply to point out the differences, but also to highlight the salient features of Chinese piracy.

TWO

Waves of Piracy in Late Imperial China

Although pirates have been active along the South China coast throughout history, the golden age of Chinese piracy appeared only in the late imperial era, roughly the sixteenth through nineteenth centuries. At that time there was an unprecedented growth in Chinese piracy unsurpassed in size and scope anywhere else in the world. In South China during the late imperial age piracy surged in three great waves: one from 1522 to 1574, another from 1620 to 1684, and the last from 1780 to 1810. The three great pirate epochs were characterized by the rise of huge leagues whose power overshadowed that of the imperial state in the maritime world. At other times, while the seas around China remained relatively calm, petty localized piracy continued unabated.

Both petty and large-scale piracy ebbed and flowed in predictable seasonal patterns according to the rhythms of climate and trade, as well as of fishing seasons and costs of food. Although piracy was a year-round operation, it increased dramatically along the southern littoral each year between the third and seventh lunar months (roughly April through August) and then dropped off precipitously during the tenth and eleventh lunar months (around November and December). As early as the Song dynasty (960–1279), as Brian McKnight has noted, most piracies were committed during "the period of fair winds that brought merchants from Southeast Asia to the ports of southern China."[1] Each spring and summer, availing themselves of the southwest monsoons, vast numbers of trading junks and Western merchantmen from the Celebes, Malacca, Borneo, Java, and Manila sailed into the South China Sea heading northward. For many fishermen in Guang-

---

[1] McKnight 1992:106.

dong, Fujian, and Taiwan, unfavorable winds and typhoons made the summer months their slack season. Also significant was the fact that food prices were the highest each year during the months from April through July in the densely populated coastal prefectures of Guangdong and Fujian, and, as one Qing scholar noted, whenever the price of rice increased so did the incidences of piracy. However, in winter, once the northeast monsoons began and fishermen were again busy with work, piracy slowed down.[2]

During the first two pirate epochs, when the imperial state banned most maritime commerce, piracy and smuggling became the chief means for conducting trade. Correspondingly, large-scale piracy was dominated by merchants who had little choice but to turn to piracy to conduct business. Besides its huge scale and deep entanglement with trade, piracy in those years also was intensely internationalized and highly politicized. The first wave was the age of the so-called *wokou* (or *wako* in Japanese) pirates, composed of Japanese, Chinese, and other foreign freebooters. Piracy was largely an inherent by-product of the Ming sea bans, which forged legitimate merchants and seamen into criminals. This was a time of great merchant-pirates such as Wang Zhi, Hong Dizhen, Wu Ping, and Xu Chaoguang, who combined trade with plunder. The next pirate wave occurred during the tumultuous Ming–Qing dynastic wars. Piracy was symptomatic of the political anarchy, economic instability, and social dislocations of the era. Many of the "sea rebels" (*haikou*) fused commerce with piracy and insurgency. The Zheng family, who took advantage of the chaos to build up a huge maritime empire, exemplified the pirates-cum-merchants-cum-rebels of this epoch. Following the collapse of the Ming dynasty in 1644, piracy and insurgency escalated out of control along the South China littoral.

The third pirate wave, between 1780 and 1810, was marked by the rise of several major pirate leagues, composed of thousands of vessels and more than seventy thousand individuals. Although petty piracy continued, nevertheless many of the smaller gangs of "local pirates" (*tudao*) were transformed into larger, more powerful fleets of "ocean bandits" (*yangdao*).[3] By that time too the nature

---

[2] See *JMZ* 91–92; He Changling 1827:85/3a; Downing 1838:1/92; Hunter 1885:14–17; Chen Maoheng 1957:47; Hucker 1974:277; Antony 1988:111; Chen Xiyu 1991:363; and Chen Chunsheng 1992:121–123.

[3] Although I use the terms *wokou, haikou,* and *yangdao* to characterize each of the three pirate epochs, the Chinese sources were never so consistent. During the first wave, though *wokou* was the term most frequently found to describe all types of pirates, the sources also use *haikou* (in this case signifying "sea traitors") to indicate

of piracy had changed significantly in China. European free-booters and the great merchant-pirates of the earlier epochs had all but disappeared; instead, this was an age dominated by commoner seafarer-pirates. As one local official, Xie Jinluan, lamented in 1804: "In the past sailors worked for merchants, but now sailors work for pirates; in the past sailors transported goods for merchants, but now sailors transport goods for pirates."[4] Cai Qian was the most notorious pirate operating on the waters around Zhejiang, Fujian, and Taiwan, while Zhu Fen ravaged the border region between Fujian and Guangdong. Further south, all along Guangdong's craggy coastline, several pirate chieftains, most notably Zheng Yi, Wushi Er, and later Zhang Bao, had formed a loose confederation that plagued the South China Sea and challenged Qing authority in the region for over a decade. Yet all of a sudden, between 1809 and 1810, at a time when these pirates were apparently at the height of their power, they utterly collapsed. With their demise the golden age of pirates in China came to an end, though piracy has never completely disappeared in the region.[5]

Piracy in Early Imperial China

Piracy is as old as ships and shipping, but just how old it is in China remains uncertain. Archaeologists have uncovered the remnants of primitive Stone Age boats along China's coast and inland river systems.[6] Perhaps the noted chronicler of pirates, Philip Gosse, was correct when he wrote that "the Chinese were practic-

---

native Chinese pirates who cooperated with "Japanese" *wokou*. In most cases the term *haikou* was used at that time to refer to powerful Chinese merchant-pirates such as Wang Zhi, Hong Dizhen, and others. By the start of the seventeenth century the term *wokou* no longer was found in the sources; instead *haikou* (in this case signifying "sea rebels") became the most commonly used term for pirates. Then in the late eighteenth and early nineteenth centuries, even more terms for pirates can be found in the sources. Besides *haikou*, we find *haidao* and *haizei* (all signifying "sea bandits"), *yangdao* and *yangfei* (ocean bandits), and several other terms. Officials at one time or another labeled Cai Qian, for example, as *yangdao, tudao* (local pirate), *daofan* (a generic term for "bandit" or "robber"), and *nizei* (rebel). In every period writers used the term *tudao* (local pirate) to denote generally small-scale, localized piracy. For useful explanations of Chinese terms commonly used for pirates see Matsuura 1995:7–10 and Yang Guozhen 1998:161–162.

[4] Cited in Chen Zaizheng 1999:75.
[5] Vagg 1993 discusses piracy in contemporary Asia.
[6] Sun Guangzhe 1989:27–33; and Ye Xianen 1989:20–24.

ing piracy before history began."[7] The first documented case, however, was that of the pirate Zhang Bolu in A.D. 109. By the fifth century, piracy had become a pervasive fact of life in the South China Sea, perpetrated by Chinese as well as Japanese and Southeast Asian corsairs. Lu Xun, who was the first pirate of any notoriety in South China, was active during the first decade of the fifth century in the waters between Guangdong and Zhejiang. Sun En, another pirate active along the southern coast at the time, was known for his perverse cruelties. Reports claimed that he and his men cannibalized victims, even forcing the wives and children of the victims to partake of the bloody feasts. As the volume of trade steadily grew over the Tang (618–907) and Song (960–1279) eras, so too did commerce raiding. Piracies were frequently mentioned in the official histories in the eleventh and twelfth centuries. In 1135, for instance, a pirate named Zhu Cong pillaged towns and shipping from Canton to Quanzhou. Then in the wake of the Mongols' abortive invasion of Japan in the next century, Chinese and other Asian pirates continually harassed coastal shipping into the early Ming dynasty (1368–1644).[8]

The Merchant-Pirates of the Mid-Ming

The mid-Ming period, during the reign of the Jiajing emperor (r. 1522–1566), was the real take-off stage for large-scale piracy in Chinese waters. Following a century of relative tranquility, beginning in the early 1520s, China witnessed a steady growth in the number of piracies along the entire coast from Shandong to Guangdong. By the 1540s many small pirate gangs had evolved into larger, better-organized fleets. Cresting in the 1550s, at a time when the Ming state was facing a serious threat on the northern frontier from resurgent Mongol armies under Altan Khan, most of the pirate activities shifted southward from Zhejiang to the seas off the coasts of Fujian and Guangdong. Characterized by officials as *wokou*, the term was used pejoratively for "Japanese pirates" but in fact was applied loosely to virtually all pirates operating along the coast of China. In reality *wokou* bands were composed of motley crews of Japanese, Chinese, Malaccan, Siamese, Portuguese, Spanish, and even African adventurers.[9]

---

[7] Gosse 1932:265.

[8] *FJTZ* 266/13b–15a; *XPXZ* *wubei*/1a; *QZFZ* 73/17b–19a; and Matsuura 1995:11–12, 17–20, 26–29, 33–35.

[9] On the *wokou* see Chen Maoheng 1957; So 1975; Tanaka 1982; Matsuura

A major underlying reason for the sudden upsurge in piracy at that time was the Jiajing emperor's determination to rigidly enforce the existing Ming sea bans and to enact tough new ones. At the start of the dynasty, the Hongwu emperor (r. 1368–1398) had set about to "immobilize the realm" by restricting both social and physical mobility. A key to his bucolic vision was the promotion of a strict quarantine on overseas travel, commerce, and contacts.[10] Thereafter the imperial court outlawed all private overseas trade, and instead vainly attempted to restrict maritime commerce within the narrow confines of the tributary system. All those caught building large ocean-going junks, trading with foreigners, traveling abroad without authorization, or colluding with smugglers were to be treated as rebels and therefore liable to capital punishment and their families to banishment. Even fishermen were forbidden from putting out to sea to fish.[11]

These prohibitions were meant to check the centrifugal forces challenging the central government and to prevent smuggling and piracy along China's lengthy littoral. But because tribute missions were sporadic and the amounts of imports and exports severely limited, they satisfied neither the commercial ambitions of Chinese nor foreign merchants. Instead of curbing illegal activities the bans actually encouraged them. Since the state proved ineffectual in enforcing its maritime policies, by the sixteenth century private, illicit trade had not only revived but was thriving up and down the coastline, and much of the dense coastal population had come to depend on it for their livelihoods. Piracy had become the most vivid expression of opposition to official maritime policies and the most vital means of conducting overseas trade.[12]

Merchant-Pirates on the South China Coast

Jiajing's enforcement of the sea bans criminalized large segments of the maritime population. Unlawful commerce inevitably led to piracy. Gradually all strata of coastal society, from fishermen and sailors to merchants and gentry, became involved to some degree or another in illegal enterprises. In the words of one

---

1995:43–79; and Zheng Guangnan 1998:177–209.

[10] Brook 1998:19.

[11] Chen Wenshi 1966. Although overseas trade was prohibited, the Ming government did not ban the coastal trade.

[12] See Higgins 1980; Lin Renchuan 1987; Li Jinming 1990; and Brook 1998:119–123.

official, "Pirates and merchants are all the same people: when markets are open the pirates become merchants, and when markets are closed merchants become pirates."[13] One of the striking features of Chinese piracy in this era was that many of the most powerful leaders, such as Wang Zhi, Hong Dizhen, and Wu Ping, had merchant backgrounds (Table 1).[14] These merchant-pirates, mixing trade with smuggling and pillaging, organized large fleets and established bases on coastal islands. They often attempted to impose some order in their world by subduing or absorbing petty gangs of local pirates who interfered with their operations. One of the most famous chieftains, Wang Zhi, actually cooperated with Ming officials to suppress pirates who disturbed trade.[15] Many pirate gangs also sought protection under the wings of influential families and local officials. Numerous merchants and gentry, though not directly engaged in piracy, collaborated with and supported pirate bands.[16]

The year 1548 marked a major shift in piracy in Fujian and Guangdong (see Table 1). Before then scores of local pirates infested the coastal waters. Their gangs were generally small and the scope of their activities limited to a relatively narrow area. After 1548 there was a significant shift in the number of *wokou* and merchant-pirate activities in the region, as large-scale piracy shifted its focus from Zhejiang southward to Fujian and Guangdong. In that year Zhu Wan, whom the Jiajing emperor had recently appointed as special grand coordinator to eradicate piracy, dispatched troops who destroyed the *wokou* stronghold on Shuangyu Island off the Ningbo coast, thereby scattering the pirates and smugglers to other points along the southern coast.[17] Every year until 1574, *wokou* pirates repeatedly raided the coast from Funing to Hainan.[18] Fujian became a "*wokou* nest," with poor villagers eagerly joining pirate bands to rob travelers, loot the houses and tombs of wealthy landlords, and parade through

---

[13] Cited in Jiang and Fang 1993:263.

[14] On these and other merchant-pirates of the mid-Ming period see Chen Maoheng 1957:129–140 and Lin Renchuan 1987:85–130.

[15] Wang Zhi was the most powerful pirate on the Zhejiang coast until his surrender and execution in 1559 (see Wills 1979:210–213; Lin Renchuan 1987:87–92; and Zheng Guangnan 1998:183–198).

[16] So 1975:34–35; Fitzpatrick 1979:5–6, 18; and Geiss 1988:490–496.

[17] So 1975:56, 66.

[18] *Ming shi* [1736] 1974:2/245–246, 8/2244–2245; *XPXZ dashi*/9b; YXTZ 19/4b; XMZ 119–120; GDTZ [1822] 1934:3/3441–3448; HLXZ 11:3a–b; and Feray 1906:372–379.

Table 1
Major Pirate Groups in South China, 1522–1574

Year	Pirate leader	Pirate identity	Main areas of activity
1522	Wu Qing	local pirate	Huizhou, Chaozhou
1523		*wokou*	Fujian, Guangdong
1525	Jiang Wensheng	local pirate	Zhangzhou, Chaozhou
1526	Wu Da, Wu San	local pirates	Huizhou, Chaozhou
1531	Huang Xiushan	merchant-pirate	Guangdong, Fujian, Zhejiang
1532		local pirates	Quanzhou
1535	Zheng Lao	local pirate	Chaozhou
1538		local pirates	Funing
1539		local pirates	Chaozhou
1540	Li Guangtou	local pirate	Zhangzhou, Quanzhou
1544		local pirates	Chaozhou
1545		local pirates	Quanzhou
1548	Li Qi, Ruan Qibao	local pirates	Quanzhou
1548–74		*wokou*	Fujian, Guangdong
1550		local pirates	Fuzhou
1553–54	He Yaba	merchant-pirate	Guangdong, Fujian, Zhejiang
1553–58	Xu Dong	merchant-pirate	Guangdong, Fujian
1555–59	Hong Dizhen	merchant-pirate	Guangdong, Fujian
1555–65	Wu Ping	merchant-pirate	Guangdong, Fujian
1554–64	Zhang Wei	local pirate	Zhangzhou
1556		local pirates	Funing
1556–58	Xie Lao, Huang Lao	local pirates	Zhangzhou
1558–62	Zhang Lian	merchant-pirate	Guangdong, Fujian
1558–63	Xu Chaoguang	merchant-pirate	Guangdong, Fujian
1560	Xie Wanguan	local pirate	Quanzhou
1561		local pirates	Zhangzhou
1561–73	Lin Daoqian	merchant-pirate	Guangdong, Fujian
1563	Li Guoxian	merchant-pirate	Guangdong, Fujian, Zhejiang
1565–69	Zeng Yiben	merchant-pirate	Guangdong, Fujian
1567	Guo Ming	local pirate	Chaozhou
1568–71	Yang Lao	local pirate	Chaozhou
1570	Xu Rui	merchant-pirate	Guangdong
1570–75	Lin Feng	merchant-pirate	Guangdong, Fujian
1571–74	Zhu Liangbao	local pirate	Guangdong, Fujian
1571–74	Zheng Dahan	local pirate	Guangdong, Fujian

Sources: *FJTZ* 267/13b–35b; *QZFZ* 73/21b–31b; *XPXZ dashi*/9b–14a; *STDSJ* 1/22–36; Chen Maoheng 1957:103–128; and Ng Chin-keong 1973:170–171.

the streets carrying placards denouncing the rich.[19] At the height of the disturbances much of the southern seaboard, for roughly two decades between 1550 and 1574, had slipped away from Ming control and into the hands of powerful pirate leagues.

Hong Dizhen, a native of Zhangzhou prefecture, was one of the first major merchant-pirates in the Fujian and Guangdong region. He began his career as a merchant and, out of necessity, smuggler before he became a pirate. Like Wang Zhi, with whom he had connections, Hong amassed a fortune in illicit trade with Japan. Around 1558, after Ming officials began harassing his family members and confiscating his ships, he began to engage in piracy for self-preservation. From offshore bases on Nan'ao and Wuyu Islands, he cooperated with *wokou* pirates to plunder towns and merchant junks in South China. In 1559 his fleet pillaged the harbors at Funing, Fuan, Sansha, and Amoy. Later that same year, after receiving promises of amnesty, he surrendered to the government, but instead of being pardoned he (like Wang Zhi before him) was beheaded.[20]

Wu Ping, who also hailed from Zhangzhou, had operated smuggling and pirate enterprises with Hong Dizhen from bases on Nan'ao and Wuyu for over twenty years before fleeing to Vietnam in 1565. Three of his associates—Xu Chaoguang, Lin Daoqian, and Zeng Yiben—perpetuated and expanded the trading network that Wu Ping had established. Xu Chaoguang, who was the adopted son of Xu Dong, began his career as a pirate chief after murdering his adopted father and taking over the gang in 1558. Until his own murder by one of his subordinates in 1563, he controlled much of the trade around Chaozhou harbor through an extensive protection racket imposed on merchant shippers. Both Lin Daoqian and Zeng Yiben benefited from Wu Ping's departure to Vietnam by expanding their bands out of the latter's dismantled organization. Lin organized a huge trading network that extended from Fujian and Guangdong to Taiwan, the Philippines, and Southeast Asia. In 1566, in collusion with *wokou* bands, he plundered Zhaoan, and in 1571 he joined forces with two Fujian pirates, Zhu Liangbao and Zheng Dahan, for a raid that took them as far south as Yangjiang county in Guangdong. In 1573 Lin fled first to Luzon and later to Thailand, where he continued for several more years as a merchant and pirate. Zeng Yiben, who

---

[19] Reid 1938:165.
[20] Chen Maoheng 1957:135; So 1975:34–35; and Lin Renchuan 1987:102–103.

came from Zhaoan, was most active in Fujian and Guangdong between 1564 and 1569. Working with *wokou* gangs, in 1567 he attacked the Huilai coast, and in 1568 he even laid siege to Canton for a week. In the next year, however, he was arrested and beheaded. After his execution, his nephew, Xu Rui, took over and ran the operation until he surrendered in 1570.[21]

Portuguese Pirates and Renegades

Offshore islands, such as Nan'ao, Wuyu, and Jinmen (Quemoy), became rendezvous for pirates, smugglers, and seafarers of all nationalities. Not only did Chinese and Japanese come to these islands to do business, but so did Portuguese and other Europeans. In this age of empire building and commercial rivalry, trade and piracy were often indistinguishable. Indeed, Western governments maintained tolerant attitudes toward piracy, even viewing it as an important auxiliary to legitimate trade. Limitless opportunities in Asia for riches, either through trade or pillage or both, attracted European exiles, renegades, and adventurers to the region.[22] They had no scruples about violating Ming sea bans. At the time that the Portuguese were establishing a foothold on Macao, their merchants not only engaged in trade but also plundered Chinese villages and carried off young children to be sold into slavery.[23]

The Decline of Wokou Piracy

Although sporadic *wokou* raids continued along the South China coast into the early seventeenth century, the number of recorded pirate incidents after 1574 rapidly diminished. Upon the death of the Jiajing emperor in 1567, the maritime bans were removed on all but the Japanese, and Chinese overseas trade was legalized but still restricted.[24] At that time several major pirate

---

[21] *FJTZ* 267/33b–35a; *STDSJ* 1/25–36; also see Chen Maoheng 1957:135–138; and Lin Renchuan 1987:99–109.

[22] Boxer 1975:314–315; Scammell 1992; and Thomson 1994:30–31.

[23] *FJTZ* 267/14b–15b; *STDSJ* 1/22–23; Reid 1938:87–91; and Brook 1998:122–123. An overview of Portugal's maritime relations with Ming China is presented in Wills 1998:335–353.

[24] In 1567 the government began licensing Chinese junks for trade with Southeast Asia; thereafter the number of licenses varied between fifty and a hundred per year. By 1620, however, the licensing system had broken down (Blussé 1988:104).

leaders were either killed in battle, were pacified by the state, or fled to Southeast Asia. Also the construction and repairs of city walls, the fortification of coastal towns and villages, and the buildup of local militia all hastened the decline of piracy after the 1570s. Furthermore, the political reunification of Japan in the latter part of the sixteenth century did much to curtail Japanese piracy in the whole region. China too began to import large quantities of silver from India and Southeast Asia, and even more from Manila and Japan (through European traders), in exchange for Chinese silks and manufactured goods. Between 1570 and 1620, the expansion of maritime commerce and monetary stability kept most people satisfied with legitimate trade and profits. With markets open, pirates again became merchants.[25]

Merchants, Rebels, and Pirates of the Ming–Qing Transition

After a respite of about fifty years, a new wave of large-scale piracy surged forth during the Ming–Qing transition between 1620 and 1684, with piracy in Guangdong and Fujian reaching a peak in the 1640s–1660s. This pirate upsurge, whose practitioners were often characterized in official accounts as "sea rebels" (*haikou*), was symptomatic of the general crisis in China that accompanied the change of dynasties.[26] Given the economic and political anarchy of this period, a clear distinction between piracy, rebellion, and trade was impossible. The Zheng family, seeing opportunity in instability, created a maritime empire in Fujian and Taiwan that was based on a combination of trade, piracy, and political manipulation. Other pirates, such as Liu Xiang, Su Cheng, and Huang Hairu, emulated the Zheng organization but on smaller scales. After the Ming collapse in 1644, there was a rise in all forms of piracy, but especially small-scale localized piracy (Table 2). European traders, with the continued support of their governments, also took advantage of the turmoil in China to pillage coastal towns and merchant junks.

By the 1620s the relative stability and prosperity of the previous several decades had been abruptly shattered. Externally, Manchu incursions on the northeastern frontier challenged Ming

---

[25] *STDSJ* 1/31–33; *JMZ* 360; also see Wills 1974:7,10; So 1975:145–146; Yang and Chen 1993:22–30; and von Glahn 1996:118–119.

[26] The best treatments in English of the Ming–Qing transition are Struve 1984 and Wakeman 1985.

Table 2
Major Pirate Groups in South China, 1620–1670

Year	Pirate leader	Pirate identity	Main areas of activity
1620–46	Zheng Zhilong	merchant-pirate	Fujian, Guangdong
1626–36	Liu Xiang	merchant-pirate	Fujian, Guangdong
1628	Zhou Sanlao	local pirate	Fuzhou
1629–30	Li Kuiqi	merchant-pirate	Fujian
1630–31	Li Zhiqi	local pirate	Chaozhou, Zhangzhou, Quanzhou
1645–50	Lin Xuexian	pirate-rebel	Chaozhou
1645–65	Su Cheng, Su Li	merchant-pirates	Huizhou, Chaozhou
1645–47	Huang Hairu	pirate-rebel	Chaozhou
1646–62	Zheng Chenggong	merchant-pirate-rebel	Fujian, Guangdong
1648	Fang Wang	local pirate	Zhangzhou
1648–61	Huang Yuan	local pirate	Zhangzhou
1649–50	Lin Sheng	local pirate	Chaozhou
1650	Wang Huizhi	pirate-rebel	Chaozhou
1653	Huang Ting	local pirate	Zhangzhou
1656	Zhang Mingzhen	local pirate	Funing
1656–63	Chen Ba	merchant-pirate	Fujian
1659	Gao Chen	local pirate	Zhangzhou
1660–61	Guo Yi	local pirate	Zhangzhou
1663	Zhou Yu	local pirate	Guangzhou
1670	Chen Kui	local pirate	Chaozhou

Sources: *HLXZ* 4a–9a; *QZFZ* 73/32a–34a; *YXTZ* 19/5a–b; *XPXZ dashi*/16b–17b; and *STDSJ* 1/38–60.

sovereignty and forced the government to commit large amounts of money and troops to defend the border, weakening its military presence along the southern coast.[27] Internally, the Ming state was fractured by corruption, factionalism, incompetence, and fiscal bankruptcy. Although the imperial court had opened foreign trade in 1567, after 1623 it once again began to intermittently prohibit maritime trade, finally banning it altogether in 1626 (except for a brief period between 1631 and 1632). At the same time the Chinese economy stagnated and then declined, in part as a result of a sudden drop in bullion imports from overseas.[28] The

[27] *MQSLWB* 7b–8a; and Shao Tingcai 1961:131.

[28] Von Glahn (1996), however, argues that the decline in silver was insufficient to adversely affect the Chinese economy. But as Robert Marks points out, von Glahn's own estimates of silver imports (p. 232, Table 23) actually support the case that there was a sharp drop in silver imports from 572.8 metric tons between 1636 and 1640 to 248.6 metric tons between 1641 and 1645, a drop of more than 40 percent (Marks 1998:142). Furthermore, silver imports dropped even further over the next ten years. On this important debate on silver imports and the "crisis of the

decrease in silver and the debasement of cash adversely affected the coastal economies of Fujian and Guangdong, which were both tied to maritime trade. During the late 1630s and 1640s, foreign trade had come to a virtual halt, and prices along the littoral soared.[29]

An unusually large number of floods, droughts, and typhoons, which destroyed crops and created food shortages, further aggravated the situation. In Guangdong there were famines every year or so between 1642 and 1665.[30] In 1648 famines and epidemics devastated the coast from Guangdong to Zhejiang. Food prices skyrocketed, and bandits and pirates appeared everywhere. So terrible was the calamity that in Xin'an county, in the lower Canton delta, men and women were sold for a peck (*dou*) of rice, and human corpses (like the one in Figure 5) were butchered for food.[31]

As the political and economic crisis deepened, social unrest increased. In addition to food riots during times of dearth, there were tenant revolts in the countryside and worker uprisings in the cities. During the 1640s mountain bandits became active throughout Fujian and Guangdong, as elsewhere in China. In Quanzhou in 1642, cultic followers of the Venerable Dipper (Dou Lao), a stellar deity who held the moon and sun in her hands and who promised aid to the poor and needy, took note of ominous signs in the heavens and rose up in revolt against the Ming dynasty.[32] The collapse of the Ming two years later signaled a further escalation of disturbances; some leaders cloaked their activities under the guise of Ming loyalism, while others pursued more personal agendas. Large roving gangs, numbering into the thousands, plundered not only villages and markets, but also walled cities. In the summer of 1645, Liu Gongxian, a Ming military licentiate (*wusheng*) from Jieyang county, Guangdong, formed a personal army, appointed officials, and raised the banner of rebellion under the dynastic title of Latter Han (Hou Han).

---

seventeenth century," see the opposing views in Atwell 1990, 1998 and von Glahn 1996.

[29] See Wills 1979:216; Atwell 1988:603–604, 631–633; Li Jinming 1990:178–179; von Glahn 1996:175; and Marks 1998:135–137, 141–143.

[30] Based on data in Qiao Shengxi 1993.

[31] QZFZ 73/12a; XPXZ *dashi*/17a; STDSJ 1/47; and P. Ng 1983:103.

[32] QZFZ 73/11b. On Dou Lao, or Dou Mu (Dipper Mother) as she was more commonly called, see Doré 1914–1938:9/107; and Maspero 1981:157. Dou Mu was, and still is, a popular deity in both the Buddhist and Daoist traditions.

Figure 5. Famine Victims Butchering a Human
Corpse. Source: China Famine Relief Fund, *The
Famine in China* (1878).

Within a month he and his band came down from their mountain
stronghold to attack Jieyang city, killing the magistrate and the
military commander. Next autumn he again raided the county
seat, this time opening granaries, destroying the jail, burning
government records, and killing more than seventy officials and
gentry leaders. Then during the terrible famine of 1648, he joined
forces with the pirate Zheng Hongkui, who had invaded the Chaozhou region in search of food and plunder. Zheng was a Ming
loyalist and the younger brother of Zheng Zhilong.[33]

---

[33] *STDSJ* 1/43, 45, 47.

The Zheng Family's Maritime Empire

By the 1640s the Zheng family, first under the leadership of Zheng Zhilong and then of his son Zheng Chenggong (better known in the West as Koxinga), had built up a sizable maritime empire, which controlled much of South China's seaborne trade. Zheng Zhilong, who began his career in the 1620s as a merchant-pirate, displayed exceptional organizational skills and an uncanny knack for manipulating governmental authorities. In 1628, when he surrendered to the Ming in exchange for a high military position, he already dominated the lucrative Fujian–Taiwan trade network from his strongholds on Amoy and neighboring islands. Official reports even claimed that no ships could sail without his permission. He levied "water fees" (*baoshui*) on merchant junks and plundered those vessels that refused to pay. Reportedly, too, many high-ranking officials in Fujian and even in the imperial court were on his payroll. He was also able to gain popular support when, after a series of droughts devastated the province, he provided food and employment to thousands of victims.[34]

In his rise to power Zheng Zhilong continually had to vie with other rival pirates and defectors within his own organization. In the 1620s his was but one of at least ten other major pirate fleets.[35] After surrendering to the Ming and receiving official titles he was able to attack his adversaries with the government's blessing and without the distractions of naval harassment. One of his most valiant rivals, Liu Xiang, had established a competing trading network with a fleet of several hundred ships and strong connections with Luzon. A native of Haicheng county, Liu was most active along the Fujian and Guangdong border. After Zheng's men killed him in 1636, officials attributed Liu's demise to the intercession of the stellar goddess, the Venerable Dipper, whom the throne thereafter recognized as a slayer of pirates.[36] After Zheng surrendered to the Ming, several of his chief lieutenants, such as Li Zhiqi, defected and formed their own gangs. Li remained active around Chaozhou, Zhangzhou, and Quanzhou until he was killed in 1631. By the late 1630s Zheng had eliminated all of his

---

[34] *XMZ* 665–667; Shao Tingcai 1961:131; also see Wills 1979:217–219; Struve 1984:87–89; Lin Renchuan 1987:113–115; Matsuura 1995:91–92; Carioti 1996:31–36; and Zheng Guangnan 1998:238–251.

[35] Lin Renchuan 1987:115.

[36] *MQSLYB* 688a–690a; Qu Dajun [1700] 1985:1/213; Matsuura 1995:93–94; and Zheng Guangnan 1998:254–257.

major rivals and had become so powerful that one official described him as "a whale swallowing up the sea."[37]

With the fall of the Ming dynasty in 1644, Zheng Zhilong wavered for another two years before finally surrendering to the Manchu conquerors.[38] Many of his clansmen, including Zheng Chenggong and Zheng Hongkui, however, continued to resist the Qing in the name of Ming loyalism. Taking advantage of the political turmoil, Zheng Chenggong expanded his power base in both Fujian and eastern Guangdong, and by 1651 he was in command of the Zheng family organization. For the next ten years his fleets had a virtual monopoly over shipping along the Fujian coast. Zheng oversaw a huge maritime empire that was financed as much by plunder and extortion as it was by trade. The core of his followers remained pirates, and he continued to obtain much of his revenues and supplies from raids on coastal areas. In 1657, for example, his forces pillaged villages in Xinghua prefecture, raping women, abducting children, and killing more than a thousand people. By 1661, after the failure of his northern campaign to take Nanjing, he was forced to withdraw his main forces to Taiwan, where he died a year later. Although his heirs continued to resist the Qing for another twenty years, the death of Zheng Chenggong began the downturn of family fortunes.[39]

Escalation of Piracy after 1644

By 1644 anarchy had spread everywhere. Once word of the fall of Beijing had reached the south, piracy quickly escalated out of control. In that year the skipper of the frigate *Surat* reported that the mouth of the Pearl River was infested with "soe many great Vessels of Rogues" that it was dangerous to venture there.[40] Some seventeen years later, Dutch traders still reported that the region was "much infested with pirates."[41] Not content with staying out at sea, pirates joined with bandits and other insurgents to

---

[37] *MQSLWB* 7b.

[38] In this instance Zheng Zhilong misjudged the Qing ruler and as a result ended up under virtual house arrest in Beijing until he was finally executed in 1661 (see Struve 1984:97–98).

[39] *XMZ* 668–671; Shao Tingcai 1961:133–139; also see Wills 1979:225–228; Struve 1984:116, 156–158, 185–188; Vermeer 1990:118–119; Matsuura 1995:95–99; and Carioti 1996:42–51.

[40] Morse 1926–1929:1/32; also see Montalto de Jesus 1926:80.

[41] Reid 1938:207.

attack inland markets and walled cities. They looted government storehouses and murdered officials and gentry leaders. Emboldened after successfully pillaging the government yamen and granary at Nandu, in Raoping county, in 1645, Huang Hairu gathered dozens of boats and led his band to attack port towns and fishing villages over the next two years in Haiyang and Chenghai counties. In 1663, Zhou Yu gathered hundreds of fishing boats to rampage the Canton delta, destroying Qing military posts and looting government yamens. Across the Fujian border in Zhangzhou, gangs of local pirates under Fang Wang, Huang Yuan, Guo Zhilong, and others rose up sporadically between 1648 and 1661, whenever Qing or Ming loyalist troops withdrew from their areas of operation.[42] Not even the powerful Zheng family could curb petty, localized piracy in Fujian after 1644.

In Guangdong two brothers, Su Cheng and Su Li, established a huge pirate and smuggling organization in Huizhou and Chaozhou between 1645 and 1665. At the time of Su Cheng's death in 1649, they commanded at least seventy vessels from their stronghold at the port of Jiazi. Although some displaced farmers had joined their band, most of their adherents were fishermen and salt smugglers. In fact, the Su brothers were leading salt smugglers on the coast, reaping an annual profit of 100,000 taels from the illicit trade. Between the mid 1640s and early 1660s, the Su organization controlled a three-hundred-mile stretch of coastline between Haifeng and Huilai counties. Unlike those pirates who associated themselves with Ming restorationism, the Su brothers identified themselves with Lin Xuexian, a pirate-rebel who attempted to establish a new dynasty in Huilai. Su Li stubbornly held on to the coastal areas in Haifeng and Huilai counties until 1664, when he was killed by Manchu troops.[43]

Dutch and British Pirate-Adventurers

By that time the Dutch and British had replaced the Portuguese as the dominant Western powers in Asia, and like their predecessors they also mixed trade with piracy. Encouraged by their sovereigns, the great mercantile companies of this era readily engaged in robbery and extortion against their Asian and

---

[42] *STDSJ* 1/45–46; *PYXZ* 22/7b–8a; *YXTZ* 19/5a–b; Vermeer 1990:112–114; Zheng Guangnan 1998:289–296; and Marks 1998:144.

[43] *HLXZ* 11/4b–9a; and Marks 1984:28–30.

European rivals. At a time when the authority of European states was still fragile, rulers did not wish to risk hostility or lose the potential services of freebooters. They brought revenue to their monarchs, public officials, and investors, and they weakened the enemies of the state by attacking their ships and settlements. Piracy, in fact, often substituted for declared war. Only the most careless pirates ended their lives on the gallows before 1700.[44]

Dutch and British traders readily took advantage of the political vacuum in China to plunder Chinese junks and coastal settlements. At times, when it was to their mutual advantage, they would join forces to attack Portuguese and Chinese ships trading in the Southern Ocean. Poorly armed junks provided easy prey for these Western adventurers. It was reported, for instance, that Dutch merchantmen robbed more than twenty-five Chinese junks within the space of a few months in the early 1620s. In 1622 the Dutch attacked Macao and then seized Penghu (Pescadores), looting and burning villages and kidnapping some fourteen hundred islanders to sell into slavery. In 1624 they occupied Taiwan, and from this base conducted trade and pirate expeditions until Zheng Chenggong expelled them in 1661. Thereafter they became engaged in a commercial war with the Zheng family, and in 1661 the Dutch plundered twenty of Zheng's ships near Fuzhou. Two years later they robbed several junks trading between Canton and Hainan. The Dutch, who were excluded from direct trade with China until 1729, actually obtained much of the silks, satins, and chinaware so vital to their trade with Japan through plunder. European freebooters continued to seize Chinese vessels in the Straits of Malacca and around the Philippines into the eighteenth century.[45]

The Suppression of Piracy and the Reopening of Trade

Once the Manchus came to power in 1644, if they regarded the European pirates as nuisances, they saw Zheng Chenggong and other Chinese pirates as serious threats to the realm. Beginning in 1652 the court promulgated a series of harsh sea bans, which

---

[44] Ritchie 1986:11–16; Pérotin-Dumon 1991:197–198; and Thomson 1994:35–39.

[45] *MQSLYB* 602a, 628b; *FJTZ* 267/38a–b; Morse 1926–1929:1/12; also see Wills 1974:35–38, 61; 1998:367–369; and Scammell 1992:649–653. By the early 1780s the region had seen the last major Western freebooter, Captain John McClary, who had plundered with complete disregard Spanish, Dutch, and Chinese merchant ships (Morse 1926–1929:2/63–64, 79).

aimed to cut off the pirates from their support on land. In rapid succession imperial decrees commanded officials in coastal areas to burn all boats, to prohibit the construction of large two-masted sea junks, and to bar the purchase of foreign-made vessels and the sale of Chinese vessels to foreigners. Chinese merchants from Shandong to Guangdong were prohibited from setting out to sea under pain of death. Even more stringent than the Ming bans, the Qing prohibited both overseas and coastal maritime trade. Still unable to curb Zheng and other pirates, between 1661 and 1662 the government adopted a scorched earth policy, forcing coastal dwellers in most of Fujian and Guangdong to relocate ten to twenty miles inland. All houses and property within the evacuation zone were destroyed, and anyone caught trying to return to the coast was beheaded. While not destroying Zheng Chenggong, these draconian measures had a devastating effect on coastal inhabitants who depended on the sea for their livelihoods. The Qing government officially severed contacts with the rest of the maritime world for the next twenty years.[46]

By the mid 1660s, the dual Qing policies of harsh maritime bans backed up with strong military force and amnesties for those pirates who surrendered began to pay off. Numerous local pirates, such as Chen Kui, as well as followers of Zheng Chenggong, particularly Shi Lang and Huang Wu, surrendered and joined with the imperial forces to fight their former comrades.[47] As the number of pirate incidents declined, in 1669 the court began allowing portions of the coastal population to return home. Then in 1684, one year after the Qing military had crushed the remnants of Zheng's heirs on Taiwan and had finally secured control over all of China, the Kangxi emperor (r. 1662–1722) rescinded nearly all of the remaining sea bans. Convinced that national security depended on the prosperity and stability of the southern coastal provinces, the imperial court legitimized the overseas and coastal junk trade and opened up several ports to foreign commerce.[48]

As the economy quickly recovered, expanded, and prospered, piracy soon diminished. Many Chinese merchants now found that

---

[46] Hsieh Kuo-ching 1932; and Ura 1954; see also Sun Guangzhe 1989:549–550; Fan I-chun 1993:239; and Huang Guosheng 2000:11–12. Although Hainan Island was not subject to this removal policy, coastal residents were nevertheless forbidden from going out to sea to fish or trade.

[47] *STDSJ* 1/60; and Wills 1979:228–229.

[48] Wills 1974:195; Viraphol 1977:55–57; Leonard 1988:230; Ng Chin-keong 1990:307–308; Cushman 1993:121–122; and Huang Guosheng 2000:18–20.

they had a vested interest to work within the system and therefore became bulwarks of support in suppressing piracy. After all, order and stability were good for both the state and business. Wealthy sea merchants began forming close ties with gentry and officials in managing port towns along the southern coast.[49] At about the same time, Western merchants began putting pressure on their home governments to suppress freebooting, and officials responded by passing stiff new anti-piracy laws and by building navies to protect their merchant ships on the oceans. European piracy soon waned in Asia and around the world. Piracy became discernable from legitimate commerce.[50]

The Seafarer-Pirates of the Mid-Qing

For most of the eighteenth century, piracy was sporadic and isolated, perpetrated by petty bands of local pirates preying on the occasional small merchant junk or fishing boat. These pirates posed no serious threat to either government or commerce.[51] Beginning in the 1780s, however, officials began noticing a sudden resurgence in the number of pirates in South China, especially around the emporiums of Canton, Chaozhou, and Amoy.[52] Piracy became such a huge problem that in 1780 the Qianlong emperor (r. 1736–1795) approved a new law specifically aimed against pirates around Canton who operated in bands of more than ten men.[53] Then over the next two decades numerous small gangs coalesced, expanded, and became better organized. Although innumerable petty bands of local pirates continued to operate in areas close to their homes, it was the large fleets of ocean bandits that came to dominate the southern coast in the first decade of the nineteenth century.

The piracy of the mid-Qing was but one of the many troubles that upset the Qing equilibrium and set in motion a long period of social upheavals culminating in the Taiping and other mid-nineteenth-century rebellions. At the end of the eighteenth

---

[49] Ng Chin-keong 1983:93–94.

[50] Ritchie 1986:138–159; and Thomson 1994:145–147.

[51] Liao Fengde 1986:198–199; Chen Xiyu 1991:359; and Matsuura 1995:109–110.

[52] See JJD (28259) QL 45.9.18; (28360) QL 45.9.27; (28881) QL 45.11.22; *GZDQL* (QL 44.5.16):47/756–758; (QL 47.11.5):53/659–660; (QL 51.10.18):62/17–18; (QL 54.4.17): 66/722; and XKTB (92) QL48.3.25, (83) QL 54.11.22, (69) QL 55.3.23.

[53] LFZZ (2825) QL 45.9.18; for a fuller discussion of this law see Antony 1988:135–139.

century, political malfeasance, fiscal crisis, and military decay plagued the dynasty. Preoccupied with the Lin Shuangwen Rebellion on Taiwan (1787–1788), the Miao disturbances in Sichuan, Hubei, and Guizhou (1795), the White Lotus Rebellion in central China (1795–1804), and the Triad uprising in Guangdong (1802–1803), as well as the Tâyson Rebellion in Vietnam (1771–1802), the Qing court at first paid little attention to the pirates along the coast. Large amounts of money and troops were diverted from coastal defense to deal with what the government considered to be more serious disturbances on land. By the time officials turned their attention to quelling the pirates, many petty gangs had already organized themselves into several menacing fleets.[54]

During these years both Guangdong and Fujian were again hit by an unusually large number of natural disasters that damaged crops and created severe food shortages. Environmental historians Tang Wenya and Xin Hong have shown that the years from 1790 to 1869 were particularly active ones for typhoons along the Guangdong coast.[55] Between 1775 and 1810, as Table 3 shows, there were twenty-nine years of famines, the most extensive and damaging were those in 1778, 1786–1789, 1795–1796, and 1809–1810. In 1795, for instance, the cost of rice shot up anywhere from double to ten times the normal cost, which in real terms meant that a peck of rice equaled five months' to two years' wages for hired sailors.[56] During the height of the pirate upheaval between 1802 and 1810, the Canton delta experienced food shortages every year except 1807. As in the past, major natural catastrophes spawned banditry and piracy.

Local Pirates and Vietnamese Privateers, 1780–1802

The large-scale piracy in South China during the mid-Qing had its origins in the 1780s, when over the next several decades many of the petty pirate gangs gradually transformed into several huge, well-organized fleets. The patronage of the Tâyson rebels in Vietnam was crucial in this transformation in Guangdong, as Dian Murray has shown, but had little effect on developments in neighboring Fujian.[57] The rebels, who needed both money and men for

---

[54] Wen Chengzhi 1842:1b; and Yano 1926:100–101.

[55] Cited in Qiao Shengxi 1993:679–691.

[56] On the wages of sailors see chapter 3. According to the Zhangpu gazetteer (*ZPXZ* 1699), in the early nineteenth century the normal price for rice in good years was approximately one tael (*liang*) per peck.

[57] The Tâyson rebellion was a massive peasant uprising led by three brothers,

their cause, actively recruited Chinese pirates. Even after the Qianlong emperor recognized one of the Tâyson leaders as "king" of Vietnam in 1788, the latter continued to pursue a risky double-edged policy of sending tribute missions to the Qing court in Beijing while simultaneously backing piratical raids along the China coast. Rebel leaders guaranteed Chinese pirates safe harbors, supplied them with ships and weapons, and rewarded them with official ranks and titles so they would engage in piracy as a means of obtaining revenue. Every spring and summer from about 1790 to 1802, when the Tâyson insurgents were finally overthrown, fleets of "boat bandits" (*tingfei*) left their bases along the Sino-Vietnamese border for Chinese waters. They returned each autumn laden with booty, which they shared with their Tâyson patrons.[58]

Encouraged by the Tâyson regime, several talented pirate leaders, such as Mo Guanfu, Zheng Qi, Wang Guili, and Wushi Er, began the long process of building huge fleets out of the numerous heretofore small independent gangs. A poor fisherman from Suiqi county in western Guangdong, Mo Guanfu had begun his outlaw career in 1787, when, after being abducted by pirates, he decided to join them. In the following year, he and Zheng Qi both received commissions as Tâyson generals to fight the royalist forces in Vietnam. By 1796 Mo commanded more than a thousand men and was promoted with the title King of the Eastern Sea (*Donghai wang*).[59] Zheng Qi, who had been born into a family of notorious pirates, had by 1800 assembled a fleet of more than two hundred vessels, the largest single force in the region at the time. In the next year he was promoted to minister of war (*dasima*) in the Tâyson regime.[60] Wang Guili, who also hailed from Guangdong, joined the Tâyson cause in 1794, took a Vietnamese wife, cut

which began in 1771 in Binh Dinh province. In 1778, with the rebels in control of much of central and south Vietnam, the reigning Lê emperor requested help from the Qing court, and the Qianlong emperor sent a military expedition to quell the rebellion. But when the rebels defeated the Chinese army, the Qianlong emperor quickly negotiated a settlement and recognized the new Tâyson regime. By 1802, however, the rebellion had been crushed. On the Tâyson rebellion, see Hall 1958:365–371; on the ambiguities of the Sino-Vietnamese relationship between 1788 and 1790, see Lam 1968; and on the rebels and their pirate connections, see Katsuta 1967:28–34; Murray 1987:32–56; and Matsuura 1995:120–123, 132–137.

[58] GZD (780) JQ 1.6.16, (1643 *fupian*) JQ 1.12.7, (1763) JQ 1.12.29, (3347) JQ 2.11.12; and *SCSX* 103/3a–b.

[59] GZD (8517) JQ 7.7.14.

[60] *DGXZ* 33/21a; and Katsuta 1967:36.

Table 3
Famines and Rice Prices in Fujian and Guangdong, 1775–1810

Year	Area of famine	Price of rice (*liang/dou*)	Area reporting price
1775	Fuzhou	1.6	Lianjiang
1776	Fuzhou		
1777	Guangzhou, Gaozhou		
1778	Guangzhou, Gaozhou, Shaoqing, Huizhou, Taiwan	4.0	Dongguan
1779	Shaoqing		
1780	Fuzhou	1.6	Lianjiang
1781	Fuzhou	1.6	Lianjiang
1784	Fuzhou	1.8	Lianjiang
1785	Huizhou		
1786	Guangzhou, Shaoqing, Huizhou, Chaozhou	5.0	Nanhai
1787	Guangzhou, Shaoqing, Huizhou	6.0	Xinhui
1788	Guangzhou, Shaoqing, Quanzhou, Fuzhou, Taiwan	3.5 10.0	Gaoming Danshui
1789	Guangzhou, Shaoqing, Hainan, Zhangzhou		
1790	Zhangzhou		
1791	Zhangzhou		
1794	Guangzhou, Gaozhou		
1795	Guangzhou, Shaoqing, Huizhou, Chaozhou, Zhangzhou, Quanzhou, Fuzhou, Taiwan	3.3 5.6 10.0	Chaoyang Taiwan Zhangpu
1796	Gaozhou, Zhangzhou, Quanzhou, Taiwan	10.0 3.0	Zhangpu Nan'an
1797	Gaozhou		
1798	Guangzhou		
1800	Guangzhou		
1802	Guangzhou		
1803	Guangzhou		
1804	Guangzhou		
1805	Guangzhou, Fuzhou	2.0	Lianjiang
1806	Guangzhou, Taiwan	6.4	Xinhui
1808	Guangzhou	4.0	Xinhui
1809	Guangzhou, Shaozhou	5.8	Xinhui
1810	Guangzhou, Gaozhou, Fuzhou	4.0	Xinhui

Sources: *STDSJ* 1/81; *LJXZ* 3/54a–55b; *ZPXZ* 1697–1699; Lian Heng [1921] 1983:1/53–55; Wang Shiqing 1958:17–18; and Qiao Shengxi 1993:546–553.

off his queue, and became a general in command of his own fleet.[61] Wushi Er joined the Tâyson rebels in the 1790s and was the last major pirate to be quelled in 1810. About 1797 the Tâyson ruler awarded him with the title Great General Who Pacifies the Sea (*Jinghai dajiangjun*).[62] Figure 6 outlines the affiliations among the major Guangdong and Fujian pirate gangs between 1795 and 1810.

At the same time, in Fujian and Zhejiang there were a number of local pirate gangs, most notably the Phoenix Tail under Zhuang Youmei, the Water Bay under Lin Yasun, and the Bamboo Yellow under Jiang Wenwu, as well as two smaller ones led by Cai Qian and Zhu Fen. Though independent, they sometimes cooperated with one another and with the Vietnamese pirates for joint raids. At other times rivalries among pirates escalated into violent confrontations.[63]

In 1800 Zhuang Youmei, Lin Yasun, and several other pirate chiefs combined with a Tâyson fleet commanded by Wang Guili for an expedition against the fishing fleets that gathered each year in late summer around Zhoushan in northern Zhejiang. Before they could put their plans into operation disaster struck. First, in August, fighting broke out between Zhuang and Lin, ending all cooperation between the two gangs. Then later that month, a violent typhoon suddenly arose and wrecked most of what remained of the pirate armada, which had anchored off the Songmen coast at a place known locally as the Hall of the Dragon King. A delighted Jiaqing emperor (r. 1796–1820), upon hearing how this "divine wind" (*shengfeng*) destroyed the pirates, immediately ordered the construction of temples in Songmen honoring the Empress of Heaven and the Dragon King (Longwang).[64] Weakened by the divine wind incident and a resurgent Qing navy in Zhejiang under Li Changgeng, many of the pirate leaders over the next two years were either killed in battle, captured and executed, or surrendered (see Figure 6).[65]

Despite the setbacks in Fujian and Zhejiang, in the spring of 1801 Zheng Qi, Mo Guanfu, and Wushi Er organized a new fleet, which set sail from Vietnam. After plundering villages on the

---

[61] T. Chang 1983:68–69.
[62] GZD (3728) JQ 3.2.19, and (10138) JQ 13.3.2.
[63] Matsuura 1995:144.
[64] GZD (5520) JQ 5.7.6; *MXTZ* addendum 1/12a–13b; and T. Chang 1983:65–68.
[65] Huang Dianquan 1958:76–77.

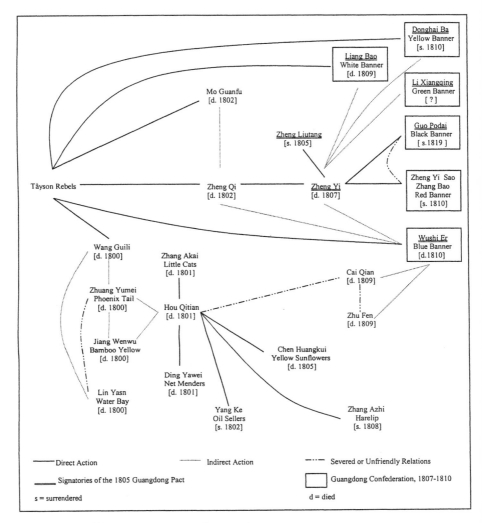

Figure 6. Affiliations among Guangdong and Fujian Pirate Associations.

Leizhou peninsula, they robbed and seized eighteen salt boats in Shuidong harbor in Dianbai county and plundered a customs office and several fishing boats in the vicinity. These incidents were followed, on September 22, during the Mid-Autumn Festival, with an attempted raid on the walled city of Dianbai. As we have seen in chapter 1, the city was saved at the last moment when a sudden storm arose, dispersing the pirates and ruining their plans.[66] Finally, before returning home that winter, they sailed unmolested all the way up the coast to Haifeng county in northeastern Guangdong, where they again plundered a fleet of salt junks.[67]

In the meantime the situation had become bleak back in Vietnam for their Tâyson supporters. By 1801 Tâyson power had diminished greatly, as royalist forces continually regained strength and reconquered territory. As the rebels' defeat became imminent, more than a thousand pirates abandoned their Tâyson benefactors and returned allegiance (*toucheng*) to the Chinese emperor.[68] After returning from their successful raid on the Guangdong coast, Mo Guanfu and several other leaders were captured by royalist troops and turned over to Qing authorities for execution.[69] These events were followed in August 1802 by the death of Zheng Qi, who was reportedly killed in battle off the Vietnamese coast.[70] By then the royalist forces had retaken Hanoi, captured the Tâyson pretender, and sent the bewildered pirates fleeing back to China.

Consolidation of Guangdong Pirates under Zheng Yi, 1802–1807

From 1802 until his death in a typhoon in the Southern Ocean in 1807, the most formidable pirate leader in Guangdong was Zheng Yi, a cousin of Zheng Qi. Both Zhengs belonged to a notorious family of professional pirates, which for nearly a century and a half were the predominant pirates in the Canton delta. They traced their beginnings to the mid-seventeenth century with Zheng Jian, who hailed from Fujian and was a subordinate of Zheng Chenggong. After Zheng Chenggong invaded Taiwan in 1661, Zheng Jian took his family to Guangdong and settled around

---

[66] GZD (6211) JQ 6.9.23; and (6212) JQ 6.9.23.

[67] GZD (7045) JQ 6.12.22.

[68] GZD (5618) JQ 6.7.19; and (6211 *fupian*) JQ 6.9.23.

[69] GZD (8517) JQ 7.7.14; Xu Wentang and Xie Qiyi 2000:35; see also GZD (8978) JQ 7.10.11.

[70] Xu Wentang and Xie Qiyi 2000:36; also see Katsuta 1967:36.

Dapeng harbor near Hong Kong to engage in fishing and extortion. Two descendants, the brothers Zheng Lianfu and Zheng Lianchang, carried on the family tradition as sea bandits. They in turn were followed by their sons, Zheng Qi and Zheng Yi, who had both joined the Tâyson rebels. After the death of Zheng Qi in 1802, Zheng Yi took command of his cousin's forces.[71]

Zheng Yi continued the work of reorganizing the disparate pirate gangs into a loose coalition that by 1804 boasted more than ten thousand followers and hundreds of junks. Using his family connections and personal relationships he was able to enlarge his influence over several important Cantonese pirate bands. In the next year, seven of the most powerful pirate leaders—Zheng Yi, Wushi Er, Donghai Ba, Liang Bao, Zheng Liutang, Guo Podai, and Li Xiangqing—met and signed a pact (*yue*) intended to impose law and order over the unruly freebooters.[72] By 1805, they were able to establish new bases along Guangdong's coast and outer islands and to extend their hegemony over most of the fishing, salt, and coastal trade, as well as over many villages, through a formal protection racket based on extortion, bribery, and terrorism.[73]

Not limiting their operations to the open seas, the pirates also made more frequent raids on coastal villages and penetrated deep into the Canton delta. In April 1803, Donghai Ba plundered several villages and kidnapped thirty people along the coast in Haikang county on the Leizhou peninsula. Other pirate bands raided markets and villages on the coast between Shicheng and Wuchuan counties. In the winter of 1805, more than three hundred pirates under Liang Bao's command attacked the Chi'ao fort in Huilai county, where they made off with cannon and other weapons before burning the post to the ground. Then in the summer and autumn, the ocean bandits pillaged several villages, markets, and forts in the Canton delta in Xinhui, Panyu, Shunde, Xiangshan, and Dongguan counties. So relentless had these piratical raids become that in 1805 several British observers lamented about the large number of villages between Canton and Macao that had been looted and burned down by pirates.[74]

---

[71] On Zheng Qi and Zheng Yi see Hu Jieyu 1959:151–152, 160–161; Xiao Guojian 1978:18–19, and 1986:153–154, 218–219; and Murray 1987:63–65.

[72] ZPZZ (1058) JQ 10.11.22; and Ye Zhiru 1989. This document is translated into English in Murray 1987:57–59.

[73] *DGXZ* 33/22b. See the further discussion in chapter 5.

[74] ZPZZ (1016) JQ 9.2.3; *Gaozhou fuzhi* 1889:49/41b–42a; *NYC* 12/25a–29b, 69a–b, 13/20b, 67b–68a; and Morse 1926–1929:3/8.

At the same time, there was an increase in pirate attacks on Western vessels trading at Canton that at times seriously interrupted trade. While pirates seldom assailed the large, well-armed Indiamen, it was open season on the smaller passage boats and lighters plying between Macao and Canton. In 1804 the East India Company reported that because piracy had become so rampant it was no longer safe to supply its ships anchored near Lintin Island. Pirates also threatened Macao on several occasions, and once, in 1804, even reduced the city to only a few days' food supply. In the next year two American merchants, en route from Macao to Canton, were attacked by pirates and narrowly escaped with their lives. Then in 1806 pirates plundered a passage boat and kidnapped Mr. J. Turner, the chief officer of the English merchant ship *Tay*.[75]

The Dominance of Cai Qian in Fujian, 1802–1809

The decimation of several major Fujian and Zhejiang gangs, as well as the demise of the Tâyson pirates, between 1800 and 1802, gave Cai Qian a chance to gain dominance in the region. He quickly moved to absorb the scattered remnants of the Phoenix Tail, Bamboo Yellow, and Water Bay gangs, whose leaders had been killed in 1800, and then he strengthened his own position by murdering a renegade subordinate named Hou Qitian in 1801. After Hou's death, his followers split into several small independent bands, but only the Yellow Sunflower and Harelip gangs survived beyond 1802 (see Figure 6).[76]

Cai Qian was born in Tongan, a coastal county near the entrepôt of Amoy, probably in 1751. Some sources described him as a rebellious youth and discontented with his station in life. Another source mentioned that he was boastful and good at martial arts. Other sources pointed out that his family was poor and that he was orphaned as a child and had to sell sugarcane to earn a living. Later he traveled around Fujian from port to port taking whatever jobs he could find. He worked intermittently as a hired laborer, cotton bower, and net mender for local fishermen. By the early 1790s, when he was already a mature adult in his forties, he became a pirate, and by 1800 commanded a gang consisting of about a hundred vessels.[77]

---

[75] Morse 1926–1929:2/424, 3/7–8, 32, 63; and Montalto de Jesus 1926:137.

[76] *XMZ* 675; T. Chang 1983:71–72; and Guan Wenfa 1994:95–96.

[77] *MXTZ* addendum 1/55a–57a; *XPXZ dashi*/19b–20a; *XMZ* 675; also see Huang

Cai Qian's wife also played an important role in his rise to power. Known to us simply as Matron Cai Qian (Cai Qian Ma), she was born in Pingyuan, Zhejiang. If Cai Qian had a reputation as a womanizer, his wife had one as the village slut. Sold to a barber by her first husband, she was later sold for a third time to Cai Qian for a large sum of money. Even after her marriage to Cai Qian, she reportedly kept a harem from among the male captives. Like her husband she too was addicted to opium. Aboard ship she proved to be a skillful and resourceful wife and a cunning and fierce fighter. According to Wang Songchen's account, she even commanded her own vessels with crews of women warriors (*niangzijun*). She died in 1804 in battle with the Qing navy off Taiwan.[78]

As Cai Qian's power increased so did the scope of his activities and his ambitions. From island bases, such as Qinjiao and Gantang, he sold "safe conduct passes" (*mianjie piao*) to fishermen and merchants and launched raids on Taiwan and along the coast from Fujian to Shandong. In 1803, for example, after a brief foray on the Taiwan coast, he sailed to Jiangsu, where he robbed thirty-six merchant junks. In the next summer his fleet plundered the Taiwanese port of Luermen and later robbed several rice junks bound for Amoy. Then in the autumn of 1804, he briefly joined forces with Zhu Fen for an expedition into Zhejiang waters, where they seized several fishing boats and a sugar junk en route to Tianjin. Soon afterward the alliance came to a sudden end when Li Changgeng, the Qing naval commander in Zhejiang, routed their joint flotilla and the two chieftains began quarrelling about the defeat.[79]

At the height of his strength, between 1805 and 1806, Cai Qian made repeated attacks on Taiwan, intent on occupying the island as his base. At this time he commanded about five thousand men and had more than a hundred ships. Receiving support from bandits and various dissident groups on the island, Cai Qian launched attacks at Danshui, Zhanghua, Luermen, and Fengshan. With apparent popular support on the island, he proclaimed himself the Majestic Warrior King Who Subdues the Sea (*Zhenhai*

Dianquan 1958:76; T. Chang 1983:72–73; Matsuura 1995:144–145; and Zheng Guangnan 1998:319–320.

[78] *MXTZ* addendum 1/56b–57a; *XMZ* 675; and T. Chang 1983:74–75. One source claimed that she died in 1809.

[79] *MQSLWB* 469a, 472a–474a, 480a, 526a–559b, 576b; *MXTZ* addendum 1/14b–15b; and *XPXZ dashi*/20a.

weiwu wang). In preparation for founding a new dynasty, he performed sacrifices to Heaven and Earth and began distributing
titles and ranks among his lieutenants, as well as among bandit
and rebel supporters. Before he could don the imperial robes,
however, his forces were defeated in 1806 in a series of battles
with the Qing military and local militia.[80]

Forced to abandon thousands of comrades on Taiwan and with
his fleet reduced to fewer than thirty vessels, Cai Qian slipped
back to Fujian. After purchasing new ships and supplies at
Shuiao, he continued for the next several years with forays around
Taiwan and Zhejiang, constantly pursued by Li Changgeng. To
make matters worse, in 1806 the navy destroyed his base on Qinjiao Island, and between 1806 and 1809 Governor-General Alinbao
imposed a strict embargo along the Zhejiang and Fujian coasts to
sever Cai's support there. As food and supplies were depleted,
the pirates had to rely as never before on plunder as their chief
source of provisions. In desperation in April 1808 Cai fled to
Guangdong, where he joined Wushi Er and Zheng Yi Sao for a
joint expedition to Vietnam.[81] After resupplying his vessels Cai
returned to Fujian that summer, only to meet with disaster. Even
the death of Li Changgeng, early in 1808, did not halt the momentum of the imperial forces, and in October 1809, Cai Qian was
killed in battle off Wenzhou in Zhejiang. Without their gallant
leader the remnants of his battered organization quickly scattered.[82]

The Rise and Fall of Zhu Fen, 1802–1809

As the Xiapu gazetteer informs us, in Fujian Cai Qian was the
most imposing pirate, and Zhu Fen was a close second.[83] Zhu was
a native of Zhangzhou in southern Fujian, and although his family
was somewhat well-to-do, he preferred to associate with rascals.
He was something of a local bully with connections to several
pirate chiefs. To avoid arrest after being reported to officials by

---

[80] *MQSLWB* 498a–b, 515a–517a, 527a–528b, 531a–b; also see Huang Dianquan
1958:78–79; T. Chang 1983:94–107; Ye Zheru 1988:833–835; Guan Wenfa 1994:99;
and Matsuura 1995:147–149.

[81] Xu Wentang and Xie Qiyi 2000:44.

[82] On these events see GZD (1944) JQ 13.r5.12, (10867) JQ 13.5.25, (11730) JQ
13.8.7; SYD, JQ 12.3.23, JQ 14.9.12; *MQSLWB* 513a–514b, 519a–b, 525b–526a, 580a,
634a; *MXTZ* addendum 1/16a–b; and *XPXZ dashi*/20a.

[83] *XPXZ dashi*/19b.

his fellow villagers, Zhu Fen, his wife, and his family fled to sea to become pirates. By 1800 he commanded a fleet of several tens of boats, calling himself the King of the Southern Seas (*Hainan wang*).[84]

Although Zhu Fen cooperated on occasion with Cai Qian and other pirates, his organization was autonomous. After breaking off the alliance with Cai Qian in 1804, Zhu plundered the area around Amoy and Jinmen. In the next year, while Cai Qian was busy in Taiwan, Zhu attacked shipping around Zhaoan and Yunxiao in conjunction with contingents from Wushi Er's fleet. In 1805 and 1808, Zhu Fen remained active on the coasts of Fujian and eastern Guangdong and made several forays around Taiwan and Zhejiang. At this time he had a fleet of more than a hundred ships and as many as four thousand followers. He was mortally wounded in battle with the Qing navy in Guangdong in early 1809. Soon afterward, his younger brother, Zhu Wo, took over what was left of the fleet and surrendered to the Qing.[85]

Zhang Bao and Guangdong's Pirate Confederation, 1807–1810

Back in Guangdong, the pirates had by early 1807 withstood the Qing extermination campaigns and had become the virtual masters of the South China Sea. Even the death of their most able leader, Zheng Yi, in that year did not stop their momentum. The leadership passed into the hands of his widow, Shi Xianggu, better known as Zheng Yi Sao (Wife of Zheng Yi), and the young and ambitious Zhang Bao. Under their combined leadership Guangdong pirates reached the apex of their strength and power.

Zheng Yi Sao, who has been described as a veritable dragon lady among the ocean bandits, had been a prostitute on one of Canton's floating brothels before she married Zheng Yi in 1801. Alongside her husband she endured the same hardships aboard a pirate vessel, and after 1802 played an important role in helping her husband consolidate his dominance over the burgeoning pirate coalition. When her husband suddenly died in 1807 she did not quietly step aside but instead maneuvered quickly to assure support from the Zheng family in her own bid for power.[86] In taking

[84] *XMZ* 675–676; also see Katsuta 1967:37–40; T. Chang 1983:166–167; Matsuura 1995:143; and Zheng Guangnan 1998:324.

[85] GZD (14382) JQ 14.5.28; *MQSLWB* 492a–b, 525a, 538b, 540a, 578a; *MXTZ* addendum 1/77a–b; and *XMZ* 676.

[86] On Zheng Yi Sao's rise to power see Murray 1981; and Zheng Guangnan 1998:305–309.

command she was assisted by the twenty-one-year-old Zhang Bao, her husband's adopted son and her paramour.

A native of the port town of Jiangmen in Xinhui county, Zhang Bao was born into a Dan fishing family. At age fifteen, Zheng Yi's gang kidnapped him while he was out fishing with his father. He quickly came to the attention of the chief, who adopted him into the Zheng family after a homosexual liaison and made him his protégé. Soon Zhang Bao was given command of his own vessel, where he ably demonstrated a knack for both seamanship and brigandage. Within weeks of Zheng Yi's death he was at the side of Zheng Yi Sao, sharing her boudoir and all the power. By 1808, Chinese and foreigner alike recognized Zhang Bao as the most dauntless and powerful pirate operating along the coast of Guangdong.[87]

By 1807 the Guangdong pirate confederation had stabilized at six large, self-sustaining fleets, each flying a separate colored banner. The Red Banner fleet, with more than 17,000 followers and several hundreds of vessels, was the most formidable. Zheng Yi Sao and Zhang Bao were its leaders. Guo Podai commanded the Black Banner fleet, which became the second most powerful group with 6,000–10,000 men and more than a hundred ships. Wushi Er, from Haikang county, led the Blue Banner fleet with its several thousand men. Wu Zhiqing, commonly called Donghai Ba or sometimes Wu Shiyizhi (Eleven-Finger Wu) because of an obvious birth defect, led the Yellow Banner fleet. The White Banner fleet's leader was Liang Bao, also known as Zongbing Bao because of his earlier commission as a Tâyson general. Finally, Li Xiangqing, who had the curious nickname of Hama Yang (Toad Rearer), commanded the smallest fleet under the Green Banner (see Figure 6).[88]

Throughout 1807 and 1808, Zhang Bao and the other chiefs had virtual control over the Guangdong coast and even many inland villages and market towns. They openly levied duties on fishermen and merchants and attacked Chinese and even foreign vessels at will. In the waters off Macao, as we can see in Figure 7, groups of pirate boats often joined forces to attack isolated merchant junks. Although the aggressive sea war (*haizhan*) in Zhejiang and Fujian had produced results under Li Changgeng and his

---

[87] Wen Chengzhi 1842:2a; also see Ye Linfeng 1970; Xiao Guojian 1995:145–158; and Matsuura 1995:141–142.

[88] *PYXZ* 22/15a–b; and Wen Chengzhi 1842:1b–2a.

Figure 7. Battling with Pirate Junks off Macao. Source: William Dean Howells and Thomas Perry, comps., *Library of Universal Adventures by Sea and Land* (1881).

successors, in Guangdong the naval campaigns were utter failures. Finally, in early 1809, a frustrated Jiaqing emperor sent in a troubleshooter, Bai Ling, who had previously served as governor of Guangdong in 1805 and more recently as judicial commissioner of Fujian in 1807. He was an old hand at dealing with pirates. Capable and experienced, he immediately set about to cut off the pirates from their sources of food and supplies on land. He not only ordered a coastal blockade, but also directed the navy to step up its campaigns and encouraged local gentry to establish militia and fortifications for self-defense.[89] The impact of Bai Ling's measures was heightened by a severe famine in 1809, which affected most of the province, especially the Canton delta.[90]

The blockade and famine created, for the first time, great hardships for these Guangdong pirates, who soon found themselves in dire need of food and other supplies. They responded by stepping up their attacks. Suddenly pirates began appearing in inland waters along the Guangdong coast searching for victuals and plunder. In June famished pirates under Wushi Er and Donghai Ba raided the ports at Xingping and Chishui in Dianbai county, and in midsummer other gangs pillaged the port of Zhanglin in Chaozhou.[91] In the Pearl River delta pirates under Zhang Bao, Zheng Yi Sao, and Guo Podai robbed towns, markets, and villages from Macao to the gates of Canton. Near Shakou Zhang Bao's band, needing food, plundered a Guangxi junk laden with grain, and a few months later they stole several thousand piculs of rice at Fojiao market. By late summer starving pirates even went ashore to help themselves to fields of newly ripened rice.[92]

Then suddenly, at the apparent height of its power, the pirate confederation totally collapsed in early 1810. The Qing embargo, naval campaigns, and militia resistance, while not in themselves enough to crush the pirates, nevertheless wore down their resistance and determination. Also in 1809, the deaths of Cai Qian and Zhu Fen, as well as the death of Liang Bao, commander of the White Banner fleet, further isolated the pirates remaining in Guangdong. With the pirates sufficiently weakened, the imperial

---

[89] GZD (13301) JQ 14.2.10, (13511) JQ 14.3.5, (14085) JQ 14.5.1; *NHXZ* 14/21a; and *DGXZ* 33/25a.

[90] *GZFZ* 81/16b; *Gaozhou fuzhi* 1889:49/44a; *XSXZ* 1879:15/4a–5a; and *Chaolian xiangzhi* 1946:283.

[91] GZD (14384) JQ 14.5.28; (19865) n.d.; and Ye Xianen 1989:225.

[92] GZD (14384) JQ 14.5.28; (14804) JQ 14.7.15; *PYXZ* 22/14b–15a; *DGXZ* 33/25a–b; and *Chinese Repository* 1834:3/73–74.

court initiated a new pacification policy, coaxing pirates to surrender in exchange for pardons and rewards.[93]

At this point the antagonisms between Guo Podai and Zhang Bao, which had been festering since Zheng Yi's death in 1807, came to a head. After a brief skirmish with Zhang Bao's fleet in January 1810, Guo Podai quickly surrendered with nearly six thousand followers. His surrender set into motion a spate of surrenders by lesser chiefs, culminating in the surrender of Zhang Bao and Zheng Yi Sao in April, with more than seventeen thousand followers. Both Zhang Bao and Guo Podai received naval commissions and were sent to fight the remaining pirates in southwestern Guangdong. That summer Donghai Ba surrendered and Wushi Er was captured and executed. What remained of the confederation quickly crumbled. For all practical purposes the high tide of large-scale piracy in China had come to an end.[94]

Although each of the three pirate waves was a unique event that grew out of distinct historical circumstances, they shared several features in common. Each wave began with upsurges in petty piracy during hard times resulting from famines, wars, or economic disruptions. Because in each case the state was preoccupied with other pressing matters—Mongols and Manchus on the northern borders during the middle and late Ming and internal rebellions and campaigns in Vietnam in the middle Qing—officials were slow to react to piracy on the southern littoral, and consequently it quickly grew out of control for several decades. In each case large pirate leagues gained hegemonic power along China's southern coast.

When large-scale piracy did subside it was as much the result of governmental policies as it was of community self-defense measures and internal dissensions among the pirates themselves. The focus of state policies was an ancient strategy known as annihilation and appeasement (*jiaofu*), a carrot and stick approach whereby military campaigns were coupled with liberal offers of amnesties and rewards. While these methods seldom eradicated the pirates, they nevertheless did severely debilitate them and

---

[93] For a fuller discussion of the pacification policies see Antony 1994.

[94] Xu Wentang and Xie Qiyi 2000:47–48. Most studies have emphasized the internal dissension between Guo Podai and Zhang Bao as the chief cause of the pirate collapse (e.g., Hu Jieyu 1959:155–156; Ye Linfeng 1970:26–34; Murray 1987:147–148; and Xiao Guojian 1995:148–149). For a recent reevaluation that challenges this assumption see Antony 1992.

caused rifts within their ranks. After surrendering, pirate leaders, such as Shi Lang and Zhang Bao, were then effectively used by the government to fight their former comrades.

Over the late imperial era the nature of piracy itself had changed. Not only did we see the disappearance of Western pirates in China's waters in the eighteenth century, but also the virtual disappearance of the great Chinese merchant-pirates. During the first two waves a major characteristic of piracy was its link with trading operations. Piracy and trade were inseparable. In the Ming and early Qing, because of the highly restrictive maritime policies, piracy became the most important and viable means for conducting seaborne trade. The sea bans had made criminals out of merchants and seafarers, who continued to trade in violation of the laws. By the eighteenth century, however, this had all changed. In 1684, the Qing court had broken with the past to legalize and even encourage sea trade. With trade open and legal, piracy was transformed. The great merchant-pirates of the earlier epochs, such as Wang Zhi and Hong Dizhen, became less in evidence, replaced in the mid-Qing by commoner seafarer-pirates, such as Cai Qian and Zhang Bao. Sharp distinctions were made between legitimate commerce and piracy.

THREE

Prosperity and Poverty in Maritime South China

Different from the land-bounded interior, South China's maritime region had its own distinct economy and social customs. The littoral attuned itself much more to the rhythms of sea, wind, and monsoon than it ever did to the rhythms of the soil. Although intimately linked to the interior, the coast supported a different and diverse sort of economic complex. If for the most part the people living inland depended on agriculture for their livelihoods, those living along the shoreline were dependent upon the sea. Though the late imperial state often regarded the sea as a pestering nuisance, by the 1680s Qing rulers had come to cautiously promote the maritime economy as vital to national security. Maritime trade brought growth, vitality, and prosperity to the entire region, but its benefits were unevenly distributed. As a result, by the late eighteenth century, South China's maritime world evidenced striking contrasts and contradictions: fabulous wealth in the midst of extreme privation, sharpening divisions and anxieties between seafarers and landsmen, and the indiscriminate mingling of respectable people (*liangmin*) with wicked villains (*jiangui*).[1]

The rise of large-scale piracy and its interconnections with maritime society in the late eighteenth and early nineteenth centuries can best be understood in this context. The social and economic changes occurring over the Qing era were unprecedented and dynamic, and although they fostered growth and prosperity, they also produced dislocation, economic privation, and social unrest. This chapter, which examines socioeconomic changes during the eighteenth century, is divided into two sections. The first explores the commercial growth and prosperity of South China's maritime economy by examining the overseas and domestic seaborne trade

---

[1] *SCSX* 12/13b.

and the fishing industry. The second section considers the contradictions of poverty amidst plenty, the gap between rich and poor, and the hardships of being a sailor and fisherman. What effect did population growth have on the livelihoods of seafarers? What sorts of misfortunes and dangers were common to work at sea? How did the division of labor and the wage system at sea sustain the uneven distribution of wealth? How did bosses, shopkeepers, and fish dealers exploit the labor of seamen? The answers to these questions help to explain the paradoxes between rich and poor in the age of prosperity.

Commercialization and Prosperity

In his *New Discourses on Guangdong*, first published in 1700, the Qing scholar Qu Dajun captured the quintessence of the most southerly of China's maritime provinces with these simple words: "Guangdong is a kingdom of water; many people need boats to make a living."[2] It was the same in neighboring Fujian, where the sea furnished more than half of the coastal population with jobs.[3] During the late imperial era, as the population leaped forward and farmland became increasingly scarce, the sea provided a natural outlet for the excess population, and consequently it steadily grew in importance. Hundreds of thousands of people found jobs as sailors on merchant and fishing junks, as well as in auxiliary occupations as traders, brokers, shopkeepers, boatbuilders, salt producers, ship's chandlers, stevedores, and the like. Maritime trade also stimulated local handicraft industries and the commercialization of agriculture.[4] As the Chenghai gazetteer neatly explained, "Farmers, artisans, and merchants all rely on boats for work."[5] For coastal dwellers the sea became their fields, their source of sustenance.[6] As early as the sixteenth century many coastal communities in Fujian and Guangdong had already become entirely dependent on the sea for survival.

---

2 Qu Dajun [1700] 1985:395.
3 Chen Xiyu 1991:269.
4 *XMZ* 644; *ZZFZ* 33/64b–65a; Williams [1895] 1966:2/61; also see discussions in Rawski 1972:57–100; Chen Xiyu 1991:266–269; and Cushman 1993:99.
5 Cited in Ye Xianen 1989:212.
6 *DBXZ* 14/43a; *FQXZ* 488; and *HFXA fengsu*/4b.

The Entrepôts of Canton, Chaozhou, and Amoy

By the end of the eighteenth century South China's maritime trading system was fully developed. The emporiums at Canton, Chaozhou, and Amoy were major distribution centers, the hubs of an enormous maritime network. Between 1735 and 1812, Guangdong and Fujian handled as much as 75 percent of China's seaborne foreign and domestic trade.[7] Canton and the entire Pearl River estuary became one of the busiest harbors in the world.[8] Besides the city of Canton itself, the delta included other major ports at Huangpu (Whampao), Macao, Jiangmen, and Foshan. In 1703, Alexander Hamilton, captain of an English merchantman, crowed about the bustling entrepôt: "There is no Day in the Year but shews 5,000 sail of trading Jonks, besides small Boats for other Services, lying before the City."[9] Chaozhou harbor, at the mouth of the Han River, accommodated several tens of ports, of which Chenghai was the most important. An early-nineteenth-century visitor described the harbor as one of the busiest and best in Guangdong. It was also Amoy's chief commercial rival.[10] At that time Amoy had more than a thousand merchant junks active in the overseas and coastal trade.[11] So prosperous was the port that it was widely known as the "city of silver." The Qing scholar Liang Zhangju wrote in 1796: "Amoy was crowded with *yangchuan* [ocean junks]. The merchants were prosperous. Beautiful scenery and splendid homes were everywhere. It was the richest city in the south."[12] When Charles Gutzlaff visited the city in 1832, he not only praised its "excellent harbour," but also declared it still "one of the greatest emporiums of the empire, and one of the most important markets in Asia."[13]

A web of trade routes linked the principal ports of Canton, Amoy, and Chaozhou with distant parts of the Chinese empire and far-flung ports around the globe. Sea-lanes spanned local, regional, and international markets. At the end of the eighteenth century, as Figure 8 shows, trade routes fanned out in all directions from these three key ports. One route went northward to

---

[7] Fan I-chun 1993:241–242.

[8] See Deng Duanben 1993.

[9] Morse 1926–1929:1/104.

[10] *CHXZ* 6/8a–b; Gutzlaff 1834:87; Matsuura 1983:627; Ye Xianen 1989:186–187, 213–214; and Ng Chin-keong 1990:312.

[11] *XMZ* 180; also see Ng Chin-keong 1983, 1990; and Chen Guodong 1991.

[12] Cited in Ng Chin-keong 1990:309.

[13] Gutzlaff 1834:176.

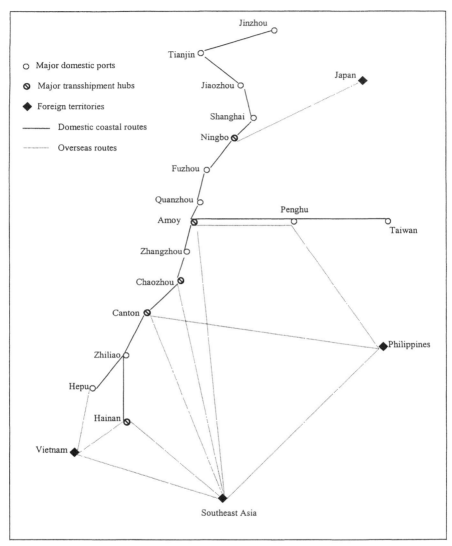

Figure 8. Domestic and Overseas Trade Routes of Canton, Chaozhou, and Amoy, 1780.

Ningbo, Shanghai, Jiaozhou, Tianjin, and Jinzhou in Manchuria. (Ningbo was the major transshipment hub for junks bound for Japan.) A southbound route hugged the Guangdong coast to the Leizhou peninsula and Hainan Island,[14] to Vietnam, and thence to Malacca or other Nanyang ports. From Amoy there were two other routes that went eastward, skipping from island to island, past Penghu and then either to Taiwan or southward to Luzon, Sulu, and insular Southeast Asia. There was also a direct route connecting Canton with Luzon.[15]

The Foreign Maritime Trade

Because of its monopoly after 1757, Canton dominated Western commerce in China. In his *Gazetteer of Guangdong's Maritime Customs*, Liang Tingnan recorded 2,530 Western merchant ships that called at Canton over a sixty-year period between 1751 and 1810. According to Liang, the number of ships grew from roughly nineteen ships annually in the 1750s to about eighty ships annually in the first decade of the nineteenth century.[16] The Western trade at Canton averaged between forty thousand and seventy thousand tons yearly.[17] The value of the trade was tremendous. In 1792, for example, Lord Macartney estimated the worth of Western imports and exports at over 12.5 million taels (*liang*), and in any given year, up to at least 1820, more silver coins than goods were imported into China by Western merchants. Anywhere from four to ten million Spanish silver dollars (*yuan*) flowed into Canton yearly from Western traders, thus pumping large sums of money into the national and local economies.[18]

In addition to the large number of Western vessels trading in China, there was also a thriving overseas junk trade that actually eclipsed Western trade in the region until at least the 1830s.[19]

[14] Hainan Island was an important transshipment hub for ships trading with the Nanyang. On the commercial importance of Hainan see Murray 1987:11–12.

[15] *XMZ* 136–150; Ye Xianen 1989:187–194; and Sun Guangzhe 1989:574–577.

[16] Liang Tingnan (1838:24/34a–40b) lists the yearly numbers of Western vessels trading at Canton from 1751 to 1838. Although slightly different, Liang's figures are generally corroborated by those of Morse (1926–1929).

[17] Ye Xianen 1989:151.

[18] Morse 1926–1929:2/152, 201, 3/2, 56, 80, 100, 102; Cheong 1965:39–42, 50–51; M. Lin 1989:224–225; and Marks 1998:180. In the eighteenth century Spanish silver dollars were a common unit of exchange all along the South China coast.

[19] Warren 1981:9; Huang Qichen 1986; Ng Chin-keong 1990:314–315; and Cushman 1993:66.

While there had been considerable trade with Japan in the first half of the eighteenth century, by the end of the century most of South China's trade had shifted to Southeast Asia. Amoy and Chaozhou dominated that trade, as Canton dominated the Western trade. The junk trade between China and Southeast Asia was conducted almost entirely on Chinese vessels or Southeast Asian vessels with Chinese skippers and crews who came mostly from the three prefectures of Quanzhou, Zhangzhou, and Chaozhou.[20] Taking advantage of the seasonal monsoons, Chinese junks trading with Nanyang ports usually left Amoy and Chaozhou during the late winter and spring and returned in the summer and early fall.[21]

Since the late Ming hundreds of large merchant junks had sailed annually from South China for the Southern Ocean. The largest ocean junks trading with Nanyang ports (like the one depicted in Figure 9) had three masts and cargo capacities of over 800 tons. Most trading ships, however, averaged between three hundred and five hundred tons.[22] In May 1795, an official of the English East India Company reported that every year there were one or two hundred large Chinese ships and about a thousand smaller craft trading with Luzon, Sulu, and other Nanyang ports.[23] While most of the large junks came from Amoy and Chaozhou, the smaller ones hailed mainly from the Canton delta and Hainan Island. These smaller vessels had carrying capacities of roughly 150 to 200 tons. During the early nineteenth century, the Chinese junk trade with Southeast Asia amounted to at least eighty-five thousand tons per year. By the 1820s, the annual value of the goods brought to Southeast Asia on Chinese vessels was over 2.4 million dollars.[24]

China's trade with Southeast Asia was based on reciprocity: manufactured goods from China in exchange for unprocessed or raw materials from Southeast Asia. Chinese exports were chiefly handicraft goods, such as chinaware, textiles, tiles, umbrellas, paper, and processed foods and fruits, which were mostly produced along the southern coast and intended for the consumption of the general public. Although some luxuries and exotic items,

---

[20] Liang Tingnan 1838:21/34a–35a.
[21] *XMZ* 178; Gutzlaff 1834:53; and Blussé 1988:112.
[22] *XMZ* 177; and Chen Xiyu 1991:157–158.
[23] Cited in Warren 1981:5–6.
[24] Viraphol 1977:180; Ye Xianen 1989:77, 151–152; Ng Chin-keong 1990:311; Cushman 1993:55–56; and Ch'en Kuo-tung 1994:207–208.

Figure 9. Ocean Junk Used in Overseas Trade. Source: John Nevius, *China and the Chinese* (1869).

such as birds nests and rhinoceros horns, were shipped from Southeast Asia to China, most of the items were bulk goods and staples of everyday life, including sugar, pepper, lumber, indigo, cotton, tin, hides, and rice.[25] At the start of the nineteenth century, China-bound junks normally carried cargoes estimated at between sixty thousand and eighty thousand silver dollars, and the net profit on these shipments when unloaded in China could go as high as triple the original investment.[26] As Gutzlaff pointed out, however, profits from the junk trade varied according to trade routes and types of goods: pepper and sapan wood netted over 100 percent profit, European calicoes about 50 percent, and sugar and tin less profit.[27]

---

[25] *XMZ* 182–184; Gutzlaff 1834:53; and Cushman 1993:75–95, 140.

[26] Warren 1981:8–9; and Chen Xiyu 1991:309.

[27] Gutzlaff 1834:134–135. Extracts from sapan wood were used in China primarily for dyeing cloth.

The Domestic Coasting Trade

In terms of size and value, the domestic long-distance and local coasting trade was even more important than the Western and overseas junk trade. Throughout the Ming period the coastal trade was generally undeveloped and confined to the area south of the Yangzi River, and only in the Qing period, after 1684, did it extend the entire coast from Guangdong to Manchuria. Fujian and Guangdong merchants also dominated the coasting trade. But unlike the junk owners in the Nanyang trade, who were predominantly wealthy merchants and gentry, the coasting trade actually involved a good many individuals with moderate or small capital.[28]

As with the overseas junk trade, the coastwise trade was seasonal: northbound boats left southern ports between the third and sixth lunar months, and southbound boats departed northern ports in the tenth and eleventh lunar months. Long-distance coastal traders made one or two round-trips up and down the coast each year, while those involved in intraregional short-distance trade made innumerable, almost continuous, trips throughout the year. During the first half of the nineteenth century there were about 5,800 Chinese coasting junks with a total capacity of 680,000 tons. Between the 1740s and 1820s, the annual value of the coastal trade was a staggering twenty-six million silver dollars. Depending on cargo and ports of call, the profits from the coasting business could be as high as 300 percent, but were normally lower.[29]

During the Qing dynasty hundreds of new ports sprang up along the coast, especially in Fujian and Guangdong, to accommodate the burgeoning maritime trade. The majority of these ports, which were relatively small in size, were involved directly in the coastal trade and only indirectly in the overseas trade.[30] Important for the promotion of trade, most of these ports were situated at or near the mouths of rivers, thereby linking the coast with the interior. Zhiliao in Wuchuan county, which is illustrated in Figure 10, was a key port in southwestern Guangdong. Inside Xianmen harbor, and protected by two forts, Zhiliao was situated at the

---

[28] Ng Chin-Keong 1983:144; and Fan I-chun 1993:101, 238, 240–241, 251.

[29] *JMZ* 104; Fan I-chun 1993:42; Viraphol 1977:197–198; Ye Xianen 1989:186–187, 213–214, 251; and Deng Gang 1997:87.

[30] See the discussions in Guo Songyi 1982; Matsuura 1983:615–627; Huang Qichen 1986:155–156; Zhu Delan 1986:408, 412; Ye Xianen 1989:223–232; and Fan I-chun 1993:103.

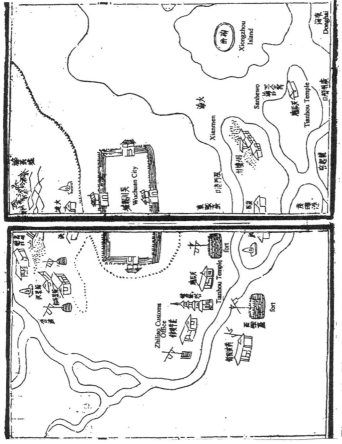

Figure 10. The Port of Zhiliao and Xianmen Harbor. Source: Liang Ting-nan, *Yuehai guanzhi* (1838).

confluence of three rivers, giving it easy access to the hinterlands of Wuchuan, Suiqi, Shicheng, and Huazhou. Zhiliao not only served as an important link to the interior, but also each autumn and winter hundreds of coasting junks from Hainan, Canton, Chaozhou, and Fujian frequented the port to conduct business. The town had hundreds of shops, a customs office, several sojourner merchant associations (*huiguan*), and numerous temples, including a huge Empress of Heaven Temple that was financed and managed by sea merchants.[31] Many other ports, such as Fengqi in Quanzhou in southern Fujian, were quite small. Fengqi was situated at the mouth of several rivers and served as an anchorage for local fishing and merchant junks.[32]

Although hundreds of large commercial junks from Amoy and Chaozhou engaged annually in the coasting trade, most of this trade was conducted in small boats with crews of fewer than fifteen men. These were usually junks with one or two masts, like the one in Figure 11, which had cargo capacities of under two hundred tons; others had capacities of only fifteen to fifty tons.[33] These vessels skirted up and down the coast from one port to the next, loading and unloading whatever was marketable or available at the time. Junks hugged the coast for the entire route from Guangdong to Manchuria, not only to take advantage of prevailing winds and currents, but also because this enabled them to visit as many ports as possible to buy and sell goods.[34] In the spring of 1749, twenty-seven merchants from Minxian, in Fuzhou prefecture, pooled their money to lease a "bird junk" (*niaochuan*) in Amoy to transport sugar up the coast.[35] After discharging its cargo at Shanghai, the ship took on another cargo of tea, which two months later was unloaded at Jinzhou in Manchuria. The captain then purchased a cargo of melon seeds and soybeans for the return trip home. But before making it back to Fujian the ship wrecked in a storm off the Ryukyu Islands.[36] It was common for junks to call at several ports to acquire sufficient cargo to fill their holds before sailing to their final destinations.[37]

---

[31] *WCXZ* 3/10a–b; *Gaozhou fuzhi* 1889:5/16b; and Yang Zhenquan 1988:11–12.

[32] *QZFZ* 8/49a.

[33] Chen Xiyu 1991:158, 176; and Cushman 1993:46–47.

[34] Chen Xiyu 1991:172; and Chen Guodong 1991:78.

[35] The "bird junks" were small swift coasting junks with up to 150-ton cargo capacity used extensively in Fujian and Guangdong (Matsuura 1983:629).

[36] Matsuura 1983:632.

[37] See numerous examples in Zhu Delan 1986; Yang Guozhen 1998:31–46; and Huang Guosheng 2000:153–154.

Figure 11. Small Double-Masted Coasting Junk. Source: A.
Colquhoun, *Across Cryse* (1883).

The regular cargoes of coasting junks consisted chiefly of bulk
items of ordinary, daily use, normally native products of the maritime provinces and Southeast Asia. Sugar was the most important
commodity on northbound junks; it was, in Gutzlaff's words, "the
staple article of export" in the south. Sugarcane was grown extensively in Fujian, Taiwan, and Guangdong, and then refined into
various grades of brown, rock, and granulated sugar. In the mid-
eighteenth century those three areas produced roughly 90 percent
of the sugar in China, about 862,000,000 pounds per year.[38] The
largest markets outside the home provinces were in Ningbo,
Shanghai, and Tianjin, where sugar was exchanged for rice and
other local commodities. In Shandong and Manchuria southbound
ships were usually loaded with beans, flour, dates, walnuts, melon
seeds, medicinal herbs, and cotton, all typical products of northern
China.[39] (See Tables 4 and 5.) Besides these products, the archival
records listed hundreds of other common items in the coastwise

---

[38] Pomeranz 2000:120–121. On the sugar industry in South China during the
Qing period see Mazumdar 1998.

[39] Gutzlaff 1834:163; Matsuura 1983:603, 609; Ng Chin-keong 1983:135–136; and
Fan I-chun 1993:257–258.

Table 4
Fujian and Guangdong Coastal Trade, 1723–1813 (northbound junks)

Port of departure	Port of call	Cargo	Year/ lunar month
Jinjiang	ᴋShanghai	chinaware, cloth, pepper,	1723/?
Shanghai	Jinzhou	sapan wood	
Zhangzhou	Jinzhou	tea, cloth	1740/6
Amoy	Ningbo	sugar	1740/6
Amoy	Shangdong	sugar, chinaware, sapan wood	1749/?
Zhangzhou	Tianjin	sugar	1749/?
Amoy	ᴋShanghai	sugar	1749/5
Shanghai	Jinzhou	tea	1749/7
Taiwan	Tianjin	sugar	1756/6
Guangdong	Tianjin	unspecified	1760/5
Zhangzhou	ᴋJiangnan	unspecified	1765/5
Jiangnan	Jinzhou	tea	
Amoy	Jinzhou	sugar	1777/6
Zhangzhou	ᴋJiangnan	sugar	1777/10
Fuzhou	Jinzhou	paper 1779/6	
Chenghai	Tianjin	betel nut	1785/6
Zhangzhou	Shanghai	sugar	1785/3
Fuzhou	Tianjin	paper boxes	1797/7
Guangdong	Tianjin	sugar	1801/6–8
Chenghai	Tianjin	sugar	1801/?
Chenghai	Rongcheng	sugar	1808/6
Fuzhou	Gaizhou	paper	1810/5–8
Taiwan	Tianjin	sugar	1813/5–8
Taiwan	ᴋShanghai	sugar	1818/5
Shanghai	Jinzhou	tea	
Zhanghou	Tianjin	sugar, pepper, sapan wood	1813/6

Note: The ᴋ symbol indicates a continuous voyage with the line directly below.
Sources: GZD (14382) JQ 14.5.28; Matsuura 1983:610–611; Chen Guodong 1991:78.

trade: cooking oil, sweet potatoes, betel nuts, opium, fresh and preserved fruits, pigs, chickens, wine, tobacco, salted fish, dried sea cucumbers, sea kelp, paper, iron nails, lumber, rattan matting, and so on. Noticeably missing were expensive luxury goods.

Trade with Taiwan also boomed. Although Amoy monopolized the trade for most of the eighteenth century, by the end of the century the Qing government had to open up direct trade from Taiwan to Fuzhou and Quanzhou because of swelling demand and smuggling. By then several thousand junks, owned mostly by Quanzhou and Zhangzhou merchants, were involved in the trade with Taiwan. The island's most important commodities, produced for export, were rice and sugar. Because the mother province suffered substantial shortages of rice, Taiwan became the granary of Fujian, with annual shipments amounting to over a

Table 5
Fujian and Guangdong Coastal Trade, 1723–1813 (southbound junks)

Port of departure	Port of call	Cargo	Year/ lunar month
Jinzhou	Fujian	melon seeds	1723/6
Shandong	Fujian	dried persimmons, walnuts, peas, medicinal herbs, flour	1740/11
Gaiping	Longxi	beans	1746/4
Shandong	Fujian	meng beans, medicinal herbs, flour	1749/11
Shandong	Fujian	meng beans, walnuts	1749/11
Jiaozhou	Amoy	meng beans, medicinal herbs, flour	1749/11
Gaiping	Zhangzhou	soybeans, raw cotton, medicinal herbs, silkworm cocoons, dried fish, dried clams, wood ears	1758/9
Guandong	Fujian	melon seeds, beans, bean cakes, silkworm cocoons, rice	1758/10
Tianjin	Guangdong	red dates	1760/10
Jinzhou	Zhangzhou	beans	1766/10
Jinzhou	Amoy	soybeans, melon seeds, flour, raw cotton, silkworm cocoons, medicinal herbs	1777/10
Jinzhou	Zhangzhou	soybeans, misc. grains	1797/11
Gaizhou	Quanzhou	beans, raw cotton silkworm cocoons, seaweed, leather goods	1801/10
Tianjin	Tongan	red dates, black dates, walnuts, pears	1801/10
Rongcheng	(Chenghai)	soybeans, bean flour	1808/10
Gaizhou	Tongan	peas, beans	1810/10
Tianjin	Fujian	red dates, black dates, raisins, rice, wine, dried fish	1813/10
Tianjin	Fujian	red dates	1813/11

Sources: GZD (14382) JQ 14.5.28; Matsuura 1983:610–611; Chen Guodong 1991:78.

million piculs. Taiwan sugar was transported not only to Fujian ports but also directly to northern coastal ports, particularly Shanghai and Tianjin. The sugar junks involved in this trade were generally the largest coasting ships, with cross beams of twenty-four feet and loading capacities of almost five hundred tons.[40]

Many coasting junks engaged in the lucrative foreign trade as well. As Professor Ng Chin-keong has pointed out, the overseas trade was an extension of the coastal trade.[41] They were

---

[40] *XMZ* 166–169; Gutzlaff 1834:201–202; also see Ng Chin-keong 1983:95–112, 131, 142; and 1990:305. For a recent overview of the history of Taiwan's shipping industry see Dai Baocun 2000.

[41] Ng Chin-keong 1983:3.

interconnected and interdependent. Several domestic hubs, besides Amoy and Chaozhou, linked up with the overseas trade to the Southern Ocean. Hainan junks regularly traded up and down the Chinese coast from Canton to Tianjin, as well as with the Nanyang.[42] Southeast Asian vessels, with their Chinese merchants, officers, and crews, also participated in the coasting trade.[43]

This interdependence between the overseas and coastwise trade can be seen in the 1723 voyage of a merchant junk from Jinjiang, the chief port for Quanzhou city. The ship, which called at Shanghai and Jinzhou, carried a cargo of chinaware, cotton cloth, black pepper, and sapan wood. It returned to Fujian with a cargo of melon seeds (see Tables 4 and 5). Chinaware was produced in upriver towns and villages from Jinjiang at Anxi and Luoxi especially for the export market. Chinaware, like other southern products such as silk, tea, and paper, was then traded in northern coastal or Nanyang ports for raw materials, such as cotton, which were sent back home to be made into cloth and then resold domestically and overseas. The black pepper and sapan wood had originated in Southeast Asia.[44] In another example, from 1713, the captain of a Fujian junk, who engaged in long-distance commerce, explained that he transported Chinese goods such as silk, rugs, gauze, and chinaware to Nanyang ports. In Siam he loaded his vessel with sapan wood, ivory, black pepper, and rice, and in Vietnam with incense and dyes, which he sold along the China coast. In Canton, Suzhou, and Hangzhou he next purchased silk and in Fujian he procured sugar to trade in Japan.[45]

Alongside the legal trade, smuggling enterprises increased dramatically in Fujian, Taiwan, and Guangdong during the late eighteenth and early nineteenth centuries. Like information regarding the smugglers themselves, however, accurate figures on the amount of illicit trade at that time remain elusive. Indirect evidence, nonetheless, suggests that smuggling accounted for a significant amount of China's seaborne trade, especially after 1800.[46] Despite the opening of new ports, commerce outstripped

---

[42] Ye Xianen 1989:188–190.

[43] Cushman 1993:22, 40.

[44] Chen Xiyu 1991:266; and Marks 1998:171–172.

[45] Zhu Delan 1986:389.

[46] Personal communication from Professor Huang Guosheng. While much has been written about Ming and early-Qing smuggling activities and about the illegal opium trade, mid-Qing smuggling and its effect on legitimate trade and the maritime economy have been sorely neglected. This is an important but complicated topic that deserves further research.

the growth of legitimate markets. Western merchants, whose trade was legally restricted to the single port of Canton, carried on a brisk clandestine trade around Macao and along China's coast, selling opium and other smuggled goods.[47] By the end of the Qianlong era, as economic competition grew increasingly fierce, more and more Chinese traders engaged in combinations of licit and illicit commerce. Smuggling allowed merchants to maximize profits by avoiding customs duties and other fees. Besides opium, contraband also included a large variety of items such as rice, salt, iron, gunpowder, silver, and even emigrants bound for Taiwan or Southeast Asia. To meet demands, innumerable small ports and bays, not officially recognized or recorded, became deeply involved in the burgeoning illegal trade with both smugglers and pirates.[48] Smuggling, in fact, went hand in hand with both the growth of legitimate commerce and the upsurge of piracy.

The Fishing Industry

The fishing industry also played a vital role in South China's maritime world. Countless numbers of people found employment either directly or indirectly from fishing, and were either fully or partially dependent on it for their livelihoods. In coastal South China more people earned their livelihoods through fishing than any other single occupation. A common saying in Guangdong ran "Seven go to fishing; three go to the plough."[49] In Fuqing county in Fujian, because the soil was too poor for farming, it was said that seven or eight out of every ten people made their living by fishing.[50] Around Amoy, where good soil was also scarce, it was typical for people to both grow sweet potatoes in the hills and fish along the coast. Most people, however, considered fishing vastly more important than farming.[51]

Most fishing was conducted close to shore in small boats with only two or three sailors (Figure 12). But there were also larger

---

[47] *WCXZ* 4/93b–94b; Morse 1926–1929:2/322, 389, 3/64; Gutzlaff 1834; and *Chinese Repository* 1836:5/339.

[48] See *XMZ* 169, 180; *JMZ* 92; *SCSX* 38/1b; *MXTZ* 8/14a–b; also see Ng Chin-keong 1983:83–84; Chen Xiyu 1991:227; and Zheng Guangnan 1998:380–381; on contraband items, see Huang Guosheng 2000:249–254.

[49] Cited in Hayes 1983:38.

[50] *FQXZ* 423.

[51] *XMZ* 644.

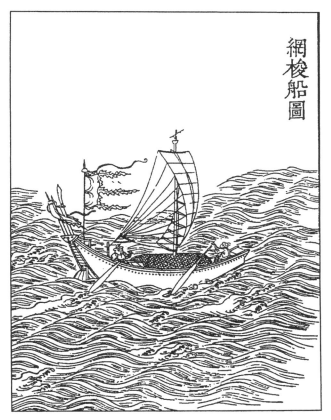

Figure 12. Small Fishing Boat. Source: *Gujin tushu jicheng* (1884).

vessels that engaged in offshore fishing. The "drag-the-wind junks" (*tuofengchuan*), though also used to transport cargo, were more commonly employed in trolling in Guangdong. The single-masted craft used in fishing normally had crews of about eleven sailors and handled burdens of about forty tons.[52] Many fishermen also sailed far from home to fish. Hainan fishing fleets, for example, regularly sailed as far away as the waters of Southeast Asia for their catch and would be away from home for months at a time. Each year during the fishing season reportedly a thousand

---

[52] Zhang and Yang 1983:114; and Ye Xianen 1989:253–254.

Fujian vessels visited Zhejiang waters to catch sturgeon and ribbon fish.[53]

Over the course of the eighteenth century there was also an expansion of pisciculture along the southern coast, as in other parts of China. In the Canton delta, particularly in Shunde county, villagers developed a unique ecosystem, which combined pisciculture with sericulture. Elsewhere coastal villagers raised fish, oysters, and clams in self-claimed sea fields, and they staked out inlets and channels close to shore with weirs for catching fish and other aquatic animals. It was the custom for men to fish and for women to gather clams and make nets.[54]

In the eighteenth and early nineteenth centuries, fishing boats too were active participants in the coastwise trade. When not fishing they often transported goods and ferried passengers inside busy harbors and between nearby ports. Although early Qing laws required that fishing boats have only one mast and prohibited them from engaging in commerce, after 1707 the government allowed Fujian fishing boats to have two masts, and after 1790 these larger craft were also allowed to carry commercial cargo.[55] The "white-hulled junks" (baidichuan), which handled up to seventy tons burden, played an important role in both fishing and merchant shipping.[56] Also, regulations in 1737, and again in 1776, allowed Fujian boats to exchange fishing and merchant licenses twice each year. Thus in the summer and fall when fishing was slow, fishing junks could register to transport cargo, and in the winter and spring when fishing was busy, merchant junks could register as fishing boats.[57] The archival records also make it clear that Guangdong fishing boats, legally or illegally, routinely engaged in commerce.

Since fishermen depended on dealers to sell their catches and on shopkeepers to purchase food and supplies, fishing also provided livelihoods for a large variety of people on shore. Da'ao, a small port in Yangjiang county, Guangdong, had several tens of shops that catered exclusively to fishermen.[58] Some villages, such

---

[53] XMZ 172; Ng Chin-keong 1983:146; Zhang and Yang 1983:68, 80–81; and Ouyang Zongshu 1998:178–181.

[54] XMZ 644; JMZ 355; LJXZ 19/19a; Chinese Repository 1836:5/343; Hayes 1983:36–37; and Mazumdar 1998:265–268.

[55] On the various, and often complicated, fishing regulations see XMZ 172–175; also see Ng Chin-keong 1983:138–139, 146; and Ouyang Zongshu 1998:121–138.

[56] XMZ 172.

[57] Ibid., 168–169; and MXTZ 5/5b–6a.

[58] YJZ 6/5b.

as those on Songshan Bay in Xiapu county, Fujian, depended solely on fishing for their existence.[59] Villagers could also earn sizable revenues from leasing fishing stations and beaches to fishermen where they could refit and careen their boats. Because fresh fish had to be salted, fishing harbors were often situated near salt fields. Thus the salt industry benefited because the demand for salted fish, traditionally one of the staples of the Chinese diet, was always great.[60]

Hardship and Poverty

The benefits of commerce were not equally shared among the coastal population. As early as the 1770s, a number of perceptive Qing officials and scholars had already begun pointing out the growing economic and material disparity separating the rich from the poor.[61] At sea the gap between the junk owners and the seamen who worked their ships was especially great. To paraphrase the words of one early-nineteenth-century writer, on the coast the wealthy became merchants and ship owners, while the poor became sailors who drifted from port to port seeking employment. Among these drifters, the writer continued, there were many individuals, "dissatisfied with their lot in life," who chose to become pirates.[62] As explained in the Amoy gazetteer, merchants went out to sea and returned home rich; for them the sea was a "money pond" (*lisou*). But sailors went to sea to support their daily needs, returning home poor and in debt.[63] Even the Jiaqing emperor once lamented how difficult it was for common seafarers to make profits without becoming pirates.[64]

Population Growth, Rising Costs, and Job Competition

While the late eighteenth and early nineteenth centuries may have been a "prosperous age" for some people, for others the period was a time of hardship and privation. At the heart of much of the distress was the population explosion. During the

---

[59] *XPXZ shanchuan*/14b; also see *FQXZ* 37; *LJXZ* 4/4b; and *QZFZ* 25/1a–b.

[60] *QZFZ* 25/1a–b; Gutzlaff 1834:169–170; Hayes 1977:38–49, 88–89; and 1983:36–37, 69.

[61] See Whitbeck 1980:109; M. Lin 1989:321–331; Will 1990:74; and Buoye 2000:48–49.

[62] Cited in Katsuta 1967:30–32.

[63] *XMZ* 231, 644.

[64] *SCSX* 88/1a.

eighteenth century China's population more than doubled. Over the course of the century the number of people living in Guangdong jumped from a little over six million to nearly fifteen million. In the core Canton delta, between 1723 and 1820, the population rose from 1.3 million to 5.3 million.[65] In the 1750s Fujian had a population of between seven and eight million, about three million of whom lived in the coastal prefectures of Quanzhou and Zhangzhou. By the 1790s Fujian's population reached at least thirteen million. At the time of the Manchu conquest of Taiwan in 1683, the island had roughly 200,000 inhabitants, but by the mid-eighteenth century the population had already shot up to about a million, a fivefold increase in just seventy years. Most of that increase was due to illegal emigration.[66] Although population growth, as several recent studies have shown, did not produce a Malthusian crisis but actually stimulated economic growth,[67] nonetheless it affected various areas and social groups in different ways. China's laboring poor were the most adversely affected.

Officials and people were gravely concerned about feeding the burgeoning population. The maritime prefectures of Guangzhou, Chaozhou, Quanzhou, and Zhangzhou not only had the highest population densities, but also suffered chronic food shortages as more and more land was taken out of food production for commercial crops to support maritime trade. In Guangdong, for example, an estimated 30 to 50 percent of the arable land was devoted to commercial crops by the late eighteenth century.[68] Around the same time two-thirds of the land for food crops in Quanzhou and Zhangzhou was too poor to grow much except sweet potatoes, and many peasants were reduced to the margins of subsistence.[69] Even earlier, in 1726, Governor-General Gao Qizhuo warned the Yongzheng emperor (r. 1723–1735) that even in years of good harvests, locally produced rice could last only six months in Quanzhou and Zhangzhou. Two years later he reported that both prefectures depended on supplies from outside the province for 60 percent of their food. Similarly, in the late eighteenth century, officials in Guangdong wrote that despite good harvests, food production in the province could not keep pace

---

[65] Ye Xianen 1988:157–158.
[66] Ng Chin-keong 1983:14–15; and Y. Wang 1986:85–87.
[67] For example, see Wong 1997; Lavely and Wong 1998; Lee and Wang 1999; and Pomeranz 2000.
[68] Buoye 2000:47.
[69] Ng Chin-keong 1983:21.

with the rising population and that food crops were insufficient to last an entire year. As a result, Fujian and Guangdong were able to feed their growing population only by importing rice from Taiwan, other provinces, and Southeast Asia.[70] Thus there existed a delicate balance between food supply and population.

Both Guangdong and Fujian also witnessed slow, relatively steady increases in the costs of food and other necessities over the eighteenth century. Inflation coupled with overcrowding. Not coincidentally, the core coastal areas had the highest food prices in their respective provinces, a fact that had a devastating effect on the laboring poor, who lived on the edge of subsistence. Any rise in food costs could push them over the edge. Each year during the spring and summer months, when grain prices were the highest in the densely populated maritime prefectures of Guangdong and Fujian, the number of pirate incidents always shot up. Also whenever there were natural disasters, such as droughts, floods, and typhoons, food crops were destroyed, prices rose, and hired laborers lost work and wages.[71] The working poor were the most vulnerable to fluctuations in food costs because they depended on their wages to purchase what they ate. A poor harvest and an increase in food prices, therefore, made it necessary for some people to sustain life by stealing.

In addition, despite the booming economy, the population explosion must have put the squeeze on employment opportunities, particularly for those people at the lower end of the social scale who sold their labor and owned very little. Rising population meant greater competition for jobs, keeping wages low at a time when the cost of living was rising. What is more, since labor was cheap and employment irregular, workers had no job security.[72] They were not totally destitute, however, for they could sometimes earn enough money from occasional work to rise just above a life of basic survival. Nonetheless, the specter of unemployment permanently haunted the lives of the laboring poor and forced them to live perpetually on the brink of disaster. For many, missing a day's work meant going to bed hungry that night.

---

[70] *MQSLWB* 23a; *JMZ* 82; *FQXZ* 40–41; see also Y. Wang 1986:86–90, 99; and Chen Chunsheng 1992:19–20, 53–58, 64–68, 156.

[71] Y. Wang 1986:102–103; Chen Chunsheng 1992:121–123; and Wong 1997:209.

[72] Y. Wang 1986:88–95; Chen Chunsheng 1992:170–179; and on hired workers and wages in the early and mid-Qing periods see Liu Yongcheng 1982:54–72; Wu Liangkai 1983; and Huang Miantang 1988.

Hardships and Dangers at Sea

Sailoring was a low-prestige occupation that did not fit neatly into the Confucian scheme of four classes: scholars, farmers, craftsmen, and merchants. Respectable people generally considered the work of common sailors dishonorable and something to be avoided by all means.[73] The sea always served as a refuge for the marginalized of society. Most seafarers, in truth, led inordinately grueling existences, with working conditions that were always risky and often unrewarding. Chinese and Western observers agreed that sailors, and fishermen in particular, were among the poorest of the poor in China. Chen Yaer was the son of a fisherman. When he was nine years old his father had to sell him to another fisherman named Lin Shitai to pay debts. Several years later, after his "adoptive father" had died, Chen had to sell the boat he had inherited because he could no longer afford repairs. He then had no choice but to hire out as a sailor for 300 cash (*wen*) per month.[74] Gutzlaff was hardly exaggerating when he wrote about the plight of Fujian fishermen: "They brave all dangers for a scanty livelihood, and suffer the severest hardships to return to their families with five dollars after the toils of a whole year."[75]

Men went to sea for various reasons. Some sought adventure or fortune, while others sailed not by choice but of necessity. There were those who could not make a go of it on land or who sought to escape the monotony of village life. Working at sea provided an important supplementary income for farmers and laborers living near the coast and was also an essential component of their overall survival strategy.[76] In 1809 an official report stated that most of the sailors hired to work on salt junks had been unemployed drifters and toughs.[77] A majority of sailors, however, made the sea their lifelong vocation, moving from port to port, seeking work wherever and whenever they could find any. Jumping ship was quite common for mobile sailors who were constantly on the lookout for better jobs. Seamen were in perpetual movement, circulating freely from ship to ship, not only between

---

[73] Diamond 1969:3.

[74] XKTB (86) QL 54.6.11.

[75] Gutzlaff 1834:417.

[76] According to Teshima Masaki and Arai Yoshio, during the first half of the twentieth century 40 percent of the Suzhou region junk crews had originally been agricultural workers, while the remaining 60 percent had combined farming with sailing (A. Watson 1972:61).

[77] *SCSX* 40/12b.

merchant junks, but also between merchant junks and fishing and pirate vessels.

Work on Chinese junks was hard and dangerous; injury and death were common. Every year countless seamen drowned after falling overboard or were crippled in job-related accidents. Sailing a ship required manual labor, consisting mainly of steering, handling rigging and sails, and, in the absence of wind, rowing and sculling. Sailors spent much time bailing water out of the holds of leaky vessels, not only in bad but also in good weather. In port sailors had to help load and unload cargo, mend sails, make rope, and careen and clean their vessels, sometimes as often as twice a month. Crews generally worked long, arduous hours, ranging anywhere from eight to twelve hours every day. They toiled both day and night. Food was often inadequate and of poor quality, and among impoverished fishermen even rice was a luxury.[78] Junks were habitually overcrowded, inordinately unsanitary, and ridden with vermin. Besides their crews, the large Nanyang-bound junks frequently, and clandestinely, transported hundreds of laborers and emigrants, thus giving these vessels the appearance of African slave ships.[79] Because the dangers and rigors of work aboard ship made sailing a young man's occupation, seamen were mostly in their twenties and early thirties. Few sailors grew old on the job.[80]

Summer and early autumn were particularly hazardous because of the numerous typhoons and squalls. According to the anthropologist E. N. Anderson, typhoon season was the most stressful time of the year for seafarers, thus a time of frequent arguments and fights.[81] In South China there was hardly a year without a severe storm.[82] Devastation was often catastrophic. Strong winds and pounding waves wrecked boats and killed and maimed innumerable people both on shore and at sea. On land storms knocked down houses and shops, disabled military

---

[78] Gutzlaff 1834:238–239, 414; and Diamond 1969:9. See chapter 7 for a further discussion of food.

[79] Gutzlaff 1834:167; also see Ye Xianen 1989:219–223.

[80] See LFZZ (2357) QL 54.3.15, (3854) JQ 2.1.27; and XKTB (96) QL 53.12.10, and (69) QL 55.3.23. For comparison, in sixteenth-century Spain, the mean age of sailors was around 28 or 29, and in general a sailor between 35 and 40 was already considered old for the job (Pérez-Mallaína 1998:78).

[81] E. Anderson 1970:33.

[82] On the frequency of typhoons in Guangdong, see Qiao Shengxi 1993:679–691.

fortifications and customs stations, and destroyed crops and animals, frequently driving the cost of food upward.[83]

Besides contending with the vicissitudes of nature, life aboard ship was not without other perils. Not only did ships wreck in storms, but also those that sailed too close to shore frequently went aground or broke up among the rocks. Even in familiar waters, as the pirate chief Huang Yasheng well understood, vessels easily ran aground. After plundering shipping in Fujian and Zhejiang in the summer of 1797, Huang carelessly sank his ship on the return voyage along the Hainan coast.[84] In an era when navigation was more guesswork than science, shipwrecks were common, especially at night. Consequently many craft anchored near shore after nightfall. But in doing so they ran the risk of pirates, who frequently took advantage of the dark to attack slumbering vessels. Darkness was a time of great anxiety for sailors.

Division of Labor and Wages

Aboard Chinese ships, crews were divided between officers and men, and work between skilled and unskilled workers. While work remained basically the same aboard all vessels, the size of crews and the compensation for labor varied according to the type and size of ships. Crews on coasting junks generally consisted of a captain and five or six subordinate officers and ten to twenty sailors. On the larger ocean junks that traded with the Nanyang, there would be a captain and as many as twenty deck and petty officers with anywhere from forty to eighty sailors, besides traveling merchants and emigrants. Smaller fishing boats and merchant junks engaged in local trade usually had only a captain, a helmsman, and fewer than a dozen sailors.[85] A hierarchy of labor determined wage scales. The lion's share of the huge profits made on commercial voyages went first to the junk owners, investors, and

---

[83] On the power and destruction of typhoons and gales see Qu Dajun [1700] 1985:11–13, 15–16; Zhu Jingying [1772] 1996:25–27; XMZ 129; CYXZ 1/7a–8a; DGXZ 4/4a–5a. Numerous pirates also lost their lives or were apprehended after their vessels were wrecked in storms; see examples in GZD (60) JQ 1.1.21; (1116) JQ 1.9.8; (2848) JQ 2.7.6; (6211) JQ 6.9.23.

[84] GZD (3611) JQ 3.1.13.

[85] Zhu Jingying [1772] 1996:15–16; XMZ 166; Gutzlaff 1834:54–55; also see Thompson 1968:184–185; Chen Xiyu 1991:161; Ch'en Kuo-tung 1994:210–211; and Dai Baocun 2000:41–42.

merchants, and next to the captains and deck officers. The common sailor received scant remuneration for his labor. Crews were paid in any combination of three ways: in space, in kind, and in cash. Over the course of the late eighteenth and early nineteenth centuries, cash wages became increasingly important, with payments based either on monthly wages or on a fixed amount per voyage. Sailors became increasingly proletarianized, in that they relied solely on the sale of their labor in earning a living.

The captain, appropriately called "ship lord" (*chuanzhu*) in South China, was an autocratic ruler aboard his ship.[86] His job was to supervise the overall operation of the vessel and determine the course and ports of call. On merchant vessels he had charge of the cargo and was responsible for obtaining the best prices. Frequently too he was the owner or part owner of the ship. If the owner did not personally travel aboard his ship, he would either appoint a family member, often an "adopted son," as captain, or hire a trustworthy skipper who also acted as the supercargo.[87] The junk on which Gutzlaff sailed from Siam to China in 1831, for example, was owned by a Chinese merchant and had about a 250-ton burden. The captain was Sin-shun, his brother-in-law was the ship's clerk, and also aboard the vessel was the captain's younger brother. After the ship reached Chenghai, Sin-shun returned home and his uncle replaced him as captain for the remainder of the trip. The ship had a crew of about fifty sailors.[88]

Whether owner, part owner, or hired employee, ship lords received huge profits on commercial voyages. Captains who were sole owners of a ship naturally received the greatest gains. On one voyage from Siam to China in 1806, the captain spent 18,250 silver dollars to outfit his ship and purchase cargo; in China he sold the cargo for 38,015 silver dollars, a gross profit of 208 percent.[89] Although hired captains received no wages, on large junks they were allotted a hundred piculs of cargo space for the voyage, which they could either fill with their own goods to trade or lease out to merchants for four to six taels per picul. They also received commissions on the goods sold by the merchants who carried cargo on their vessels; for every hundred taels captains could

---

[86] Besides ship lord in South China, other designations for sea captains included *chuanzhang* (ship master) and *chuhai* ([one who takes the ship] out to sea).

[87] Ng Chin-keong 1983:149; and Cushman 1993:103.

[88] Gutzlaff 1834:67, 98.

[89] Chen Xiyu 1991:309.

receive anywhere from 20 to 50 percent commission. Each illegal emigrant smuggled to Siam paid the captain eight silver dollars; to Taiwan, anywhere between two and five silver dollars.[90]

Deck officers were usually more experienced and older seamen, often men in their fifties.[91] Large ocean junks typically hired several deck officers for each voyage. The captain normally took no part in navigating his ship, leaving that job to one or two mates (*huozhang*). The latter were highly skilled mariners whose duties included charting the ship's course and maintaining the compass and the sand hourglass. Their skills were highly guarded secrets. Each mate had cryptic route books, called "water ways" (*shuijing*), which were handed down to them and copied.[92] These highly skilled mates were second in command and received substantial remuneration, generally two hundred silver dollars and fifty piculs of cargo space per voyage.[93] Other deck officers on large junks included one or two clerks (*caifu*), who oversaw the loading and unloading of cargo and kept account of the money; a boatswain (*zonghan*), who assisted the mates and summoned the rest of the crew to duty; and one or two helmsmen (*duogong*), who handled the steering. Clerks and boatswains received a hundred silver dollars and fifty piculs of space and helmsmen fifteen piculs of space without monetary wages.[94] Alternatively, helmsmen on some ships were paid wages of about eight hundred cash per month instead of receiving space.[95]

Besides the deck officers, large trading junks also had four or five petty officers and their assistants, who were in charge of the anchor, of the rigging for the sails and the masts, and of the ship's boat or sampan. Generally, they did not receive wages but got nine piculs of cargo space.[96] The large ships also employed other highly trained specialists: a carpenter (*yagong*), who was responsible for all repair work; a lookout (*yaban*); and one or two stewards (*zongpu*), in charge of the ship's food, stores, and firewood. All junks, large and small, had a religious specialist, called the

---

[90] Ibid., 310–311; Cushman 1993:103; and *MXTZ* 8/14a–b.

[91] Chen Xiyu 1991:162.

[92] Thompson 1968:191 n. 34.

[93] Chen Xiyu 1991:312.

[94] *XMZ* 178; *JMZ* 97; Gutzlaff 1834:55; Chen Xiyu 1991:312; and Cushman 1993:104.

[95] XKTB (83) QL 54.7.22, and (103) JQ 9.2.23.

[96] *XMZ* 178–179; *JMZ* 97–98; Gutzlaff 1834:55; Chen Xiyu 1991:312; and Cushman 1993:105.

"incense burner" (*xianggong*), whose job was to burn incense and paper money twice each day as offerings to the deities of the sea.[97] Compensation for this latter group was roughly the same as for petty officers.[98]

Finally, the rest of the crew on large junks was composed of several tens of ordinary sailors (*shuishou*), who were under the direction of the officers. Sailors were unskilled and untrained laborers who did most of the heavy, dirty work of heaving, pulling, and hauling. The youngest and least experienced seamen were generally assigned the most menial chores as apprentices (*zeku*), who cleaned the hold and deck, or as cooks, who were notoriously unskilled at their task. Ordinary sailors received no cash wages but were granted a small space, only five to seven piculs, in which to sleep and store their personal belongings and any goods they wished to trade.[99] Typically, on junks with a 5,000-picul (350-ton) burden, this meant that each sailor was allotted a mere 0.14 percent of the total available cargo space. On many fishing boats too, sailors were not paid wages but only received a portion of fish. According to Barbara Ward, around Hong Kong in the 1970s, a sailor's share was only about 4 percent of the total catch.[100] It is unlikely that conditions were any better in the mid-Qing.

Whereas sailors working on the larger vessels received no monetary wages, those working on smaller coasting and fishing junks were commonly paid only cash wages. For ordinary seamen wages were terribly low, remaining relatively constant throughout the eighteenth and early nineteenth centuries at about two hundred to four hundred cash per month.[101] In 1787, before becoming a pirate, Chen Yabian, who was only fourteen years old at the time, took a job as a cook on a fishing boat for wages of two hundred cash for a voyage.[102] Given the rising costs of living over this period, the real wages of seafarers actually fell. The amount of money they earned was barely enough for a single person to make ends meet, let alone support a family (a major reason why few

---

[97] *XMZ* 179; and Gutzlaff 1834:59.

[98] Dai Baocun 2000:44.

[99] XKTB (91) QL 53.12.3; *XMZ* 179; *JMZ* 98; Gutzlaff 1834:55–56; and Dai Baocun 2000:44.

[100] Ward 1985:15.

[101] XKTB (285) QL 38.11.10, (97) QL 39.3.1, (93) QL 53.9.13, (86) QL 54.6.11, (83) QL 54.7.22, (77) JQ 4.3.16, (78) JQ 11.8.22. See also Mazumdar 1998:58.

[102] XKTB (91) QL 53.12.3.

sailors were married). Income barely kept up with providing the daily necessities of life. Hired sailors in mid-Qing South China made only enough money to buy a cattie *(jin)* of rice each day and not much else.[103]

Work at sea was seasonal and unpredictable, and therefore beyond a sailor's control. Finding year-round employment was always difficult. In South China many sailors working on overseas and coastwise merchant junks had trouble landing jobs during the summer, when most ships were already out at sea. After returning to port sailors expected to be laid off for days, weeks, or even months. Work on fishing boats was also seasonal, depending on the catch and region, but in general the winter and early spring were the busiest seasons.[104] According to Hiroaki Kani, Hong Kong fishermen spent only 120 to 150 days each year in actual fishing.[105] There were always employment gaps for fishermen and other seamen, times throughout every year when they could find little or no work.[106]

Given such harrowing existences, how could seafarers manage to survive? Exploitative bosses, shopkeepers, and fish dealers would regularly give sailors and fishermen advances on their wages or shares, without which they would have been unable to buy food, supplies, and other necessities. Because on most junks the owners or captains provided crews with only minimal amounts of rice, seamen had to procure for themselves all other items needed for a voyage.[107] Fish dealers gave advances to fishermen on their catch, and in return the fishermen had to sell their fish to those same dealers, who then took a commission on the sale price of the fish and also collected payments on loans. According to E. N. Anderson, among the fishermen he studied in Hong Kong, their greatest expense was paying interests on loans

---

[103] Wu Liangkai 1983:25–26; Chen Chunsheng 1992:172. My calculations are based on the following: in the mid-Qing an adult male consumed approximately one cattie of rice per day (E. Anderson 1970:74; and Y. Wang 1986:88), and the normal price of rice rose from about five cash per cattie in the 1780s to twelve cash per cattie in the early 1830s (XKTB (14) QL 48.7.26, (74) QL 53.6.5, (22) JQ 9.7.8; and *Chinese Repository* 1835:3/471).

[104] Zhang and Yang 1983:81, 94–96; Ng Chin-keong 1983:146; and Chen Yande 1997:71.

[105] Kani 1967:70.

[106] See, for example, the comments of Jiqing in GZD (1212) JQ 1.9.29; and Bai Ling in YZD (40) JQ 15.4.18. For the complaints of seafarers themselves see GZD (857) JQ 1.7.5; (2109) JQ 2.3.3; and (8158) JQ 7.5.27.

[107] Gutzlaff 1834:56.

to shopkeepers and dealers, who took away almost all of the profits of their clients. Fishermen, who took it for granted that they would be cheated, had a saying: "the fish dealer's catty has eighteen ounces," when it should have only sixteen.[108] Most fishermen and seamen, therefore, found themselves in a vicious cycle of borrowing money and paying loans that kept them forever in debt and poverty.[109]

Prosperity and poverty went hand in hand with the upsurge of piracy in the mid-Qing era. Maritime trade and fishing not only provided hundreds of thousands of people in coastal South China with seafaring jobs and other auxiliary occupations, but they also provided the necessary conditions for expanding piracy. Visible wealth, in terms of the huge amounts of goods and money being transported by ships, provided greater opportunities and greater temptations for people to commit crime, especially for those living in or near destitution. Poverty, exploitation, and the hardships of making an honest living forced many seafarers to turn to piracy and other illegal enterprises.

---

[108] E. Anderson 1970:76–79.
[109] Kani 1967:44; and Ward 1985:16–17, 27–33. See also the discussion in Rediker (1987:125–127) on pay advances to eighteenth-century Atlantic sailors.

FOUR

Fishermen, Sailors, and Pirates

In the fall of 1788, Liu Yaer and thirteen other men were arrested for piracy. In his deposition Liu said that he and ten companions had formed a gang because of "increasing difficulties in finding work and earning an honest living." All of the men were fishermen and hired sailors from Xin'an, Xiangshan, Xinning, and Yangjiang counties in Guangdong. Because Liu had a boat and had been the one to suggest banding together as pirates, he took command. He was thirty-two years old, married, but had no children. The ages and family backgrounds are known for nine others. Their ages ranged from twenty-four to forty-seven *sui*, with five in their twenties, three in their thirties, and one in his forties. Of these nine men six were single. All of the gang members, including Liu, claimed that one or both of their parents were dead, and only two said that they had elder brothers. During questioning, it also came out that Liu and four other men had been involved on and off in other previous piracies. The remaining three arrested men had been abducted from their fishing junks by Liu's gang and coerced to work for their captors.[1]

The above case points out three salient features that characterized Chinese piracy in the late eighteenth and early nineteenth centuries: one, most pirates were poor fishermen and sailors who could not depend solely on honest work to sustain their lives; two, most gang members were occasional not professional pirates; and three, gangs usually included a number of captives who had been forced to serve the pirates aboard ship. In fact, captives, who frequently outnumbered actual pirates, especially during the heyday of pirate disturbances between 1795 and 1810, were of vital importance to the growth and development of large-scale piracy in the mid-Qing era. Both groups of pirates and victims had similar

---

[1] XKTB (69) QL 55.3.23.

socioeconomic backgrounds in that most were single males who came from fishing, sailing, and other water-related occupations. They were mostly young adults and highly mobile in their activities. On the one hand, as people living and working on the margins of respectable society, seafarers were predisposed to part-time piracy as a means of supplementing other work; on the other hand, as residents of the maritime world, they were also the prime targets for attack and abduction by pirates. The archival records clearly show that there was no simple dichotomy between petty and professional pirates, as other scholars have alluded, but rather a more complex arrangement between professional, occasional, and (what I call) reluctant pirates. This chapter shall examine in greater detail each of these points.

Social Backgrounds of Pirates and Victims

Although individuals became pirates for a variety of reasons and under different circumstances, nevertheless in their confessions convicted pirates reiterated one central theme: "poverty and hardships in making a living" (*pinku nandu*). In 1799, Wang Zhiyin, governor of Fujian, put it this way: "People are not born [sea] bandits, but drift into brigandage because they can no longer support themselves."[2] Bai Ling later elaborated in a memorial written in 1810 to the Jiaqing emperor. Pirates were originally people living on shore, he explained, but because they could not find employment they could not adequately support themselves. They therefore put out to sea to become pirates and secure a livelihood through crime. As he put it, they were doltish, simple people who were ignorant of the laws, and so turned to piracy as a means of survival. In another memorial written several weeks later, he reiterated that when people lacked the resources to maintain themselves and their families, the fear of starvation drove them to outlawry.[3]

At times pirates felt compelled to publicly justify their motives. In 1809, for instance, they posted notices in both Macao and Canton explaining that they had become outlaws because officials had "tyrannical hearts" and squeezed the poor out of all their earnings.[4] A year later, on the eve of Zhang Bao's surrender, pirates

---

[2] He Changling 1827:85/32a.
[3] SYD, JQ 15.3.23; and YZD (40) JQ 15.4.18.
[4] Cited in Murray 1987:166–167.

presented a formal petition to Bai Ling that explained their position:

> Originally we were humble people and good subjects, but we became pirates for a variety of reasons. Because some of us were not careful in making friends, we fell among the robbers. Others among us were unable to secure a livelihood or were kidnapped while trading on the lakes and rivers. Still others because of having committed some crime joined this watery empire to escape punishment.... In addition, as a result of the famines of the last several years, people had nothing with which to maintain their livelihood and as time went on could not help but pillage in order to live. Had we not resisted officials and soldiers, our lives would have been in danger. Therefore, we violated the laws of the empire and wrecked trade. This was unavoidable.[5]

These notices say much about the plight of the poor and their worry about securing decent livelihoods. Both notices were written during the height of the pirate disturbances in Guangdong and at a time of severe food shortages and high prices caused by famines. There was clearly a close correlation, at least in the minds of the authors, between piracy and the cost of food.

For the years 1780 to 1810, we have information (Table 6) on the occupational backgrounds of 427 convicted pirates: 73.8 percent had aquatic occupations while 26.2 percent had nonaquatic occupations. Pirates, like seafarers in general, were overwhelmingly of humble birth. Most were unskilled workers. As we have noted in the previous chapter, most of the occupations listed in the table provided only subsistence livelihoods, and the people who engaged in those occupations usually lived uneasily on the margins of respectable society. They were China's laboring poor and disaffected, those people recurrently singled out by officials as "poor misfits" (*pin bushoufen*). Unemployment and chronic underemployment forced many mariners and other workers into a life of crime at sea. While poverty and despair were powerful motives for joining up with pirates, nevertheless, the vast majority were not idle vagabonds but rather working-class people who were unable to make ends meet from their normal jobs. For many people piracy was a necessary supplement to their regular jobs.

---

[5] The original Chinese text is in Ye Linfeng 1970:109–110; my translation is based on Dian Murray's (1987:172–174), but differs slightly from hers. Other translations are in Charles Neumann 1831:69–73 and in Thomas Chang 1983:240–244. Although there is controversy over the authorship of this second document, it is nevertheless a fair representation of pirate sentiments.

Table 6
Occupational Backgrounds of Pirates, 1780–1810

Aquatic occupations	Number	Percentage
Fishermen	213	
Hired sailors	78	
Grass cutters	11	
Other seamen	13	
Total	315	73.8

Nonaquatic occupations		
Hired laborers	31	
Porters	20	
Woodcutters	18	
Peddlers	15	
Merchants	9	
Soldiers	5	
Dismissed lower-degree holders	3	
Dismissed yamen clerks	2	
Others	9	
Total	112	26.2

Sources: XKTB, QL45–JQ 16; GZD, QL46–JQ14; ZPZZ, JQ 10–JQ 16; and *MQSLWB* 468b–564a.

Fishermen and hired sailors were the largest source of pirate recruits, together accounting for 68.2 percent of the total in Table 6. Arrested pirates, who had backgrounds as fishermen, almost uniformly complained to authorities that they had become pirates in the first place because fishing conditions were poor and they had no way of making an honest living.[6] Drifting about freely from place to place they grabbed whatever work they could get, whether licit or not. Mobility was a salient feature of seafaring life, as it was for other marginalized groups in late imperial China. In a survey of 123 cases, in 81 instances (94 percent) fishermen and sailors told authorities that they fished or worked in areas outside their native counties.[7] As David Ownby has shown in his study of

---

[6] See examples in GZD (857) JQ 1.7.5; (3749) JQ 3.2.29; (1496), JQ 1.11.18; (2109), JQ 2.3.4, (8158) JQ 7.5.27; ZPZZ *(falü* 75) JQ 3.11.19; and *MQSLWB* 474b, 484b, 487a, and 569b.

[7] XKTB, QL 45–JQ 16; GZD, QL 46–JQ 14; ZPZZ, JQ 10–JQ 16; and *MQSLWB* 468b–564a.

Chinese secret societies, movement and violence were central features of society along the southeastern coast in the eighteenth century. Violence contributed to mobility just as mobility contributed to violence, and both were aggravated by the population explosion, which created fierce competition over jobs and resources.[8]

Dan boat people were often singled out in the sources as an ethnic group prone to piracy. According to the Qing writer Deng Chun, they had "violent temperaments and were good at being [sea] bandits."[9] A number of chieftains, such as Zhang Bao and Guo Podai, were sons of Dan fishermen. Because Dan seafarers both worked and lived on the seas, they were the most vulnerable to pirate attacks, and because of their poverty and marginalization they were more willing to engage in illegal activities. Many became pirates not by choice but by necessity. For example, in 1798 Chen Heshe, a Dan fisherman from Dongguan county, gathered a gang of fourteen men in three boats and became pirates because fishing was so unprofitable that they could no longer make a decent living.[10] Numerous kidnapped fishermen and sailors actually chose to remain among the pirates rather than return to their former occupations.

Besides fishermen and sailors, pirates were also recruited from people in other walks of life. Hired laborers, porters, woodcutters, and peddlers were the most likely recruits among the nonaquatic occupations mentioned in Table 6, together comprising 19.7 percent of the total. A number of merchants, particularly those, such as Yang Yazhang, who had failed in business, also joined pirate gangs.[11] Huang He, who was a defrocked collegian (*jiansheng*), became one of the clerks in Wushi Er's organization, and Li Yingfang, a dismissed county clerk, joined with the pirates and later became a chieftain in charge of ten boats.[12] Zhou Feixiong was a doctor, opium dealer, occasional pirate, and petty thief; later he had helped to arrange the surrender of Zhang Bao in 1810, for which service the government rewarded him with a minor post in Macao.[13] According to Turner, there were even a few men among the pirates who were "of decent appearance" and with some

[8] Ownby 1996:13–17; also see Antony 1988:187–188.
[9] Cited in Chen Xujing 1946:112–115.
[10] ZPZZ (*falü* 75) JQ 3.11.19.
[11] GZD (2845) JQ 2.7.6.
[12] ZPZZ (1121) JQ 15.7.12; and NYC 13/68a.
[13] DGXZ 33/21b; and XSXZ 1827:8/60b.

money, and at least one man who spoke a little English and acted as an interpreter for the pirates.[14]

Unlike in the heyday of Ming or early-Qing piracy, we find no well-to-do merchants and no gentry holding high degrees among these Chinese pirates of the early nineteenth century. Table 6 lists only nine merchants, none too well off, and three dismissed holders of lower degrees. It can be argued that most well-established merchants were no longer attracted to active participation in piracy because trade was open and the profits were usually large enough from legitimate commerce (or perhaps smuggling). The majority of successful, wealthy merchants, therefore, shared the same view of piracy as did the state: it was a reprehensible crime against society and ruinous to business. When merchants and gentry did become involved in piracy, it was normally indirectly as fences and receivers. Peasants and tenant farmers were also conspicuously absent from among the list of pirates. As Thomas Chang has suggested, their skills were not particularly suitable for seamanship and "their attachment to the land created a lifestyle vastly different from that of the pirates."[15]

Although the evidence is somewhat fragmentary (only 184 cases), we can nonetheless venture a few tentative remarks concerning the personal and family backgrounds of convicted pirates. They ranged in age from a youth of fourteen to a man of sixty-eight *sui*, with the highest concentration between the ages of twenty-one and thirty-six. The mean age was 29.7 *sui*. As for family backgrounds, pirates tended to be unmarried (discounting the taking of mates from among the captive women), and from small, often broken, families. Most pirates were what the literature called "bare sticks" (*guanggun*), unmarried males who lacked steady jobs. Such displaced men, who were unproductive and highly mobile, had neither a position nor a stake in society, and had much free time on their hands.[16] While some pirates returned periodically to their homes to share their loot with family members, others had no families or homes. And many of those with families refused to return home for fear of being arrested.

Who were the victims of piracy? Most victims, of course, were aboard junks or in coastal towns and villages when they were robbed or abducted by pirates. One of the documents I uncovered

---

[14] *Chinese Repository* 1834:3/81–82.

[15] T. Chang 1983:232.

[16] See Hsiao 1960:455–457; and Perry 1980:59–60.

in the Qing archives affords us a rare glimpse into the backgrounds of a group of thirty-three victims kidnapped by pirates in 1797. There were twenty-six males, three females, and four children. In all but one instance the victims were fishermen and their family members. Among this group were members of a Dan boating family: Mrs. Liao, née Zhu, who was twenty-eight years old, and her three year-old son, the youngest of the victims. The family, who came from Zhaoan county in Fujian, was transporting tea to sell in the market at Zhangzhou when they were attacked by Wu Yaer's gang. Mrs. Liao was raped and kept by one of her captors. Unfortunately the document does not say what happened to her husband; we can presume that he had been killed or drowned. Another boy, Li Yatian, who was eleven years old, had been abducted while fishing along the coast near his home in Taiping county in Zhejiang. The oldest of these victims was Li Yazhan, who was forty-four; he was a fisherman from Raoping county in eastern Guangdong. Most of these victims came from small families, usually consisting of two or three members, and they were highly mobile.[17] The evidence suggests that there was little difference between pirates and victims with respect to age, family background, and mobility.

Becoming a Pirate

People generally became pirates in one of three ways. Some individuals had joined pirate gangs of their own free will (*touruhuo*); some originally had been abducted before joining a gang (*beilu ruhuo*); and others had been forced against their wills to join and aid pirates (*beixie fuyi*). The great pirate chiefs Cai Qian and Zhu Fen, driven perhaps as much by lust for riches and power as for adventure, became pirates by their own choice. For the cousins Zheng Qi and Zheng Yi, who were born into the trade, piracy had been a family business for several generations. In 1807, while he was being held prisoner by pirates, Turner frequently witnessed groups of five, ten, and even twenty men coming to enlist as pirates of their own accord.[18] In some cases, people were enticed into joining gangs by monetary inducements. For instance, Fu Bangjing was paid three silver dollars and Lin Yajiu four silver dollars to join pirate gangs. Others were offered boats,

---

[17] LFZZ (3854) JQ 2.1.27.
[18] *Chinese Repository* 1834:3/81.

weapons, women, or positions of authority if they became pirates.[19]

A number of people evading justice fled to sea to become pirates. Huang Kuei, who had been kidnapped by Cai Qian and later arrested and sentenced to penal servitude, escaped and fled back to sea to join Wu Liu's band. Liang Taizheng, a Shunde native, had committed a robbery on land in 1805, and afterward ran off to sea to avoid arrest. Fan Yuanchang had been arrested and sentenced to penal servitude for snatching a sack of money from a traveler, but he later escaped and joined the pirates. Chen Wuzhao was a deserter from the army when he entered Wushi Er's gang.[20] In the wake of the suppression of the Lin Shuangwen Rebellion on Taiwan in 1787–1788 and the Triad uprising in Guangdong in 1802–1803, a number of fugitive secret society members reportedly became pirates.[21] The sea had always served as a refuge for the lawless and criminal elements in society.

Probably most people began their criminal careers, however, after being abducted and then willingly joining bands. Governor-General Bai Ling believed that in Guangdong nine out of every ten pirates had originally been abducted; and a modern scholar, Guan Wenfa, claimed that 80 percent of the Fujian pirates had been kidnapped before becoming pirates.[22] Indeed, many of the major pirate leaders, such as Mo Guanfu, Wushi Er, Guo Podai, and Zhang Bao, were "recruited" in this manner. Whenever pirates abducted someone, they would first try to coax the person into voluntarily joining the gang. Often captives willingly became pirates, as was the case with Zheng Yasu and Zheng Atu, two fishermen who, after abduction by Guo Podai's men, decided to remain with the outlaws. Later Guo Podai appointed both men as captains of their own vessels. It was not uncommon, too, for kidnapped victims who had at first refused to later join the gang, working their way up the ranks from cook to lookout and then to full-fledged pirate. The longer someone stayed aboard a pirate vessel the more likely he would participate in crimes and the more likely he would be willing to remain as a pirate.[23]

---

[19] See, for example, GZD (3749) JQ 3.2.29; (3728) JQ 3.2.19; XKTB (136) QL 46.3.25; and (147) JQ 14.4.23.

[20] *MQSLWB* 483b; ZPZZ (*falü* 76) JQ 4.8.27; GZD (14385) JQ 14.5.28; and (11082) JQ 13.r5.25; for other examples see GZD (465) JQ 1.4.14; (981) JQ 1.7.29; and *MQSLWB* 492a–b.

[21] *DGXZ* 20b–21a; and Ljungstedt 1835:111.

[22] ZPZZ (1120) n.d.; Guan Wenfa 1994:97.

[23] GZD (11447) JQ 13.7.5; (11709) JQ 13.8.5; (8978) JQ 7.10.11; (12311) JQ 13.10.27;

Individuals also were frequently "adopted" into the pirate profession. The practice of adoption of both sons and daughters was common among South China's mariners, especially among the wealthy sea merchants who frequently adopted sons (*yizi*) from among the poor, raising them to captain their ships on risky trading voyages.[24] Pirate chieftains likewise used the same device to increase their own followings with loyal subordinate officers. Zheng Yi, for example, used this method quite frequently, taking as adopted sons not only Zhang Bao and Guo Podai, but also a number of other young men who had been abducted.[25] In another case, in 1795 Zheng Qi kidnapped a twelve-year-old boy named He Song and made him an adopted son. When He got older, Zheng Qi awarded him with a bride from among the captive females and gave him 7,000 silver taels to return home to Fujian to establish a store as a front for recruiting more men and for handling stolen goods. In 1801, at the youthful age of eighteen, He was given command of three ships, but in the following year he was apprehended by Guangdong authorities and promptly beheaded.[26] Sometimes parents, in need of money, sold their sons to pirates. Lin Zhi, a poor fisherman from the port of Maxiang, sold his fifteen-year-old son to Cai Qian, who raised him as his own flesh and blood and trained him in the pirate profession.[27]

In many cases, too, pirates forced kidnapped victims to become pirates against their will. Under such circumstances they became reluctant pirates. Undoubtedly many captives became pirates the hard way, that is, by first being physically abused or by working their way up the ranks from prisoner, to cook, to lookout, and then full-fledged pirate. On one occasion, as reported by Richard Glasspoole, who had been held for ransom by pirates for over two months in 1809, pirates captured nine rice boats, and since their captives had put up no resistance, they were allowed to become pirates. When four of them refused, they were tortured until they either "died or complied with the [pirate's] oath."[28] In other cases, male captives, such as Wu Yasheng, were first sexually abused by

(14385) JQ 14.5.28; XKTB (217) JQ 7.3.19; (87) JQ 12.8.3.; and *NYC* 13/12a–b.

[24] *XMZ* 652.

[25] GZD (15315) JQ 14.9.3; also see Ye Linfeng 1970:16.

[26] GZD (8052) JQ 7.5.12; and for other examples see GZD (5050) JQ 5.2.15; (6266) JQ 6.9.29; XKTB (92) JQ 11.6.15; and (86) JQ 14.1.17.

[27] GZD (9668) JQ 13.1.6.

[28] Glasspoole 1831:114–115.

pirates before giving in to their demands that they join with them. This was not an uncommon method of recruitment.[29] Besides outright kidnapping, pirates recruited gangs by coercion and threats as well as by trickery. In September 1796, Chen Dehong, a fisherman from Yangjiang who owned a boat, formed a gang of pirates with three other fishermen and their crews. Fifteen crewmen were willing to join, but Zhou Yaer and ten others refused to become sea bandits. Chen and the others had to threaten their lives and force them to go along.[30] In other instances pirates would hire sailors on legitimate pretenses, but once at sea, they would reveal their true intentions, leaving hired sailors little choice but to cooperate. Liang Guida had formed a pirate gang of fourteen men in late 1796. Thinking he had too few men, he then hired another eleven hands who believed that they had signed on as sailors on a fishing boat. After leaving sight of land, Liang explained his real intents and compelled the eleven sailors to become pirates.[31] Some men also were coerced to participate in crimes because their family members were held as hostages. After capture it was common practice for pirates to separate family members, keeping women and children as prisoners below decks or on different vessels in order to force their menfolk to cooperate.[32]

Professional Pirates

Certainly not everyone became a pirate because of poverty or out of necessity. There were those people, both men and women, whose motives went beyond mere survival to crime for profit. For them piracy was a vocation, a way of life. They were fully committed to crime and relied solely on the spoils of their endeavors for their livelihoods. As career criminals they depended on the structures of organized gangs for their daily support. At the end of the eighteenth century, with the increase in the number of piracies, and especially the upsurge in large-scale piracy, there was a corresponding increase in professional piracy, but at no time did it

---

[29] GZD (1656) JQ 1.12.11; also see GZD (827) JQ 1.6.25; (857) JQ 1.7.5; (1392) JQ 1.11.1; (2531) JQ 2.3.4; and (2845) JQ 2.7.6.

[30] GZD (1176) JQ 1.9.21; also see WJD, JQ 16.5.23.

[31] GZD (2109) JQ 2.3.4; see also GZD (292) JQ 1.3.10; (1392) JQ 1.11.1; and (3749) JQ 3.2.29.

[32] GZD (8978) JQ 7.10.11; ZPZZ (1016) JQ 9.2.3; and (1058) JQ 10.11.12.

come to eclipse occasional piracy. These hardened criminals included the "great pirates" (*judao*) Zheng Yi, Wushi Er, Zhang Bao, Cai Qian, and Zhu Fen, their subordinate officers, and many ordinary gang members. Many hard-core pirates had such names as Tiger Heart Liu, Black Pig Zheng, Cut Nose Lin, and Scabby Zhou.

Wushi Er was the archetypal professional pirate, one of the earliest pirates to emerge in Vietnam in the 1790s and the last major pirate to be subdued in 1810. Born Mai Youjin in the small fishing village of Wushi (hence the sobriquet) in Haikang county in southwestern Guangdong, he began his criminal career as a petty thief and blackmailer in port towns along the coast. After being kidnapped by pirates he decided to become one himself, and soon afterward joined the Tâyson rebels in Vietnam. By 1797 he commanded a gang (*huo*) of roughly a hundred men and had three vessels. Around this time the rebel ruler awarded him with the title the Great General Who Pacifies the Sea. After the Tâyson defeat in 1802, he returned to Chinese waters, and by 1805 Qing officials reported that he had become the most fearsome pirate in western Guangdong with a fleet (*bang*) of eighty to ninety junks. By the time of his capture in 1810, he commanded a great fleet (*da bang*) of over a hundred vessels and several thousand pirates.[33]

At that time too Wushi Er oversaw a vast criminal network centered on the waters off Hainan Island and the Leizhou peninsula and branching outward as far away as Chaozhou and Zhangzhou. Each year his fleets took in profits of several thousand taels from plunder and extortion, making it necessary for him to employ a small bureaucracy of scribes to write blackmail letters and to keep accounts of the loot, as well as of weapons and provisions. Over the years he had slowly built up his organization by cultivating kinship and native-place relationships (*guanxi*) with subordinates and followers. His formidable Blue Banner fleet was divided into eight squadrons, organized around a central core of family members (his elder brother, Wushi Da, and younger cousin, Wushi San) and other career pirates from the Leizhou region (Long Yuandeng from Haikang, Yang Pianke and Chen Yaguang from Suiqi). In extending his network into eastern Guangdong he relied on Chaozhou natives Zheng Yaozhang and Zhou Tian, who had joined Wushi Er's gang in 1807 after being kidnapped. Through these two subordinates, and others such as Zhang Ruisui

---

[33] GZD (3728) JQ 3.2.19; and (10138) JQ 13.3.2.

and Cheng Linyuan, natives of Chaozhou and Zhangzhou respectively, Wushi Er was able to collaborate on joint ventures with Zhu Fen and Cai Qian.[34]

Because in South China many women made their homes aboard ship and worked alongside their menfolk, it was not unusual to find females among these ocean bandits. While most ordinary gang members remained unmarried, some pirate captains reportedly had five or six wives on board their junks as well as other family members. One chief named Huang Shengzhang kept his whole family with him at sea: his mother, wife, two sons, four other female relatives, and a servant girl.[35] A number of women pirates had married, either voluntarily or by coercion, into the pirate profession and apparently willingly lived and died as outlaws. Several female pirates even became powerful chieftains, such as Zheng Yi Sao, leader of the formidable Red Banner fleet, and Cai Qian Ma, who commanded several pirate vessels with crews of women warriors. In Fujian a female pirate known as Qi Sao (Seventh Elder Sister-in-law) commanded a fleet of some twenty ships.[36] The wife of the pirate Chen Acheng, whom we know only by her surname Li, took part in more than ten robberies at sea; after their arrest her husband was put to death and she was made the slave of a military officer.[37] In one contemporary account, during a sea battle with the imperial navy in 1809, the wife of a pirate, with cutlasses in both hands, fought bravely and wounded several soldiers before a musket ball cut her down.[38]

Women who lived aboard ships and worked alongside men inevitably enjoyed more freedom than their counterparts living on shore, and this fact surely made it easier for, and perhaps even encouraged, some seafaring women to participate in piracy. Women, too, may have been more willing to become pirates because they were much less likely than men to receive the death penalty for involvement in capital offenses.[39] I have not come

---

[34] Ibid.; ZPZZ (1058) JQ 10.11.22; (1121) JQ 15.7.12; SYD, JQ 14.9.12; and JQ 16.3.15.

[35] *MQSLWB* 465a.

[36] T. Chang 1983:169.

[37] GZD (1047) JQ 1.8.19.

[38] Neumann 1831:24.

[39] In general, women were punished less severely than men for committing the same crime. Notable exceptions were those cases where women were convicted of adultery or of murdering their husbands, parents, or in-laws.

across in the archives any instances of female pirates who were
executed for piracy; indeed, the most severe penalty was exile into
slavery, as was the case of woman Li above. In most instances,
however, women who were arrested in piracy cases were simply
returned home to their families under bond.

These and other women pirates were able to survive in a man's
world by proving themselves as capable as (and sometimes more
so than) men in battle and in their duties as sailors. They were
not merely tolerated by their male shipmates but were, in many
cases, actually able to exercise leadership roles aboard their junks.
Their example offered an important alternative image of womanhood in late imperial China that contradicted and challenged ideal
Confucian constructs.[40]

Occasional Piracy

One of the outstanding characteristics of mid-Qing piracy, even
at the height of large-scale piracy in the early nineteenth century,
was that most gang members were not career criminals. Rather,
they were occasional pirates.[41] They were, by and large, unorgan-
ized amateurs, lacking any particular criminal skills. While professional pirates made crime a full-time occupation and subsisted
entirely on the fruits of their crimes over an extended period of
time, occasional pirates did not rely on crime as their sole source
of livelihood. They did make piracy an important, even essential,
part of their overall survival strategy, but they also engaged at
least part of the time in lawful occupations, as fishermen, sailors,
laborers, and the like. Such men either joined pirate gangs during
periods of lawful employment to supplement honest wages, or
went on temporary sprees of criminality during intervals between
periods of legitimate work. For many individuals piracy was, in

---

[40] Female pirates, of course, were not the only example of women who turned
Confucianism on its head; throughout Chinese history one can find examples of
women warriors, bandits, and rebels (see, for instance, Naquin 1976:84–85; Perry
1980:67n; and Xiaolin Li 1995:111–145).

[41] Although Dian Murray (1987 and 1997) and Thomas Chang (1983) have attempted to equate the petty piracy before 1802 with part-time, occasional piracy,
and the large-scale piracy between 1802 and 1810 with professional piracy, I argue
that no such clear-cut distinctions can be found. Both professional and occasional
piracy were common throughout the entire period, even within the huge pirate
leagues.

the words of Robert Ritchie, "an interlude in an otherwise normal life."[42]

Along the southern coast of China were villages that had long-standing traditions of combining fishing, smuggling, wrecking, and piracy.[43] A number of villages and bays were so infamous that route books, some dating back to the Ming dynasty, warned their readers to stay clear of those places. In those coastal areas, where the population was dense and villages in close proximity to one another, intervillage strife over fishing grounds or water rights was a common occurrence. On the Quanzhou coast, for instance, it had long been a customary practice for feuding villages to rob each other's oyster traps and fishing nets and to abduct rival fishermen and their family members for ransom.[44] Another "evil custom," so common along the southern littoral that it prompted the state to enact preventive legislation, was for villagers to take advantage of storms to plunder vessels in distress.[45] Numerous Chinese and aborigine villages along the west coast of Taiwan, an area lined with dangerous shoals and having frequent shipwrecks, had reputations for wrecking as late as the end of the nineteenth century. For them wrecking was a community enterprise and tradition.[46] Indicative of the greatly increased opportunities for plunder provided by the growth of maritime trade, by the late eighteenth century many coastal communities came to depend on wrecking, smuggling, and piracy as much as, or even more than, on legitimate sources for their sustenance.

In the mid-Qing, as was true in earlier times, it was not unusual for fishermen and other seafarers to oscillate between legitimate pursuits and piracy. For many mariners, such as Liu Caifa and Chen Yatian, piracy served to augment otherwise irregular work and meager earnings. Liu was a native of Raoping, in eastern Guangdong, and he had joined a gang of pirates in October 1795. After plundering a junk, he used his share of the loot to purchase his own boat and resumed fishing for a while. In December he and several other fishing companions formed a new gang and robbed a junk near Chenghai.[47] Chen Yatian, a Fujian native, likewise joined a pirate gang in the summer of 1794, and

---

[42] Ritchie 1986:123.

[43] *XMZ* 175; *JMZ* 92; *DGXZ* 33/28a–b; and Huang Dianquan 1958:76.

[44] *MXTZ* 8/14b.

[45] Ibid., 11/2a; and ZPZZ (*falü* 75) JQ 3.9.23; (*falü* 76) JQ 4.8.27.

[46] See Pickering 1898:176–193.

[47] GZD (981) JQ 1.7.29.

after being wounded in a raid, he returned home to recuperate. When he recovered he resumed fishing. Then in the following spring, he joined another gang of pirates. Arrested in September 1796, he was promptly beheaded after trial.[48] Piracy was indeed a regular and integral component in the life cycles of many mariners.

For fishermen and sailors it was easy to make the transition to pirate. They had mobility, the sorts of occupations, and the most important tool of the trade—a boat—all of which allowed them to slip in and out of ports without much notice. The archival records are replete with accounts given by arrested pirates who tell how they availed themselves of unforeseen opportunities to rob unsuspecting vessels that happened to pass nearby while they were out fishing. This was apparently true of Chen Qiyi. In 1789, he and sixteen companions set out to fish in their small boat, but when they came across a passage boat anchored in a remote spot offshore, they did not hesitate to plunder it. Later they resumed fishing.[49] In the early nineteenth century there were many stories about how fishing fleets—the "companions of the net" (*gupeng*) in Guangdong and the "fishhook boat gangs" (*diaochuanbang*) in Fujian—while out fishing would take advantage of their strength in numbers to attack lone vessels.[50] As late as the 1830s, it was still common practice for Fujian fishermen to spend several months each year off the Zhejiang coast, where they engaged in both fishing and "occasional piracy."[51] Because seafarers were often away from home and the constraints of community and government for variable periods of time, they found it easy to engage periodically in piracy.

Gangs were also essentially transient in nature. They formed, splintered, and reformed, apparently with ease, and individuals did not necessarily spend many years associated with the same group of men. Even after pirate groups became more permanent and professional after 1802, membership in gangs actually remained open and flexible. In 1807 Turner reported that although in some cases pirates were allowed to come and go as they pleased, "lately the [pirate] chief refused to permit any to

[48] GZD (1091) JQ 1.8.30; and for other cases see GZD (67) JQ 1.1.21; (780) JQ 1.6.16; (981) JQ 1.7.29; XKTB (92) JQ 11.6.15; and (86) JQ 14.4.17.

[49] GZD (56944) QL 54.4.17; and for other examples see GZD (137) JQ 1.2.9; (1091) JQ 1.8.30; (1279) JQ 2.r6.21; *MQSLWB* 487a; and WJD, JQ 16.5.23.

[50] See Chen Xujing 1946:112–115; and Zhang and Yang 1983:72–74.

[51] Gutzlaff 1834:238.

join him for a term less than eight or nine months."[52] Fishermen, sailors, and laborers would sign on to pirate vessels during slack seasons when honest living and legitimate jobs were hard to come by. They worked aboard pirate ships as they would on fishing and merchant junks. Piracy was treated like any other job. Jumping ship and switching gangs were common. Even among professional pirates there was a high degree of mobility between gangs. One pirate boss named Qi Benyin, for example, easily switched from Cai Qian's to Zhu Fen's band after the former met a setback in Taiwan.[53]

Aboard pirate vessels crews typically consisted of a diverse mix of men, some whose criminal activities may have begun a few weeks earlier and others who were hardened criminals of many years. In one band, for instance, Guang Henghe had been a pirate for nearly three years, while Rong Yachun, who was a fisherman, had joined the gang only two months before their arrest in 1809.[54] In another band one man had been a pirate for over ten years while most of his comrades had been active pirates for only a few months or from two to three years. Several of the new recruits recently had been fishermen or hired sailors and had joined the gang during a period of seasonal unemployment.[55] In general, the archival evidence suggests that most of the men convicted of piracy only had been at it for a year or less before being apprehended and brought to trial. Cases like that of the great pirate chieftain Wushi Er, who remained a pirate for more than twenty years, were rare.[56]

Reluctant Pirates and Captives

In the mid-Qing the crews aboard nearly every pirate vessel were composed of both actual pirates (*zhengdao*) and their captives (*beilu zhe*). The actual pirates, who included both professional and occasional pirates, were full-fledged gang members who perpetrated violent crimes on both sea and shore and shared

---

[52] *Chinese Repository* 1834:3/81.

[53] *MQSLWB* 538b; see other examples in GZD (3459) JQ 2.12.1; *MQSLWB* 429b; and ZPZZ (1121) JQ 15.7.12.

[54] GZD (14561) JQ 14.6.19.

[55] XKTB (85) JQ 5.2.12.

[56] There was at least one other instance of a pirate chief named Huang Deren who remained an outlaw for more than twenty years before surrendering in 1800 (GZD [4825] JQ 5.1.24).

equitably in the spoils. They were the culprits who boarded their victims' boats or broke into their homes to rummage and rob, who assaulted or killed their victims, and who kidnapped and raped men, women, and children. According to Qing law they were genuine criminals who had to be punished in the most severe manner, either death by imminent decapitation and exposure of the head (*zhan lijue xiaoshi*) or, in the most heinous cases, by slow dismemberment by slicing (*lingchi*).[57] Because of the upsurge in piracy, the Jiaqing emperor, in 1796 and 1797, ordered provincial officials to henceforth execute convicted pirates immediately after trial in accordance with an extraordinary judicial procedure known as summary execution by royal mandate (*wangming xian-xing zhengfa*).[58] Afterward the severed heads were sent to the localities where the crimes had been committed and placed on pikes or in cages for public exposure. Even the recovered corpses of pirates had their heads cut off and were similarly displayed along the coast.[59] Throughout these years the spectacle of decapitated heads dangling in the air in port towns and marketplaces must have been a ubiquitous sight along the southern coast of China.

The captives were kidnapped victims whom pirates held either for ransom or to serve them aboard their vessels. Pirates routinely compelled a certain number among their captives to participate in crime, thereby making them unwilling accomplices or reluctant pirates. Officials considered them as criminals (*fan*) and, therefore, also deserving punishment. During the height of the pirate upheaval between 1795 and 1810, captives outnumbered the actual pirates by three to one. I have collected from the Qing archives information on 9,600 individuals who were arrested in connection

---

[57] *HDSL* 619/2a–b; and *DQSL* (QL 60.7.6):1482/6a–7a. Although not a literal translation, I use the term "imminent" rather than the more conventional "immediate" to describe the *lijue* executions. To characterize the executions as immediate is misleading because they were never carried out immediately, but rather had to await the approval of the emperor, which could take months. A more appropriate meaning of the term *lijue* is "imminent" because the sentence was impending and almost certain to be carried out once approval was received from the throne.

[58] See GZD (263) JQ 1.3.5; and (2631) JQ 2.6.16. Normally all capital cases had to be reviewed and approved by the emperor before executions could be carried out. The summary executions by royal mandate allowed certain high-ranking provincial civil and military officials to bypass the regular time-consuming procedures so that executions could be carried out right after trial (usually at the provincial level) in those cases considered too serious to be delayed.

[59] See, for example, GZD (67) JQ 1.1.21; (465) JQ 1.4.14; (1656) JQ 1.12.11; (2531) JQ 2.5.29; (3728) JQ 3.2.19; and (12312) JQ 13.10.27.

with piracy between 1795 and 1810 in Fujian and Guangdong: only 2,803 men (29.2 percent) were actual pirates, while 6,797 individuals (70.8 percent) were captives. Based on this archival data, captives can be further divided into three groups: one, those forced to be accomplices in the commission of crime (1,918 men or 20.0 percent); two, those compelled to help the pirates in various tasks aboard ship (3,102 people or 32.3 percent); and three, those held as prisoners below decks (1,777 individuals or 18.5 percent).[60] These figures are presented in Table 7.

Why did the pirates keep so many captives? It is impossible to understand the rise, growth, and longevity of the great pirate leagues without taking into account these large numbers of kidnapped victims. In fact, large-scale piracy in the mid-Qing depended on the procurement of ever increasing numbers of captives. Not only were the ransom payments for kidnapped victims important sources of revenue, but even more important, captives were also essential sources of labor, indeed exploited forced labor, for the pirates. Many more captives, in fact, were kept to do forced labor than were held for ransom. On pirate junks, while work was the same as aboard any other Chinese vessel, it was less intense because pirate ships were usually greatly overmanned, and most of the tedious and mundane tasks of sailing a ship were forced upon the captives.

Those captives who did all the hard, manual labor aboard ship and who were often forced to participate in criminal activities generally went unrewarded. The actual pirates did not count captives as members of the gang, and therefore they had no right to a share of the spoils. In the Liang Guida case mentioned above, Liang formed a gang of fourteen men in 1796 and coerced another eleven men into joining him. Near the Dongguan coast they plundered Chen Jinxing's fishing boat of 195 silver dollars, 4,000 copper cash, five pecks of rice, a wooden oar, and a brass gong. After the robbery Liang set the eleven coerced "pirates" free on

---

[60] This quantitative evidence has to be used with caution. Piracy was after all a capital crime, and therefore the fabrication of depositions by persons arrested in piracy cases was a matter of fact. It was also a matter of concern to officials, who did take precautions to prevent abuses. Elaborate judicial procedures, including interrogations and cross-examinations of suspects and witnesses, as well as multiple case hearings and reviews, all attempted to assure fairness and justice according to the law. Many men had unquestionably been kidnapped and forced to serve pirates aboard their vessels, but perhaps not as precisely as the statistics indicate. Nevertheless, the overall pattern suggests a reality that is undeniable.

Table 7
Persons Arrested in Fujian and Guangdong Piracy Cases, 1795–1810

Actual pirates		Captives	
	Accomplices	Helpers	Prisoners
2,803	1,918	3,102	1,777
29.2%	20.0%	32.3%	18.5%
2,803		6,797	
29.2%		70.8%	

Sources: GZD, JQ 1–14; ZPZZ, JQ 10–16; LFZZ, JQ 2–15; WJD, JQ 8–16; and *MQSLWB* 468b–564a.

shore without any recompense and then divided the loot among the original fourteen pirates into fifteen shares with himself taking two shares as leader. Each share was worth thirteen dollars, 200 cash. The leftover 1,000 cash and rice were put in reserve for later use. As for the wooden oar and brass gong, Liang also claimed these as his own. Once the loot had been divided the gang dispersed. On occasion Cai Qian also conscripted fishermen without paying them any compensation to transport provisions and munitions from shore to his island bases.[61] Such captives were treated the same as slave laborers.

Whenever pirates plundered a vessel or raided villages, they would compel a number of captives to either act as lookouts (*bafeng*) or remain aboard the pirate vessel to help handle and receive the loot (*jiedi zangwu*) as it was passed to them from the victim's boat or home. By such acts, in the eyes of Qing officials, they became accomplices in crime and were punished with banishment as the slaves of military officers in Manchuria and, after 1802, in Xinjiang.[62] Chen Kaifa and seven other companions, who had all been abducted by Zheng Qi, were first ordered to perform simple chores for their captors, but later they were each forced *once* to handle the booty or act as lookouts.[63] However, once a

---

[61] GZD (2109) JQ 2.3.4; and *MQSLWB* 526b; for other examples see GZD (981) JQ 1.7.29; ZPZZ (1120) JQ 15.4.14; (*falü* 164) JQ 10.5.20; XKTB (135) JQ 9.2.19; (145) JQ 9.3.14; (58) JQ 10.11.3; and (209) JQ 16.10.3.

[62] *HDSL* 619/28b–29a; and Wu Kun 1871:49/18b–19b.

[63] GZD (8978) JQ 7.10.11; also see *MQSLWB* 464b–465a, 499b, and 529b–530a; and GZD (7452) JQ 7.2.21.

captive had committed a second crime, as lookout or handler of booty, even if he had been coerced, the law treated him as no different from an actual pirate and therefore he too would be sentenced to death. The longer one remained aboard a pirate vessel the more likely he was to participate in more than one crime. Hence, when Yang Fengke was convicted for helping pirates "handle and receive booty *twice*," despite his claims of having been kidnapped and coerced to act against his will, he nonetheless was summarily beheaded alongside other cutthroat pirates.[64]

Another group of captives, in fact the largest number, was composed of individuals who had been forced to do various menial tasks aboard pirate vessels, such as hauling in ropes, weighing anchor, cooking, brewing tea, washing dishes, bailing water, cleaning the hold, and so forth. They did the dirty, exhausting work of common sailors. For their acts the Qing Code punished them with three years of penal servitude and one hundred strokes of the heavy bamboo.[65] After pirates kidnapped Li Xingyi off the Xinning coast, his captors forced him to bail water and burn incense for them. Cai Yaying, a blind man abducted from a fishing boat, was ordered to give massages to the pirates.[66] One eyewitness pointed out that people who had been kidnapped for ransom, but could not pay the demands, were forced to work for the pirates. In some cases they were allowed to work off their ransom, and after about five years of service were set free. Many, however, were afraid to return home because they had been involved in several crimes, and therefore remained with the pirates.[67]

There was yet another group of captives coerced to serve the pirates in another manner: women and men who were forced to have sex with their captors. Although men made up the majority of captives, there were also women and children. According to Glasspoole, the most lovely female captives were reserved for the wives and concubines of pirate chieftains; others remained untouched and were held for ransom; the most homely were simply returned to shore. Women who were not ransomed were later sold to the crew as "wives" at forty dollars a head.[68] Among the

---

[64] GZD (7452) JQ 7.2.21 (emphasis added).
[65] *HDSL* 619/28b–29a; and Wu Kun 1871:49/18b–19b.
[66] GZD (1092) JQ 1.8.30; and GZD (1302) JQ 1.10.15.
[67] Glasspoole 1831:114–115.
[68] Ibid., 113; see also *Chinese Repository* 1834:3/72, 80–81.

women prisoners, of which there were 218 mentioned in the archival case records used in this study, a little more than half had been raped and kept (*jiansu*) as wives or mistresses of pirates. Apparently some women were held for ransom, others kept as sex slaves for their captors. For these latter women and young girls, sex was a form of forced service. For instance, after robbing and murdering their husbands, pirates abducted, raped, and forced Mrs. Deng, née Li, and Mrs. Deng, née Zhou, to mate with them.[69] In another case, the pirate chieftain Wuchuan Si had abducted a Western woman, known to us only as A-lan, whom he kept aboard his ship for several years to satisfy his sexual whims.[70] Understandably a number of captive women bore the children of their pirate masters: Huang, née Su, bore two sons of the pirate Huang Zhenggui; Luo, née Zhong, bore the son of pirate Luo Xingda; and Wu, née Yang, gave birth to a son and a daughter of the pirate Wu Xinzhi.[71]

Pirates abducted not only women but also men and boys to serve their sexual needs. Because homosexual activities were common aboard pirate ships, it should not be surprising that a number of male captives, especially among adolescents, fell victim to the sexual abuses of their captors. Yet among the captives only 298 (9.6 percent) admitted to the authorities that they had been sodomized (*jijian*). Surprisingly few men used this ploy in the hopes of reducing a certain death sentence to penal servitude. Why there was such underreporting is difficult to explain. Perhaps the stigma and shame of rape—of being a penetrated male—was too great to admit.[72] The kidnapping and trafficking of men, women, and children for sex were ubiquitous aspects of piracy.

Finally, there were numerous men, women, and children who were held prisoners by pirates, usually below decks on ships (*yajin cangdi*). Prisoners held for ransom would normally be released when ransoms were paid. Not all prisoners, however, were held for ransom; a significant number of captives were also retained as a sort of reserve labor force to be put to work for the pirates as needed. Ye Zhengzhu, a sailor from Suiqi county, was abducted

---

[69] GZD (7452) JQ 7.2.21; also see LFZZ (3854) JQ 2.1.27; and GZD (1448) JQ 1.11.10.

[70] GZD (3347) JQ 2.11.12.

[71] GZD (6266) JQ 6.9.29.

[72] See my discussion in chapter 7, and for a general discussion of homosexuality among Guangdong pirates see Murray 1992.

in July 1796. At first he was imprisoned below deck, but later the pirates forced him to serve as cook. In another case, Li Achu, a native of Zhaoan county who was kidnapped by Cai Qian's gang in 1804 while fishing near Penghu, had refused to become a pirate and so was locked up in chains below deck with some twelve other men. In his deposition Li described how one by one over a period of several months the pirates dragged people from the ship's crowded hold and forced them to assist with sailing the vessel.[73] As long as kidnapped victims were held as prisoners below deck and did not aid the pirates in any way, Qing law did not hold them culpable for any crime and, once rescued by the authorities, they were released and sent back home.[74]

Not all captives, however, passively submitted to the wills of their captors. In 1807, Lin Qicheng and fourteen other kidnapped victims who were being held for ransom managed to kill their captors in their sleep and then escape. Two years later, Yang Zuoxing and several companions who had been forced to serve the pirates as cooks and lookouts mutinied and fled to freedom. In at least one case a female captive led a revolt against her captors. Miss Liang, a spirited Dan boatwoman, had been kidnapped, raped, and kept by the pirate captain Chen Yasheng. Because of his cruelty and perversity, she led the other captives in killing Chen and several gang members. After surrendering to officials she was rewarded with twenty taels of silver, in spite of the fact that she had "lost her virtue" (*shijie*).[75]

As the archival records clearly show, most of the people arrested in connection with piracy in Fujian and Guangdong had actually been victims who were abducted by pirates. Some were kept as prisoners and held for ransom, while others were forced to serve their pirate captors in a variety of ways. Large-scale piracy in the mid-Qing could never have developed in the ways that it did nor lasted as long as it did without the systematic use of forced labor of captives. For the pirates they were essential sources of revenue, conscript labor, and recruits. Even many of the actual pirates originally had been kidnapped victims. Little separated victims from criminals. All were potential ocean bandits.

---

[73] GZD (1116) JQ 1.9.8; and XKTB (321) JQ 11.2.7.

[74] Zhu and Bao 1834:14/22a.

[75] GZD (15316) JQ 14.9.3; (12783) JQ 13.12.17; and (13115) JQ 14.1.25. For other cases see GZD (13115) JQ 14.1.25; (13250) JQ 14.2.5; (14382) JQ 14.5.28; and (15316) JQ 14.9.3.

Whether actual pirates or captives, most of the individuals caught up in the piracy cases used in this study had common backgrounds as fishermen and sailors. As members of China's laboring poor, they shared similar hardships in making a living and the same fears of inescapable poverty. These were people who were highly mobile, unattached, and living on the edge, where etiquette and propriety seldom prevented violence and predation. Evidently those individuals who willingly committed crime, if even occasionally, did not share the same values espoused in Qing law and observed by respectable society. Although most seafarers did not become professional pirates, large numbers of them nevertheless did engage in occasional piracy as an important part of their overall survival strategy. Piracy was a rational response to unemployment and chronic underemployment. It was just another aspect of the mariner's life. Although dangerous it could also be rewarding. Pirates, who engaged in all sorts of criminal activities, did so not only to make ends meet but also for profit. During the first decade of the nineteenth century, when large-scale piracy reached its peak, powerful pirate leagues, using intimidation and brutal force, came to dominate much of the South China coast.

FIVE

Pirate Brutality and Hegemony

On July 10, 1809, Governor-General Bai Ling memorialized the throne about a naval engagement with Zhu Fen's fleet that had taken place near the island of Nan'ao earlier that year. It was an important victory for the government forces: hundreds of pirates were reported killed or drowned and more than twenty of their vessels were captured or sunk. Soldiers apprehended some thirty-seven suspects involved in piracy, including one Wang Pao. According to Wang's deposition, he was a native of Chenghai county in Chaozhou prefecture. In the summer of 1808 he had signed on as a sailor aboard a coasting junk owned and registered to Huang Yuanxing, also from Chenghai. The ship, skippered by the owner's two younger brothers, Huang Yaer and Huang Yawu, had a crew of more than forty sailors. After an uneventful voyage of several months the ship arrived in late winter at its final destination, the port of Rongcheng on the Shandong peninsula. Once the cargo was sold, the Huang brothers purchased soybeans and bean cakes, took on a passenger whose surname was Gao, and then set sail for the return trip to Guangdong.

Before reaching home, on February 5, 1809, Wang's ship was plundered off the Zhaoan coast by five or six pirate junks belonging to Zhu Fen's band. After firing cannons and muskets the pirates, with knives and sabers in hands, came alongside the merchant junk and boarded it. In the ensuing struggle Wang and several comrades were wounded, and Huang Yaer and seven other crewmen were killed and thrown overboard. When the smoke had settled the pirates had control of the ship and began apportioning the surviving victims aboard the pirate junks. Huang Yawu, the passenger named Gao, and eleven sailors were held for ransom, while one victim, Cai Azhao, was put ashore to report to Huang Yuanxing, the ship's owner, with the ransom note. The pirates tried to force Wang Pao and another twenty sailors into serving them, but when they refused they were put below decks as prisoners.

Afterward the pirates joined up with the main body of Zhu Fen's fleet at Cusha near the Guangdong border. The fleet sailed a few days later for Chaozhou waters, but on February 9, near Nan'ao, they engaged the navy in a fierce battle in which Zhu Fen was mortally wounded by cannon shot to his left eye and throat. The next day soldiers captured Wang and some thirty other men, who were promptly turned over to the Nan'ao subprefect for initial questioning. At about the same time Cai Azhao and Huang Yuanxing reported the case to the Chenghai magistrate.[1]

While we would be hard pressed to find a typical pirate incident, the above case is representative of many others found in the Qing archives. According to Qing law a pirate was someone who plundered on rivers and oceans, as well as anyone using boats to pillage coastal villages and towns. Piracy was rarely a single crime, but as in the case above, a compound of offenses, including robbery, assault, murder, kidnap, and extortion. In this chapter we will look more closely at the above offenses, as well as at the use of brutality and protection rackets by pirates to gain dominance over large sections of South China's seafaring society.

Pirate Modi Operandi

Pirates would attack any vessel, but only when they felt assured of success. They preferred easy targets that put up little resistance, even if the spoils were scant. Like most of the ships they robbed, the pirate junks also stayed close to shore and seldom attacked vessels far out at sea. They would regularly lie in ambush behind crags or hide among fishing fleets awaiting their quarry.[2] Stationary targets made easier prey than moving ones. Night attacks were common. Often, as in the depiction in Figure 13, pirates would use smaller craft, such as rowboats and sampans, to launch attacks on larger ships at anchor or becalmed. Pirates also used their sampans for raids on coastal villages and for expeditions along inland rivers.[3] Although, by the early nineteenth century, the pirates had organized themselves into

---

[1] GZD (14382) JQ 14.5.28.

[2] Brown 1861:15. This section has also benefited from the discussion in Murray 1987:80–89, 91–98.

[3] *MQSLWB* 474b.

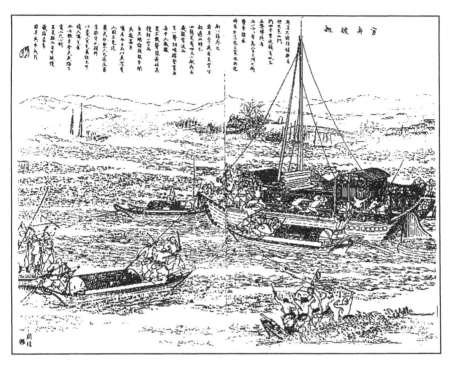

Figure 13. Pirates in Sampans Attacking Junk at Anchor. Source: *Dianshizhai huabao* (1884).

several huge leagues and fleets, the normal operational unit was a single vessel or perhaps several vessels.

Pirates used a wide variety of ships and weapons, which they obtained by capture or by purchase. In battling the ocean bandits, naval war junks had to face swifter, more maneuverable pirate vessels, ranging in size from 15 to 200 tons, with the majority averaging between 70 and 150 tons. One typical pirate craft, as illustrated in Figure 14, was the "open-the-waves junk" (*kailang-chuan*), so named because of its ability to cut swiftly through the water. These vessels carried crews of about thirty to fifty men.[4] Other popular vessels, such as the one depicted in Figure 15, were specially outfitted with both sails and oars for greater speed and maneuverability. Such craft had shallow drafts so they could sail close to shore without fear of running aground.[5] The largest pirate

---

[4] Audemard 1957–1971:1/58; Murray 1987:169; and Matsuura 1995:106–109.
[5] XMZ 175; and Audemard 1957–1971:1/61.

Figure 14. "Open-the-Waves Junk" used by Pirates.
Source: *Gujin tushu jicheng* (1884).

junks usually had twelve six- or eight-pound guns (some of these
had been manufactured in the West), and had crews of up to two
hundred men armed with swords, lances, and muskets. Smaller
boats, such as the sampans and rowboats, carried lighter
weaponry and fewer men.[6] The pirates could usually outgun the
navy because the heaviest cannonballs that it used were only one
catty, while the pirates used shot weighing between thirteen and
fourteen catties.[7]

---

[6] *Chinese Repository* 1833:2/241–242; and 1834:3/70; also see Audemard 1957–
1971:8/68–69; and T. Chang 1983:193–194.

[7] Wei 1979:94; Guan Wenfa 1994:96; and Matsuura 1995: 129–132.

叭喇唬船圖

Figure 15. Small Pirate Junk with Sail and Oars.
Source: *Gujin tushu jicheng* (1884).

While the most tempting prizes may have been the large trading junks of the Southern Ocean, they were usually well defended
and thus difficult targets. One such craft, called trough junks (*caochuan*), were sturdy double- or triple-masted ships with crews of
roughly eighty sailors. They sat high out of the water, making
boarding by pirates difficult, and their hulls were shielded with
layers of ox hides and fishing nets to deflect cannon shot. They
also went armed with cannon and other weapons, frequently
exceeding the legal limits set by the Qing state.[8]

---

[8] Ye Xianen 1989:196, 251–253.

Often deception was necessary when pirates hoped to plunder large, well-armed trading junks. In 1808, for example, when Zhang Bao decided to plunder a large merchant junk laden with goods from Tonkin, he needed to devise a ruse because he knew he "could not take her by force." He therefore ordered his men to steal two boats and to disguise themselves as ferrymen so that they could come up close to the junk without being suspected. As they came aside their victim, however, the ruse was discovered, and the junk's crew was able to fend off the attackers.[9]

Nevertheless, whenever those ships appeared vulnerable, pirates would attack, and on some occasions pirates seem to have overtaken their victims without much trouble. When attacking another vessel the pirates would run their boats alongside the victim's ship, fire a volley of cannon or musket shot, then shower the ship with "a great quantity of stink-pots" to set the sails on fire. Once the victim's ship was disabled, the pirates would jump aboard with their knives and spears to take command, as in the case presented at the start of this chapter.[10] In early November 1795, Liang Xuancan's gang, consisting of a crew of twenty-three pirates, plundered a Fujian merchant junk loaded with sugar, pears, and dates. Liang imprisoned the master and crew below deck and sailed off with his prize back to Vietnam.[11] In October 1805, pirates seized a large ocean junk near Macao carrying thirty thousand piculs of rice and a cargo valued at more than twenty thousand taels.[12] After procuring a fleet of great-ocean-crossing junks (*da hengyang chuan*), which had crews of roughly two hundred men, Cai Qian was successful in attacks against the large rice and sugar junks plying between Taiwan and mainland ports.[13] Such large prizes were worth the risk and effort.

More frequently, however, it was the smaller, more mundane coasting and fishing vessels that succumbed to pirate attacks. Typically, most maritime victims were tiny vessels with crews of fewer than ten, and often only two or three men. These vessels were generally poorly, if at all, armed. Even relatively small gangs could handle these boats. Their cargo, as described in chapter 3, consisted chiefly of ordinary goods such as sugar, rice,

---

[9] Neumann 1831:22–23.

[10] ZPZZ (*falü* 83) JQ 12.4.26; and Brown 1861:75.

[11] GZD (137) JQ 1.2.9.

[12] Murray 1987:83.

[13] *MQSLWB* 474a, 483b, 490a, 522b, 526b, 528b, 531b, and 578b; also see Huang Dianquan 1958:87–88; and T. Chang 1983:82–83.

sweet potatoes, peanuts, betel nuts, pigs, salted fish, cloth, and the like. Occasionally there would also be small stashes of opium, sycee, silver dollars, and copper cash.[14] These items, not the treasure chests of gold and jewels, were the typical spoils of pirate plunder. Pirates attacked these vessels perhaps as much for their cargo as for their men, who, as we have seen, were frequently abducted and forced into service.

As an operational technique, pirates frequently disguised themselves as merchants, gentry, officials, and soldiers for raids on inland rivers and market towns. According to the Panyu gazetteer, "crafty pirates" sometimes tried to pass themselves off as local gentry in order to take charge of government cannon that were used by militia units combating pirates. At other times they seized official craft and pretended to patrol the rivers, so that villagers, thinking themselves secure, would relax their defenses. Then suddenly the pirates would attack and loot those places without encountering staunch resistance. On still other occasions they disguised themselves as itinerant merchants or healers in order to spy on local communities. Such tactics caused so much confusion, the gazetteer continued, that villagers became distrustful and suspicious of all strangers. On at least one occasion, we are told, soldiers who landed to buy provisions were mistaken for pirates and butchered by the villagers.[15]

While pirates usually kept some of their plunder—especially foodstuffs, fresh water, weapons, and gunpowder—for their own use, they would sell most of the rest of their booty to other boatmen or in markets. Lin Ating's gang robbed a boat hauling thirty baskets of salted fish, which Lin sold to a fisherman for twenty silver dollars; later his gang robbed another boat with a cargo of peanuts, which was sold for forty silver dollars.[16] Chinese pirates, like their Western counterparts in the early eighteenth century, devised a share system for splitting up booty: gang leaders normally got double shares while the rest of the gang (but excluding captives) received one share each.[17] Usually the smaller, less permanent gangs split up their loot after each heist. Alternatively, particularly among the larger, more permanent gangs, all loot was

---

[14] See examples in GZD (4602) JQ 4.5.29; *MQSLWB* 469b, 474b, 480b; also see Murray 1987:82.

[15] *PYXZ* 22/16a–b.

[16] GZD (1496) JQ 1.11.18.

[17] On Western pirates see, for example, Rediker 1987:107, 264.

put into a common fund and then later, usually at the end of a campaign, divided into shares and distributed among the gang.[18] The earnings of individual pirates from just a single successful raid were generally much higher than the monthly wages of sailors on fishing and merchant junks. For indigent seafarers this was incentive enough for becoming pirates. Though an exceedingly dangerous business, piracy could be quite profitable.

Robbery, Kidnapping, and Rape

The most common offenses committed by pirates were robbery and kidnapping, which were also frequently attended by other violent acts such as assault, murder, rape, and sodomy. Robbery and kidnapping normally went hand in hand: when pirates seized a ship or village they routinely abducted a number of victims. As we have seen, while pirates held some kidnapped victims for ransom, they held others to provide services. According to the Xin'an gazetteer, pirates would "abduct wealthy hostages for ransom and press the poor into becoming pirates."[19]

A contemporary Qing poem, "A Song on Ransom," vividly depicts the harrowing experience of abduction by pirates:

> At sea, pirate ships, often a hundred-odd in number,
> North, east, south, and west wait for passing guests.
> In an encounter, the sounds of cannon fire shake the sky,
> And myriad pirates shouting in unison swarm on board.
> Everyone turns pale, grows sick with fear,
> As daggers fall as white as snow,
> They loot the cargo thoroughly and seize the passengers;
> They feign furious anger at prisoners brought on board.
> The captives scrape and bow on seeing the pirate chieftain.
> The pirate chieftain, his head wrapped in a lichee-colored kerchief,
> Interrogates both rich and poor, who beg for their lives:
> The ransom for each is set at ten thousand or one hundred in gold.
> With a great shout, he orders paper and brush
>   for carefully penned notes,
> Demanding a hundred items to be delivered within ten days,
> And should the deadline be missed, the hostages will be
>   disemboweled.
> Letters are sped off to their closest kin,
> Who pawn clothing and personal belongings, beg for loans.

---

[18] See GZD (981) JQ 1.7.29; and (9147) JQ 7.9.3.
[19] Cited in Xiao Guojian 1978:19.

> Concealing their bitterness, they devise means to solve
>   the problem,
> If only lives can be saved, no need to discuss impoverishment.[20]

Pirate chiefs, who grilled captives to assess their worth, determined the amounts of ransom according to family background and ability to pay. Frequently, pirates specified that payments be made in both money and goods, especially nautical equipment, food, and weapons.

Although in most cases pirates released captives after the ransom was paid, this was not always the case. Occasionally pirates would not only keep their hostages but also abduct those people sent to pay the ransom.[21] If ransom demands were not met on time, hostages were sometimes executed. In one case, for instance, the younger brother of a man named Xu Ze was kidnapped and held for ransom by pirates on Jinmen Island. After being notified, Xu Ze agreed on the place and time to pay the money, but was delayed a day in delivering it because of a storm. Since he did not make the deadline, the pirates killed his younger brother, but Xu Ze still had to pay the ransom to recover the corpse for proper burial.[22]

It was not unusual for pirates, whenever they had the chance, to abduct Westerners. On December 7, 1806, J. Turner, the chief mate of the English ship *Tay*, and five Lascars were abducted just outside Macao and held by pirates for five and half months before being released for a ransom worth about six thousand dollars. The pirates received two thousand dollars in cash, three chests of opium, and five thousand pieces of matting for sails. The ransom had been raised by the Western and Chinese merchants at Canton, each contributing half the total.[23] Three years later a gang associated with the Red Banner fleet kidnapped Richard Glasspoole and six other British seamen off Macao. The pirates had originally demanded a ransom of seventy thousand dollars. Eleven weeks and three days later, a ransom of forty-two hundred dollars was paid in cash; besides money, the pirates also received "two bales of superfine cloth; two chests of opium; two casks of gunpowder;

---

[20] Cited in T. Chang 1983:251.
[21] *NYC* 13/9b.
[22] *JMZ* 195.
[23] *Chinese Repository* 1834:3/69–70; and Morse 1926–1929:3/32, 63.

[and] a telescope."[24] Afterwards Glasspoole and the others were released.

Not only were people abducted and held for ransom, but so were vessels and their cargo. In 1796, a week before the lunar new year, Liu Caifa's band seized a boat near Chenghai and held its cargo of beans for a ransom of 130 dollars. In another case, Lin Daoban's gang, in 1800 near Amoy, captured a cargo junk laden with sugar, which he retained until the owners paid him a ransom of 350 dollars. The cargo actually was worth more than twice the ransom.[25] Some pirate chieftains reportedly employed specially trained appraisers to make accurate assessments of the market value of captured ships and goods.[26]

Sexual violence against women as well as men was a regular feature of the pirate's trade. In one case a certain Miss Feng, who had been kidnapped by Afang's gang in 1796, testified that she had been repeatedly gang-raped.[27] Apparently, too, pirates specifically targeted some women for their own individual sexual pleasure. One woman, surnamed Zheng, while out fishing, was seized and raped by the pirate Dianbai Chen; and another woman, surnamed Li, was snatched from shore and raped by Cai Fusi. Four other gang members raped four captured males.[28] In Vietnam two women who sold rice to pirates were carried off and gang-raped; members of this same gang also abducted and sodomized four seamen.[29] In many cases the rape victims would be released after the assault, but in other cases they were kept aboard ship to continue to serve the pirate crew. The rape and mistreatment of women was apparently done in wanton disregard of the stipulations in several pirate codes. In Guangdong, for instance, one pirate code specifically stated: "When captive women are brought on board, no one may debauch them; but their native places shall be ascertained and recorded, and a separate apartment assigned to them in the ship; any person secretly or violently approaching them shall suffer death." Cai Qian also reportedly had similar rules forbidding gang members from violating captive women.[30]

---

[24] Glasspoole 1831:125; also see Morse 1926–1929:3/117, 122; and Miller 1970: 126.

[25] GZD (1496) JQ 1.11.18; and XKTB (78) JQ 6.10.9.

[26] T. Chang 1983:210.

[27] GZD (1047) JQ 1.8.19.

[28] GZD (1448) JQ 1.11.10.

[29] GZD (2845) JQ 2.7.6.

[30] *Chinese Repository* 1834:3/73; and T. Chang 1983:233–234.

Murder, Mutilation, and Dismemberment

Not surprisingly, since the crimes committed by pirates were normally violent, they frequently ended in the death of victims. Sometimes pirates would murder a portion of the victim's crew to intimidate the rest into submission.[31] At other times they would murder the entire crew to assure their silence. When Guo Lianghuo's gang plundered a boat off the Xiangshan coast in April 1809, the pirates not only robbed it of 550 taels of silver and its cargo, but also killed the victims by tying them up and throwing them overboard, thereby ensuring that no one reported the crime to the authorities.[32]

Pirate brutality could reach extremes. Normally when victims offered no resistance, they would only be robbed, perhaps kidnapped.[33] But for those victims who resisted, the pirates sometimes ruthlessly murdered a part of the crew and cruelly mistreated the rest in addition to robbing them. After a sailor defied and cursed him, the pirate chief Xie Yaer immediately cut him down and threw his mutilated corpse overboard for the fish to eat. In another case pirates murdered fifty-seven sailors and threw their bodies into the sea.[34] When one of the passengers on a Chaozhou merchant junk tried to resist the pirate Chen Laosan, the latter had the poor man quartered and dismembered, and then had his heart and liver mixed with wine for the pirate gang to eat. A week later, when Chen's gang plundered a fishing boat, the helmsman who had resisted suffered the same fate.[35] Cai Qian and his wife reportedly indulged in cannibalistic orgies in which they devoured the hearts and livers and drank the blood of executed captives.[36]

During the inland raid in the Canton delta in 1809, wrote Glasspoole, one chieftain offered a bounty of ten dollars for every head his cutthroats brought him. Some pirates, eager for the money, returned to their boats with five or six severed heads, tied by their queues and slung round their necks.[37] In the village of

---

[31] GZD (9147) JQ 7.9.3.

[32] WJD, JQ 16.5.23; also see *MQSLWB* 480b.

[33] See GZD (1967) JQ 2.2.7; (9073) JQ 7.10.24.

[34] GZD (1967) JQ 2.2.7; and (9147) JQ 7.9.3.

[35] GZD (2779) JQ 2.r6.21. Edward Brown, who had been abducted by Chinese pirates off Vietnam in 1857, also described how his captors had brutally killed the master of a Chinese merchant junk by cutting him into pieces and then drinking his blood (1861:29).

[36] *MXTZ* 235.

[37] Glasspoole 1831:118–119; this story is also recounted in *GZFZ* 81/20a.

Sanshan in Panyu county, after three days of heavy fighting against militiamen, the pirates burned the village to the ground, cut off the heads of the murdered villagers, and suspended them on nearby trees as a warning to others not to resist.[38]

Whenever pirates captured naval war junks or patrol boats, even if there was no resistance, they often killed the entire crew. The victims would first be tortured and cut to pieces and thrown overboard. Turner vividly described the torture and execution of two captured naval officers. One man had his feet nailed to the deck and was beaten with rattan whips until he vomited blood, "and after remaining some time in this state, he was taken ashore and cut to pieces." The other officer "was fixed upright, his bowel cut open, and his heart taken out"; afterward the pirates soaked the heart in wine and ate it. Such atrocities, Turner commented, had a great psychological affect on the imperial forces, which dared not attack pirates unless assured of victory.[39]

However horrifying and repulsive, pirate cruelty must nevertheless be judged in the context of the times and in relation to official behavior. For pirates and seafarers, the image of a brutal state was heightened by the bloody executions of hundreds, perhaps thousands, of people on the coast each year. Pirates followed the example of officials. State executions themselves were not pretty sights, but rather veritable theaters of horror meant to impress the public. In death-by-slicing the criminal was bound to a cross and then cut either into 120, 72, 36, or 24 pieces (Figure 16). In some cases, as a gesture of imperial clemency, the body was sliced into eight portions only. One witness gave this graphic description of the punishment of twenty-four cuts:

> The first and second cuts remove the eyebrows; the third and fourth, the shoulders; the fifth and sixth, the breasts; the seventh and eighth, the parts between each hand and elbow; the ninth and tenth, the parts between each elbow and shoulder; the eleventh and twelfth, the flesh of each thigh; the thirteenth and fourteenth, the calf of each leg; the fifteenth pierces the heart; the sixteenth severs the head from the body; the seventeenth and eighteenth cut off the hands; the nineteenth and twentieth, the arms; the twenty-first and twenty-second, the feet; the twenty-third and twenty-fourth, the legs.[40]

---

[38] *GZFZ* 81/20b.
[39] *Chinese Repository* 1834:3/71–72.
[40] Gray 1878:1/59–60.

Figure 16. Death-by-Slicing. Source: *Dianshizhai huabao* (1884).

On occasion emperors ordered other cruel executions, as was the case in 1808 of a servant who had killed his master. The murderer was executed before his victim's grave and, by order of the Jiaqing emperor, his heart was ripped out and presented as a sacrificial offering to pacify the dead man's ghost and to serve as a warning to others.[41]

It was an age of awful brutality. The conscious use of terror, by the state and by pirates, constituted a recognizable display of awesome power and authority over the weak and powerless. For the pirates (as will be discussed in chapter 7) the bloody sacrifice also took on magicoreligious significance, which they believed empowered them with supernatural strength to vanquish their foes.

---

[41] Waley-Cohen 1993:337–338.

Protection Rackets

With the emergence of several large fleets at the start of the nineteenth century, piracy became an increasingly powerful force in the region. During those years all vessels operating in Chinese waters were liable to pirate attacks unless they bought safe-conduct passes. This form of extortion, which dated back to at least the mid-Ming *wokou*, was a major source of pirate income. The practice had become so pervasive by 1809, explained Bai Ling, that the pirates were "like ants attaching themselves to honeycombs."[42] To avoid attack, merchant junks and fishing craft paid protection fees to the pirates, who in return issued passports or certificates guaranteeing impunity to the purchaser. Such "tribute" was regularly collected semi-annually or annually. The whole system became highly institutionalized with registration certificates, account books, full-time bookkeepers, and collection bureaus.[43]

In Fujian, Cai Qian squeezed merchants to purchase "tickets" (*piaodan*): in some cases, large ocean-going junks were charged four hundred silver dollars when departing ports and eight hundred silver dollars when they returned, and in other cases, ships were charged percentage fees (*choufen*) based on their size and cargo. Fishermen paid fishing fees (*yugui*), but at somewhat lower rates.[44] Some Western merchants also paid protection fees to the pirates so their ships would avoid trouble.[45] By 1809 this sort of tribute system had become so widespread all along the South China coast that few vessels dared to venture forth without passes.[46]

Even the government's monopolized salt trade was affected. By 1805 pirates virtually controlled Guangdong's salt trade. Salt boats en route to Canton, Nayancheng memorialized, purchased passports from pirates at a standard rate of fifty dollars per hundred sacks of salt. Once they purchased the passports, the pirates escorted the salt fleets to assure that other gangs did not attack them. Those salt merchants who refused to pay the protection fees were persistently plundered. In the same year he reported

---

[42] GZD (14804) JQ 14.7.15.

[43] GZD (13513) JQ 14.3.5; *DGXZ* 33/22b; and Zhang and Jiang 1983:64.

[44] *MQSLWB* 483b–184a, 487a–b, and 559a; and SYD, JQ 8.3.3; also see Huang Dianquan 1958:88; and Zheng Guangnan 1998:337–338.

[45] Hu Jieyu 1959:153.

[46] Glasspoole 1831:108; also see T. Chang 1983:188; and Liao Fengde 1986:203.

that pirates had burned sixty or seventy salt junks at Dazhou market, had plundered another seventy in Dianbai harbor, and robbed yet another twenty at the port of Shuidong. "It is clear," he explained, "there is nowhere that ocean bandits do not attack our [salt] fleets." By the end of the year, only four of the 270 salt boats had not succumbed to the extortion racket.[47]

The pirates also extended their tribute system inland to villages and markets along the coast. During the fishing season, Fujian pirates regularly sailed to Zhejiang around the Zhoushan archipelago to collect "harbor fees" (*aogui*) from fishing markets and local fishermen.[48] In Macao and Canton the pirates established their own "tax bureaus" for collecting extortion and ransom payments.[49] Towns and villages situated near large forts or otherwise strongly defended were normally spared from attack. All others, unless they bought protection from the pirates, were vulnerable to looting and burning. The pirates used extortion to obtain not only money, but also food, weapons, and other necessities.[50]

In the autumn of 1809, Richard Glasspoole witnessed a pirate expedition that went up the west branch of the Pearl River to "levy contributions" on villages and towns. The pirates first passed a large town about three or four miles from the entrance of the Bogue, which was tributary to the pirates. The townspeople "saluted them with songs as they passed." Next they came upon a village that had not yet been levied, and therefore they sent representatives ashore to demand a tribute of ten thousand dollars annually. After some negotiating, both parties agreed to a sum of six thousand dollars, payable on their return trip downstream. In this way the village was spared destruction. From several of the other villages under their protection, the pirates received money, sugar, and rice, as well as a few roasted pigs.[51]

Other villages were less fortunate. Glasspoole described the plight of one village that decided to resist:

> October the 1st, the fleet weighed in the night, ... and anchored very quietly before a town surrounded by a thick wood. Early in

---

[47] *NYC* 11/42a–b; 12/31b; SYD, JQ 10.11.5; and JQ 10.11.9; see also Morse 1926–1929:3/8.

[48] GZD (6575) JQ 6.11.1; (9400) JQ 7.11.6; (10866) JQ 13.5.25; and (14513) JQ 14.5.9.

[49] *Chinese Repository* 1834:3/82–83.

[50] GZD (14804) JQ 14.7.15; (1513) JQ 14.9.3; *DGXZ* 33/21b–22a; and *Chinese Repository* 1834:3/70–71.

[51] Glasspoole 1831:107–112.

the morning the Ladrones [the Portuguese term for pirates] assembled in rowboats, and landed; then gave a shout, and rushed into the town, swords in hand. The inhabitants fled to the adjacent hills, in numbers apparently superior to the Ladrones. We may easily imagine to ourselves the horror with which these miserable people must be seized, on being obliged to leave their homes, and every thing dear to them. It was a most melancholy sight to see women in tears, clasping their infants in their arms, and imploring mercy for them from those brutal robbers! The old and the sick, who were unable to fly, or to make resistance, were either made prisoners or most inhumanly butchered! The boats continued passing and repassing from junks to the shore, in quick succession, laden with booty, and the men besmeared with blood! Two hundred and fifty women, and several children, were made prisoners, and sent on board different vessels. . . . The town being plundered of everything valuable, it was set on fire, and reduced to ashes by the morning.[52]

About a hundred women were eventually ransomed and returned home, while the rest were sold to the pirates as "wives." In early November the pirates attacked another town, which was protected by a small fort. After overcoming heavy resistance, the pirates entered the town, slaughtered everyone they could find "without regarding age or sex," and then looted and burned the town to the ground.[53] Needless to say, many villages decided not to resist the pirates.

In general, the pirates appeared to have been fairly honest in keeping their part of the deal. It was once reported that when a fishing boat that had previously purchased a passport was mistakenly attacked, the pirate chief not only made his men return the stolen property, but also made them pay the victim five hundred dollars in damages.[54] A reputation, on the one hand, of fair treatment toward those who paid tribute and, on the other hand, of extreme cruelty toward those who did not contribute and also resisted, worked to discourage opposition and made merchants and fishermen much more amenable to the demands of the pirates.

During the first decade of the nineteenth century Fujian and Guangdong pirates were able to broaden their activities from the water to the land. Powerful pirate chieftains, such as Zheng Yi, Wushi Er, Zhang Bao, Zhu Fen, and Cai Qian were able to

---

[52] Ibid., 116–117.
[53] Ibid., 117.
[54] *Chinese Repository* 1834:3/71.

establish niches on shore through formal systems of bribery and extortion. Piracy became a significant and pervasive force in the region at that time. The pirates were able to penetrate the structure of local society through the establishment of "tax bureaus," which regularly collected tribute. Extortion, mainly in the form of a protection racket, was the most direct and effective way that the pirates exercised hegemony over an area. Through the systematic use of extortion, bribery, and terror, the pirates gained a firm hold over coastal villages, towns, and markets, as well as over fishing and shipping enterprises. In fact, they constituted a level of control over South China's maritime society that operated independent of that exercised by officials and local elites.

SIX

Piracy and Seafaring Society

Like all seafarers, pirates too relied on others for their survival. Cut off from land by their life on the seas, they ultimately depended upon people on shore for victuals, water, matting, rope, spars, and tar, as well as gunpowder, weapons, and information. Pirates also needed help for disposing of their booty. Boats had to be beached and careened every several months for cleaning and repairs. Those who aided pirates became partners in crime, and the state ruthlessly hunted them down and prosecuted them with a vengeance. The worst thing that could happen to pirates, as officials well understood, was to be cut off from their sources on land. By extending their operations inland, pirates entrenched themselves in local villages and made contacts with a wide cross section of local society. They built up a huge network of accomplices that included fishermen, merchants, soldiers, gentry, and officials, as well as bandit gangs and sworn brotherhoods. This chapter examines pirate bases and the black markets that served them, as well as the various people on shore who aided them and came to depend on them, at least in part, for their own livelihoods. The final section of this chapter discusses the effect of piracy on local economies.

Pirate Lairs and Black Markets

Pirates established bases just about everywhere. Contrary to conventional wisdom, they were not only in remote, thinly populated peripheral areas or along borders where jurisdictions were imprecise. Rather, "pirate nests" could be found in core areas, some of which were close to the seats of state power, and they were in these areas not only during the heydays of large-scale piracy but at most other times too.[1] More often than not lairs were

---

[1] For example, even after the decline of large-scale piracy in 1810, later

situated near lucrative trade routes. While some strongholds were on out-of-the-way coasts and offshore islands, others were near busy ports and even military camps. These bases provided regular anchorages and hideouts where pirates returned after an expedition to rest and refit. In choosing their bases, pirates favored areas in protected harbors with plenty of fresh water and firewood and with easy access to both friendly populations and prey. Although many of these camps were impermanent, others became fortified strongholds where pirates settled their families and stockpiled their loot.

Giang Binh (Jiangping), a Vietnamese market town on the Chinese border, had long been a major smuggling and pirate base.[2] As Figure 17 shows, the port was not only isolated but also protected by mountains and thick forests; thus communication by land was almost impossible. Even as late as the 1820s, only one Qing military fortification guarded the entire area. In addition, the many nearby craggy islands offered perfect hideaways for pirates and smugglers and were in easy reach of the town and its black markets. Taking refuge across the border was an important pirate strategy.

By the 1790s Giang Binh was a bustling border town, which boasted a population of more than two thousand households, including both Vietnamese and Chinese. A large Vietnamese squatter population settled on the sandy shoals at the entrance to the harbor. Many of the residents specialized in handling stolen goods and provisioning pirates. It was well known that merchants and traders from Guangdong and Guangxi frequented the town specifically to buy stolen merchandise. Giang Binh served not only as refuge for pirates and other "unregistered rascals" (*wuji feitu*) evading Qing justice, but it also attracted large numbers of fishermen, sailors, laborers, and porters who came in search of work. These were the sorts of men who provided a steady pool of new recruits for the pirates. Giang Binh and its environs remained one of the most important pirate strongholds until 1802, when the royalist forces that defeated the Tâyson rebels destroyed it.[3]

---

nineteenth-century officials such as Lu Kun and Zhang Zhidong continued to complain about pirate bases in the Canton delta and around Chaozhou (*Guangdong haifang huilan* 1/5a–b; and *Guangdong haitushuo* 26a–b).

[2] *GZDQL* (QL 28.12.24):20/200–201. Also see the discussion on Giang Binh in Murray 1987:18–20.

[3] GZD (465) JQ 1.4.14; (1334) JQ 1.10.19; (1656 *fupian*) JQ 1.2.11; ZPZZ (*falü* 78) JQ 4.9.5; and *Guangdong haifang huilan* 26/1b–2a.

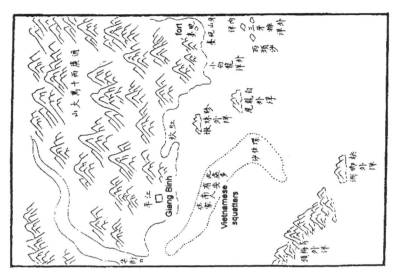

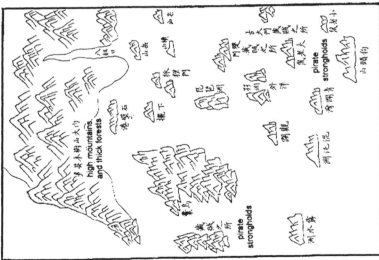

Figure 17. Giang Binh and the Surrounding Coastline. Source: *Guangdong tongzhi* (1864).

After 1802 the pirates had to find refuge in Chinese waters and establish new bases. In western Guangdong, Wushi Er, Donghai Ba, and Zheng Yi set up permanent camps in Guangzhou Bay on Donghai and Xiongzhou Islands, and west of the Leizhou peninsula on Weizhou Island (see the map in Figure 3). These areas were somewhat remote but near busy sea-lanes. There the pirates found safe anchorages and places where they could sell their loot and purchase provisions.[4] In 1805, Governor-General Nayancheng reported that peasants from as far away as three hundred *li* would travel to villages on Donghai Island to sell their rice to pirates because they paid more than market prices. On the secluded shores of Guangzhou Bay and on Xiongzhou Island, pirates built shanties where they settled their families and conducted business with nearby villagers.[5] Weizhou had paddy fields, plenty of fresh water, and firewood that supported both the pirate and local squatter communities on the island.[6] When a military expedition attacked Weizhou in 1808, the soldiers apprehended more than 500 men, women, and children: 223 were "pirates" (including 128 kidnapped victims who performed menial chores for their captors); 56 were victims the pirates held for ransom; 150 were unregistered farmers living unlawfully on the island; 72 were hired laborers and beggars; and 3 were individuals who fenced stolen goods or handled ransom payments for the pirates.[7] Despite repeated attacks from soldiers, pirates continued to maintain bases in these areas throughout the first decade of the nineteenth century.

A number of pirate bases were also situated on the many islands in and around the entrance to the Pearl River, the gateway to Canton. This core area, which had always provided shelter for pirate and bandit gangs, was the most heavily fortified in Guangdong; but despite the military presence, pirates easily found refuge in many places. Along the myriad waterways of Dongguan, Panyu, Shunde, Xiangshan, and Xinhui counties pirates set up camps with easy access to markets and to the sea.[8] Governor-General Bai Ling was dismayed over the numerous pirate haunts around such vital spots as Humen, Yaimen, Jiaomen, and Macao.[9]

---

[4] *SCSX* 39/11b–12a, 22b; *GDTZ* 1864:124/18a–b; and *Gaozhou fuzi* 1889:19/41b.
[5] *NYC* 12/90b–92a, 13/1b.
[6] Neumann 1831:11–12; and *SQXZ* 6/5a–b.
[7] GZD (11082) JQ 13.r5.25.
[8] *GDTZ* 1864:123/3b; and *XHXZ* 1/12b–14a.
[9] Wen Chengzhi 1842:3a.

Dayushan (Lantao Island), an island near Hong Kong, had remained the headquarters for pirates since at least the Ming dynasty. It had long boasted a thriving population of pirates, smugglers, and fishermen. The pirate Zheng Liangchang built a stronghold in the mountains behind the Tianhou Temple, and from this vantage point his gang commanded the entire harbor. At the start of the nineteenth century, this same area continued to serve Zheng Yi, Zhang Bao, and other pirates.[10] On Hong Kong Island Zhang Bao constructed two stockades, which he fortified with cannon and other weapons. He also had a base on nearby Changzhou Island, among the fishing harbors, where he reportedly cached his booty in a small cave.[11]

Zhu Fen and other pirates established bases along the Guangdong and Fujian border. Undeterred by several government fortifications, Nan'ao Island had repeatedly provided pirate lairs since the Yuan dynasty. During the southern monsoons pirates regularly found shelter and supplies on three small islands, known collectively as Sanpeng, off the Chaozhou coast. Another nest was near Zhanglin on Fangjishan Island, the site of a famous Tianhou temple.[12] Zhu Fen had his most important strongholds near the port of Yunxiao and on Tongshan Island in Zhangzhou prefecture in Fujian.[13]

Cai Qian had important bases around Amoy and Jinmen and in Lianjiang and Xiapu counties. At Fuquan, just across from Jinmen on the mainland, pirates had a camp where they careened their boats and traded with local fishermen. Liaoluo Bay, although protected by two military posts with more than 135 soldiers, was nonetheless a favorite anchorage for fishing, merchant, and pirate junks.[14] In 1805, Cai Qian established bases off the Lianjiang coast on Gantang and Qinjiao Islands, where he sold booty and careened and refitted his junks. His pirates put up sheds where they made and mended sails and manufactured gunpowder. They procured food and other materials either through trade or "harbor fees" imposed on nearby fishermen and merchants. On the islands Cai Qian stockpiled food, weapons, gunpowder, bamboo matting, and other materials. Within a year, however, soldiers

---

[10] *XSXZ* 1827:8:56b; Hunter 1885:84; and Xiao Guojian 1978:18–19.

[11] Hu Jieyu 1959:151. Today Zhang Bao's cave is a popular tourist attraction for Hong Kong visitors to Changzhou Island.

[12] *GDTZ* 1864:123/35b–36b; and *Guangdong haifang huilan* 1/1a–8a.

[13] *MQSLWB* 537a; and *YXTZ* 8/18b.

[14] *JMZ* 101–103; and *MXTZ* 8/11b.

attacked and burned these bases to the ground.[15] Further north along the coast near the customs office at Sansha in Xiapu county, Cai Qian established a lair on Mazu Bay.[16] All of these bases were situated either at the entrances to ports or along trading routes.

Officials frequently mentioned friendly port towns and villages where pirates, smugglers, and bandits regularly congregated to sell booty and purchase supplies. Up and down the coast there were many well known ports that catered to illegal commerce: Sanhewo, Bohuo, Liantou, and Baimiao in Gaozhou prefecture; Anpu in Chaozhou prefecture; Meizhou, Baisha, and Duxin in Zhangzhou prefecture; Chongwu, Pengwei, Shage, Futou, and Wubao in Quanzhou prefecture; Guzhen, Shuiao, Xiahu, and Yanting in Funing prefecture; and Suao and Donggang on Taiwan.[17] Sanhewo (illustrated in Figure 10) was a friendly village near the entrance to Xianmen harbor and across the strait from the pirate base on Xiongzhou Island. The village, which boasted a famous Empress of Heaven temple where all passing boats stopped to worship, was near the walled city of Wuchuan, several military fortifications, and the entrepôt of Zhiliao.[18] Some areas were so frequented by pirates that they were labeled "pirate bays" (zei'ao) on maps.[19] Figure 18 shows one such pirate bay near Shuliang harbor in Lufeng county, Guangdong; it was situated between the two military batteries at Zhelang and Shishitou.

One of the most famous pirate and smuggler rendezvous was Macao. It was the Tripoli of the Orient—an international meeting place for desperados and misfits. In his history of Macao, Sir Anders Ljungstedt explained that "vagabonds, gamblers, thieves, etc. entertain the expectation of hiding themselves easily in a place where the jurisdiction is divided, and the tenor of the laws variously applied; the influx of these pernicious dregs of nations, is therefore constant and great."[20] Here was the natural place for pirates to meet and socialize, to recruit new gang members, and to conduct business. Not surprisingly, Zhang Bao made Macao a headquarters for his extortion operations. There, and in Canton and several other towns, he established his "tax bureaus" for

[15] MQSLWB 525b–526b, 559a.

[16] MQSLWB 536b; XPXZ shanchuan/14a.

[17] GZDQL (QL 21.6.17):14/644; MQSLWB 508a; YXTZ 8/18b; WCXZ 4/91b–92a; DBXZ 7/2b; XPXZ shanchuan/15a; and JMZ 91–92.

[18] WCXZ 3/11a, 4/91b–92a.

[19] Guangdong haifang huilan 1/1a–8a; and Chinese Repository 1834:12/481.

[20] Ljungstedt 1835:108.

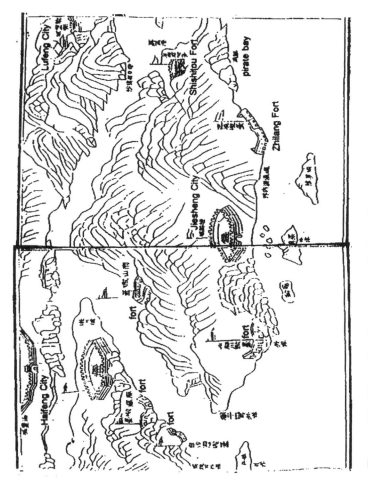

Figure 18. "Pirate Bay" along the Lufeng Coast. Source: *Guangdong haifang huilan* (N.d.).

collecting the protection fees paid by merchants and fishermen. Pirates also used these bureaus for handling ransom payments.[21]

The numerous inns, shops, brothels, and gambling dens that dotted these coastal marts were the favorite gathering places for pirates, smugglers, and thieves, as well as for ordinary sailors and fishermen. Bai Ling reported that "wicked coastal people" often moved to offshore islands to open stores specifically to trade with pirates and smugglers.[22] Two petty merchants, Chen Ping and Chen Bai, pooled their money and opened a rice shop in Chenghai as a front to trade with pirates.[23] Occasionally pirates set up their own shops to sell stolen goods. In 1795, as mentioned earlier, Zheng Qi gave his "adopted son," He Song, a captive female as his bride and seven thousand taels of silver to return home to Zhaoan, Fujian, to establish a store to front booty and collect ransom payments.[24] Seafarers and pirates met in these places not only for drink and amusement, but also to buy and sell licit and illicit goods, exchange information, and recruit gangs.[25]

Wicked People and Worthless Fellows

Everywhere along the coast officials found "wicked people" (*jianmin*) and "worthless fellows" (*lanzai*) who willingly collaborated with pirates by providing them supplies and services. Provincial officials in Fujian and Guangdong repeatedly emphasized the importance of cutting the pirates off from their suppliers on shore as the first step in eradicating piracy. Bai Ling put it most succinctly: without rice and gunpowder there would be no pirates.[26] On the coast officials initiated staunch measures to search for and arrest villagers, fishermen, and merchants who sold food, weapons, and other supplies to pirates. Between 1780 and 1810 several thousands of these "illicit aiders" (*tongdao jifei*) were arrested and prosecuted in South China.[27]

---

[21] *Chinese Repository* 1834:3/82–83; and Morse 1926–1929:2/68.

[22] GZD (14560) JQ 14.6.19.

[23] *MQSLWB* 493a.

[24] GZD (8052) JQ 7.5.12; also see GZD (9668) JQ 13.1.6.

[25] SYD, JQ 12.10.26; *MQSLWB* 306a–b; *SCSX* 99/2a–b; Katsuta 1967:42; and T. Chang 1983:32.

[26] GZD (14890) JQ 14.7.23.

[27] See, for example, *SCSX* 38/1b; *NYC* 12/43a–b, 67a–69b; ZPZZ (1133) JQ 10.5.16; GZD (1764) JQ 1.12.30, and (19806) JQ 14 (complete date missing). I use the term "aiders" here because it is closer to the original Chinese term used to describe individuals who not only acted as fences and receivers but also as sup-

The penalty for aiding pirates varied from wearing the cangue for several months to capital punishment, depending on the seriousness of the offense and the degree of participation of the offender.[28] As the pirate menace continued to grow after 1780, however, the government tried to deter piracy by imposing the harshest penalties on aiders. For instance, Yang Yawo was arrested in 1799 in Guangdong for fencing goods stolen by pirates. Because Governor-General Jiqing feared that the stipulated penalty of wearing the cangue was too light and that Yang would be back to his old ways before long, he received permission from Beijing to increase the sentence to three years of penal servitude plus one hundred strokes of the heavy bamboo. Furthermore, to assure that Yang would not aid pirates again, officials were ordered to resettle him in an area far removed from the coast after he served his term.[29] In another case in 1809, when Xiao Shique sold watermelons to pirates, instead of receiving the normal penalty of penal servitude, the court increased his penalty to banishment into slavery in Heilongjiang.[30] In one case a Qinzhou fisherman, Yang Pinfu, who sold rice to pirates on three occasions, was summarily beheaded as a warning to other would-be aiders.[31]

Despite the harsh punishments, pirates, who were known to pay high prices for provisions, had little trouble finding suppliers.[32] When the pirates did not go to them, suppliers went looking for the pirates. As the censor, Yan Lang, made known to the throne, fishermen would set out to sea on the pretext of fishing but would actually seek out pirates to sell them food and munitions.[33] Junks carrying weapons, ostensibly for their own protection, frequently sold them instead to pirates and later, after returning to port, reported that they had been plundered. Aiders and pirates often had prearranged rendezvous and signals. When pirates fired their cannon, one official reported, the fishing and small trading junks understood that it was safe to sail out to trade.[34] All along the southern coast thousands of ordinary people

---

pliers for the pirates.

[28] An extensive discussion of the laws on aiding pirates is in the [Xingbu] *Shuotie* 1811:*ce* 11.

[29] ZPZZ (*falü* 76) JQ 4.4.17.

[30] *SCSX* 40/8b–9a.

[31] ZPZZ (1136) JQ 12.5.20.

[32] *DGXZ* 33/21b; *MQSLWB* 559a–b; and Yano 1926:103.

[33] SYD, JQ 11.11.10; and Liang Tingnan 1838:17/14b–15b.

[34] *SCSX* 38/1a–2a.

depended on combining fishing and aiding pirates to earn their living.[35]

What supplies they obtained directly from plunder were never enough to satisfy the daily needs of pirates out at sea. They depended on contacts on shore for most of their food, water, firewood, and cooking oil.[36] Take the case of Zeng Yasi. In February 1805, while fishing off the Xin'an coast, he was approached by the pirate Huang Yasi, who proposed that Zeng assist the pirates in buying food. Amenable to the idea, Zeng immediately returned to his village, where he borrowed eight silver dollars to purchase a small pig from Chen Yasan. Zeng then went to nearby Yantian market and bought four large earthen containers of wine, as well as one picul, five pecks of rice. Two days later he transported the supplies to Huang Yasi, who rewarded him with eleven dollars and requested that Zeng buy more food. Once again Zeng returned home. Accompanied this time by a friend, Li Yunlian, the two men set out on March 2 with thirty dollars for Danshui market in neighboring Guishan county. There they purchased ten piculs of rice as well as several other items. When two days later they brought the supplies to Huang, he paid them a total of forty-four dollars, allowing each man to make a nice profit of seven dollars.[37]

Pirates also needed naval supplies such as cannon, guns, gunpowder, ships, sails, rope, and iron. In the summer of 1805, yamen runners arrested Wu Laozhang in Haikang county for selling iron to pirates, and another man for selling charcoal.[38] In 1807 soldiers apprehended Chen Peiju and Xu Zhanfang when they tried to sell a junk to pirates.[39] Zhu Pan, a member of Zhu Fen's gang, gave Wu Hou, from Zhaoan county, two hundred silver dollars to buy gunpowder. Wu used a hundred dollars to buy fifty *jin* of gunpowder and pocketed the remainder of the money.[40] Cai Qian, in 1806, paid thirty silver dollars to Lin Cancan and Zhou Wanwan for sails.[41]

---

[35] *MQSLWB* 526a; also see GZD (13252) JQ 14.2.5; (13252) JQ 14.2.5; and (15313) JQ 14.9.3.

[36] See cases in ZPZZ (1133) JQ 10.5.16; GZD (10724) JQ 13.5.8; (11244) JQ 13.6.15; (13252) JQ 14.2.5; (13005) 14.1.13; (15186) JQ 14.8.23; and *MQSLWB* 485b, 487b, 525b–526b; 559a–b.

[37] ZPZZ (1133) JQ 10.9.5.

[38] *NYC* 12/51a–52b.

[39] SYD, JQ 12.12.2.

[40] *MQSLWB* 559b.

[41] GZD (10484) JQ 13.4.13.

Besides selling food and weapons to pirates, aiders also sold their services. Cai Qian hired carpenters, sail makers, and blacksmiths to build and repair junks and manufacture weapons.[42] Jiang Ayao, who was well acquainted with the pirate Chen Atong, accommodated gang members in his house and received rent.[43] Lin Zongji was arrested in Lianjiang for feeding and harboring in his restaurant a local pirate named Chen Fudao and three gang members.[44]

Other people helped pirates by selling safe-conduct passes and collecting tribute and ransom payments. On October 30, 1805, soldiers in Xinning county arrested Li Yide and another man for aiding pirates. Li owned a small boat and made a living by peddling salted fish. He confessed that in December 1801, the pirate Dashi Er had kidnapped him and demanded a ransom of fifty silver dollars. Li agreed to pay the money, and afterward became quite friendly with the pirates. In February 1802, he became Dashi Er's agent for collecting tribute payments from coastal villagers. On behalf of the pirates, Li went around to sixty-seven shopkeepers in one market demanding that they contribute two thousand copper cash each as well as wine and food. He collected a total of 134,000 cash, of which he took out 20,000 cash for himself. He later helped pirates procure rice, pigs, oil, wine, and opium, for which he received seventy silver dollars. At his trial Li received a sentence of imminent strangulation in accordance with the substatute on "wicked scoundrels who clandestinely transport rice to the outer ocean to aid pirates."[45] Aiding pirates, although lucrative, was risky.

Pirates needed to find not only people to sell them food and supplies, but also fences and customers for their booty. This neither was a problem. Lin Atang and Lin Aqian, for example, sold stolen peanuts for pirates, for which each received a commission of three dollars.[46] In another case, in 1805, a group of men and women were arrested for fencing stolen property and selling rice to pirates. Arrested were Li Yasan, Zhou Hesheng, his stepmother, née Zheng, and four other people. Ms. Zheng was the younger sister of the pirate Zheng Yi.[47]

---

[42] *MQSLWB* 531b, 536a.
[43] Ibid., 522b.
[44] Ibid., 533b.
[45] XKTB (121) JQ 10.12.11.
[46] GZD (981) JQ 1.7.29; also see *NYC* 12/51a–52b.
[47] ZPZZ (1133) JQ 10.5.16.

Pirates, too, depended on collaborators on shore to act as their ears and eyes (*ermu*) and as guides for inland operations.[48] Pirate chiefs often sent ashore gang members, disguised as gentry or peddlers, to gather information on the comings and goings of merchant and fishing junks. Such spies colluded with paid informers on land.[49] When pirates raided the Canton delta in 1809, He Zongpei acted as Guo Podai's spy and guide. Previously He had twice sold rice and wine to Guo's men, and then later guided the pirates on a raid of a Shunde village, even pointing out a wealthy kinsman, whom he resented, to kidnap for ransom.[50] In another case, pirates paid a fishmonger named Zhang Lianke ten silver dollars for each report he made to them about the movements of merchant junks around the port of Leizhou.[51] The success of pirate ventures often depended on the intelligence they obtained through networks of collaborators and spies. Information became a valuable commodity and was sold to pirates like everything else.

While most of the aiders were ordinary sailors and fishermen, a few local gentry, wealthy landowners, and merchants, tempted by apparently easy profits, ventured to aid pirates.[52] One of the most notorious cases was that of Lin Wu. He was a wealthy merchant and ship owner who had purchased a minor degree in Chaozhou prefecture and had built a large fleet of merchant vessels. To safeguard his business he willingly cooperated with Zhu Fen and other pirates in the region, first paying them protection money and afterward acting as their agent in collecting port fees (*ganggui*) from other merchants. He also procured provisions and cannon for the pirates.[53]

In another case, Lin Ban, who was a merchant from Chenghai, owned a shop in Zhanglin and merchant junks that traded with Vietnam and Siam. In 1802, and again in 1803, Lin was responsible for several homicides. At the same time he began collaborating with pirates. In August 1803, for example, he purchased a hundred sacks of black pepper from Fujian pirates for 520 dollars and then resold the pepper for a hefty profit. Later that month he

[48] *DGXZ* 33/21b; *XSXZ* 1827:4/62b, 88a; 8/56b.

[49] GZD (3347) JQ 2.11.12; (6793) JQ 6.11.28; *PYXZ* 22/16a–b; and Neumann 1831:36–37.

[50] GZD (15313) JQ 14.9.3.

[51] GZD (6211 *fupian*) JQ 6.9.23; and (6793) JQ 6.11.28.

[52] *MQSLWB* 492b–493b; GZD (15187) JQ 14.8.23; and *DGXZ* 33/25b.

[53] ZPZZ (1135) JQ 11.5.6; (1135) JQ 11.5.25; LFZZ (3848) JQ 11.7.16; and *SCSX* 79/10a.

paid 232 dollars for five cannon, which he then sold to pirates. He continued his dealings for another year before being finally arrested, tried, and executed.[54] In general, the gentry and merchants who became involved with pirates were also involved in other criminal activities, and, in fact, much of their wealth had been acquired through unlawful dealings.

More alarming to the higher officials in Beijing was the collaboration between pirates and local officials, yamen underlings, or soldiers. Although it was their appointed duty to apprehend these criminals, instead they supplied them with information in exchange for bribes. In 1800 the Jiaqing emperor complained of the widespread practice among lower officials along the southern coast of taking bribes, colloquially referred to as "salaries from the sea" (*haifang*), and also issued new orders denouncing "low-ranking military officers who ignored bandits and succored wicked people."[55] The problem became so pervasive in Chenghai county among yamen runners and clerks that in 1806 even the magistrate himself decided to get involved to enjoy a share of the profits.[56] In Fujian local pirates had a standard practice of dividing their plunder into three equal shares among yamen underlings, soldiers, and themselves.[57]

Poorly paid soldiers were particularly notorious for selling their weapons, gunpowder, and information on naval deployments to pirates.[58] Official reports stated that on Nan'ao Island sailors on naval patrol boats routinely sold food and weapons to pirates for as much as ten times the normal cost.[59] Three military batteries along the Dianbai coast had to be shut down and the soldiers sent back to their battalion headquarters because of "incompetency," a euphemism for colluding with ocean bandits and smugglers.[60] All of these bases were near harbors frequented by pirates. In fact, as we have already noted, many pirate bases were close to military camps.

In 1804 Guangdong officials memorialized the throne about an "extremely reprehensible" case. Sergeant Luo Mingliang had been

---

[54] ZPZZ (1133) JQ 10.6.26; and *NYC* 12/15a–b.

[55] *DGXZ* 33/19b; and Leung 1977:156.

[56] *DQSL* (JQ 11.7.8):164/10a–b; and SYD, JQ 16.r6.19.

[57] T. Chang 1983:31.

[58] *GZDQL* (QL 51.7.4):61/59a–62b; *NYC* 11/29a–b; SYD, JQ 11.11.10; and *SCSX* 38/17a.

[59] Katsuta 1967:40.

[60] *DBXZ* 7/2a–3a, 13/15a–17a.

arrested for colluding with pirates and other undesirables. Because Wanshan, the island where he had been stationed, was remote and food and other necessities consequently scarce, Luo decided to open a rice shop with several local residents. They sold to anyone who had the money, "no matter if they were honest folks or criminals." As a result Luo and his partners came into contact with pirates who patronized their shop. Luo's nefarious operation was finally uncovered by the authorities after a tip-off that he had taken a bribe and subsequently released a pirate named Du Yafa who had been handed over to him by nearby villagers. In an edict the emperor approved the governor-general's request for Luo's immediate beheading, a punishment witnessed by the assembled soldiers and villagers on the island.[61]

Pirates, Bandits, and Brotherhoods

Among the worthless fellows who aided and colluded with pirates were members of inland bandit gangs and sworn brotherhoods. Pirates maintained close ties with various bandits and secret-society members along the coast, who in turn helped pirates to procure food and weapons, and fence their booty, and who occasionally assisted them in raids on villages and markets.[62] During Cai Qian's raids on Taiwan in 1804 and 1806, he depended on support from local bandits such as Hong Silao and Wu Jinqiu.[63] In Guangdong pirates returned to Hainan Island during the autumn slack season to rest and refit. On shore "society bandits" (*huifei*) protected and succored them and provided them with detailed information about prospective targets on both land and sea.[64] Secret societies in both Fujian and Guangdong were also instrumental in helping pirates regularize their extortion racket on the coasting trade and salt monopoly.[65] Officials were dreadfully afraid of conspiracies between pirates and secret societies, especially in the several years after 1787 and 1802, when the Triads were involved in massive uprisings in Taiwan and in the Canton region.[66]

---

[61] *SCSX* 38/15b–16a.

[62] See *NYC* 12/30a–31b; *SYD, JQ* 7.4.18; *GZD* (8052 *fupian*) *JQ* 7.5.12; *LZFZ* 21/56a; and *SQXZ* 2/20a. Also see the discussion in Zheng Guangnan 1998:310–315.

[63] Huang Dianquan 1958:78–79.

[64] *CZFZ* 19/27a–28a.

[65] T. Chang 1983:34; and Murray 1987:86–87.

[66] See *DGXZ* 33/20b–21a; and Antony 1988:348–350.

One of the most famous cases of this period involved the notorious Lufeng society bandit Li Chongyu. Official records described him as "a man of moderate wealth who liked to loaf about and spend money freely." After Li organized a Society for Filial Sons (Xiaozihui), ostensibly to collect money to cover the funeral costs for the deceased parents of members, officials arrested and sentenced him in 1798 to penal servitude for swindling fellow villagers. Before arriving at his place of detention, Li escaped and fled to sea, joining up with a gang of pirates. Eventually he made his way back home to Jiazi, a bustling port town on the Lufeng coast, where he formed a new gang and cultivated close relationships with several petty officials and yamen underlings and soldiers. He changed his name to Li Jingxing and purchased a *jiansheng* degree, thereby joining the ranks of the local gentry.[67]

Later, probably in 1804, he organized a Heaven and Earth Society (Tiandihui) with a Haifeng bandit named Shi Chenglian.[68] By then Li had more than several hundred followers who addressed him as elder brother (*dage*), the common appellation of a Triad boss. About the same time, in either 1803 or 1804, Li opened a rice shop that actually was a front for buying and selling stolen property from pirates such as Lin Yafa, Zhu Fen, and Wushi Er. Li also operated a gambling den and brothel and engaged in a host of other criminal activities including robbery, kidnapping, extortion, and local feuds.[69]

An upshot of the collaboration between Li Chongyu and his secret-society and pirate connections was an abortive attempt to attack the military battery guarding Wutuwei harbor. On the night of September 16, 1805, several of Li's cronies, including the pirate chief Zheng Wuzhu (Black Pig Zheng), gathered a gang of some forty pirates and local thugs at Meilong village. From there they planned to proceed on foot toward the fort. But before they got too far they were spotted by local militia, who were able to turn them back. Zheng Wuzhu and a number of his followers were apprehended, but the rest of the band fled to their ships. Getting wind of the attempted raid, county civil and military officials quickly assembled local braves and hired a small fleet of

---

[67] SYD, JQ 11.1.27, and JQ 11.2.16; and *SCSX* 38/18b, 48/17b, 98/22b–23a.

[68] *HFXA yishi*/33b; and *HZFZ* 18/17b–18a.

[69] *NYC* 14/1a–b, 17b–25b, 36a; ZPZZ (*falü* 163) JQ 10.7.12; and SYD, JQ 11.8.18, and JQ 11.9.13.

fishing boats to pursue the pirates, but they escaped.[70] Also in the fall of 1805 rumors abounded that Li Chongyu had more than ten thousand followers and was planning an uprising, but nothing came of this because he soon surrendered to Nayancheng in December in exchange for a pardon.[71]

Piracy and Local Economies

How did piracy affect local economies? On the one hand, legitimate commerce naturally suffered at the hands of predacious pirates. Direct losses included the loss of capital in the form of ships and cargo and of labor with the kidnapping, wounding, and killing of crews. The large-scale piracy of the early nineteenth century incessantly upset the normal operations of trade. Some scholars argue that piracy disturbed the junk trade with Southeast Asia for about thirty years.[72] British merchants in Canton in 1804, 1806, and again in 1809 reported that the disruptions in trade resulted in a dearth of goods and thereby caused the prices of rice and salt to skyrocket. At times pirate disturbances resulted in sluggish markets and low prices for Western imports.[73] In March 1806, for instance, because pirates obstructed shipments of rice from Taiwan, the Canton authorities were fearful of food riots or other more serious disturbances arising from increased costs.[74]

Indirect losses included capital outlays for protection against pirates. Much of the cost for construction of fortifications, casting of cannon, and hiring of local braves and ships came from contributions of Chinese and Western merchants, as well as local gentry and villagers. In 1805 and 1809, for example, the Canton Hong merchants reportedly contributed several hundred thousand taels to the defense efforts.[75] The estimated cost for protecting Macao from 1804 to 1810 was more than 480,000 taels.[76] These expenditures, of course, were lost for the use of direct productive activities. Disruption of trade and loss of capital meant not only economic stagnation but also a slump in the already glutted labor market as well as a further lowering of wages. Unable to find

---

[70] *HFXA yishi*/33b; and *Chaozhou zhi dashiji* 2/31a.
[71] *HZFZ* 18/18a.
[72] Leonard 1984:82; and Blussé 1988:151.
[73] Morse 1926–1929:2/290; Liao Fengde 1986:202; and Murray 1988:242.
[74] Morse 1926–1929:3/37.
[75] Ibid., 3/10, 122.
[76] Montalto de Jesus 1926:246.

gainful employment, seafarers and others whose livelihoods were tied to maritime trade had to seek alternate incomes, including either joining or aiding pirates.[77]

Yet on the other hand, piracy also stimulated trade, albeit illicit trade. The tens of thousands of pirates were eager customers who paid above market prices for goods and services. Pirates needed to be fed, clothed, and entertained, and their ships had to be regularly provisioned and refitted. "Fresh water, rice, and other items," as Governor-General Jiqing explained in 1796, "all must come from shore."[78] Although the scale of the pirate trade is impossible to gauge, nevertheless it must have pumped large amounts of money and goods into the local economies in exchange for necessities and services. Pirates contributed to the accumulation of local capital. Coastal dwellers, fishermen, yamen underlings, and soldiers eagerly traded with pirates in order to supplement their regular earnings and in hopes of securing substantial profits. If some individuals became pirates as part of a survival strategy, then others willingly broke the law to aid pirates as part of their survival strategy.

Black markets sprang up all along the coast to handle booty. Illegal businesses thrived. The establishment of markets specifically to handle stolen goods was clear indication of weaknesses in the structure of normal, legal markets. Pirates and smugglers performed important services by redistributing goods to areas where they otherwise would not have arrived, and they did so at bargain prices. They brought the prices of goods within the reach of a wider public while at the same time they expanded the network of distribution. Piracy allowed marginalized fishermen, sailors, and petty entrepreneurs, who had otherwise been excluded, to participate in the wider commercial economy. The pirates, in their own cant, referred to this trade as simply "a transshipping of goods."[79] Black markets also tended to perpetuate piracy. Once pirates generated supplies of goods for sale at discount prices, buyers were attracted to these entrepôts that arose to handle the trade in stolen property.[80]

---

[77] See the discussion in J. Anderson 1995.
[78] *SCSX* 38/1a–b.
[79] Neumann 1831:15.
[80] See the discussion in Starkey 1994:69–70.

SEVEN

The Cultural World of Seafarers and Pirates

For the most part, pirates shared with other seafarers a common culture that was substantially different from that of peasants, merchants, gentry, and officials living on shore. Many landsmen would have agreed with Li Guangpo, an early Qing scholar-official, who was perplexed and wary about the sea. For him it only meant trouble:

> Nothing is more dangerous than water except seawater, which is all the more unpredictable. It is a vast expanse stretching to heaven, and nothing can measure its length. What is more, the boats of wicked scoundrels are like froth floating on the sea and are impossible to apprehend.[1]

Social customs highlighted and nurtured differences. Even after the Dan boat people were "emancipated" by the Yongzheng emperor in 1729, they still were discouraged from residing on land, holding government office, or wearing silk clothing. Land dwellers looked down upon seafarers and refused to let their daughters marry them. Written accounts depicted them as uncouth and vile. They were regarded as a sort of subhuman species living beyond the pale of civilization; some writers even claimed that Dan sailors had webbed feet and could breathe underwater like fish.[2] Such attitudes and stereotypes only furthered mutual mistrust and rifts between the two worlds of land and water.

It was not only the dominant society on land that demarcated sharp cultural boundaries; mariners too deemed themselves a separate group. Popular sayings among Dan boatmen—such as

---

[1] He Changling 1827:83/1a.

[2] See Qu Dajun [1700] 1985:485–486; *Guishan xianzhi* 1783:15/9a–10a; and Gray 1878:2/283.

"on water a dragon, but on land a worm"—emphasized their confidence and virtuosity at sea but discomfort and maltreatment once on shore. The dominant institutions and customs on land, such as lineages, ancestral halls, and written genealogies, were of little importance to seafarers. "Water people" consumed the same kinds of food and drink, amused themselves with the same pastimes, and shared similar religious beliefs and ritual behaviors. They did not worship earth gods but rather gods of the sea, and they expressed themselves with their own unique speech. Mariners wore distinctive clothing and had peculiar hairstyles. Women who went to sea did not bind their feet, and they lived and worked alongside the men aboard junks. The habits, lifestyles, and worldviews of seafarers embodied their rough-and-tumble sojourning existence.[3]

The cultural world of seafarers and pirates both mirrored and mocked dominant society on land. Seafaring culture enveloped not just the wooden world of sailors aboard ship, but also the dockside inns, brothels, and gambling dens they frequented when in port. It was a culture of survival forged by the rigors and dangers of work at sea. This chapter explores maritime culture, beginning with the material features of the habits and lifestyles of ordinary seamen and proceeding to discuss their distinct speech, amusements, sexual habits, and religious beliefs and rituals. It ends with an examination of the magicoreligious rites of cannibalism among pirates.

Habits and Lifestyles

The ship was a self-contained world with too little space on board and too much space outside.[4] Most junks were overcrowded and exceedingly uncomfortable. Often they were the dwellings of extended families, where parents and children, and the wives and children of married sons, all lived together. Hired sailors were also housed and fed with the rest of the family aboard ship.[5] Men, women, and children had to compete for the limited space with rats, fish, gear, food, drinking water, cargo, and baggage. While the captain had a small cabin at the rear of the vessel, sailors had

---

[3] See discussions in Chen Xujing 1946; Kani 1967; Diamond 1969; E. Anderson 1970 and 1972; and Ward 1985.

[4] See Rediker 1987:158–161.

[5] Ward 1985:15; and Chen Yande 1997:71.

to sleep either in poorly ventilated compartments below deck or exposed to the elements on deck. On pirate ships each member of the crew was allowed only a small berth of about four square feet where he slept and stowed his belongings. Captives were even more cramped, as Turner explained, with sleeping space "never more than about eighteen inches wide and four feet long." Aboard any ship there was little privacy. Awake or asleep one was always in the company of family and workmates.[6] The restricted living quarters on junks ensured a compact communal social life that was both bonded and bounded by numerous restrictions and limitations. The vastness of the oceans simply added to the isolation and detachment from other people and the dominant society on land.

The living conditions and habits of fishermen, sailors, and pirates aboard ship differed very little from one another. They all wore simple but distinct clothing, as we can see in Figure 19. Cotton was the preferred fabric because it was cheap and sturdy and could withstand the rigors of rough work and salt water. Clothes lacked adornments and were loose fitting so as not to hinder or slow down work. Most seamen possessed few articles of clothing, and what they had usually lasted for several years. They seldom wore shoes. Although ordinary pirates dressed like other sailors, their leaders were often more ostentatious. Zhang Bao and other pirate chieftains snubbed polite society by regularly wearing flamboyant purple or red silk gowns.[7]

Everyone aboard ship also had to stomach the same poor diet day after day. The usual fare consisted mainly of water and rice with some salted fish and dried vegetables. Only on rare occasions, such as New Year's day and certain religious celebrations, did they eat fresh vegetables, fruit, pork, and poultry. Rats, which were common aboard most vessels, were considered a delicacy. Whereas on land these rodents were specifically raised for the tables of the wealthy, the poor tended to eat wild rats whenever they could be caught. In times of scarcity pirates, like other impoverished mariners, ate whatever they could find. One eyewitness recounted how during one particularly difficult period, they "lived three weeks on caterpillars boiled with rice"; and in fact, he went on to say, "there were very few creatures that they will not

---

[6] *Chinese Repository* 1834:3/70; also see Glasspoole 1831:127–128; Gutzlaff 1834:55–56; Kani 1967:24–25, 54; and Diamond 1969:43.

[7] *Chinese Repository* 1834:3/74.

Figure 19. Chinese Boatman. Source:
Dianshizhai huabao (1884).

eat." It was not unheard of for sailors on long voyages to run
short of food and starve to death.[8]

Seafarers, even when they came from different regions and
spoke different dialects, nevertheless conversed with one another
in a common language of the sea. Seamen needed their own occupational argot, which included many technical terms used in sailing a ship, as well as descriptions of various weather conditions.
Their speech, considered vulgar by outsiders, was direct and
unpretentious. It was a working-class language with its own
vocabulary and cant, fused with cursing and swearing, which
bespoke their defiance of polite society. As one Western observer
put it: "Their curses and imprecations are most horrible, their

---

[8] Glasspoole 1831:128; and Gutzlaff 1834:56, 98, 167; the dietary habits of
Chinese during this period are described in the *Chinese Repository* 1835:3/457–471.

language most filthy and obscene."[9] Their crude talk and profanity reflected the sorts of values stressed by sailors: masculinity, strength, and independence. Mastering the peculiar language of the sea was elemental to the socialization process aboard ship, creating the basis for a solidarity and a collective consciousness common to all seamen. Pirates, who, of course, were fluent in the seaman's tongue, developed their own unique argot of crime. The distinctive speech of mariners, mostly incomprehensible to landsmen, further highlighted their estrangement from dominant society on shore.[10]

Confined by a grueling workload and the cramped space aboard ship for most of the time, seamen were limited in their diversions. Aboard ship, when not hard at work, sailors spent most of their free time sleeping, eating meals, and washing and mending clothes. They amused themselves as best they could with song, card games, and plenty of hard liquor. Some sailors—and even fishermen—relaxed by fishing, while others passed the time by telling stories or reciting ditties. The pirate Guo Podai, who kept a library on board his junk, was often found reading poetry and historical romances.[11]

In port seafarers and pirates would often dawdle away their time visiting opium dens, gambling parlors, and brothels. As Charles Gutzlaff observed, sailors came from the "most debased class of people": addicted to fighting, whoring, gambling, drinking, and opium smoking, they spent their money just as fast as they made it.[12] Religious festivals, such as the one illustrated in Figure 20, provided relaxation and relief from the drudgery and monotony of daily life. They offered everyone a cheap form of

---

[9] Gutzlaff 1834:61.

[10] See XKTB (92) QL 48.3.25; Zhu Jingying [1772] 1996:16; *LJXZ* 2/35b; and *MXTZ* 7/11a. E. Anderson (1970:6–8) describes the "language of the water" of Hong Kong boat people; my observations have also been informed by conversations and interviews with seamen in Hong Kong in December 1990 and in October 1994, in Chaozhou in December 1990, and in Jilong (Keelung) in June 1996. The contemporary Taiwanese writer Liao Hongji, himself a fisherman, in a story titled "The Language of Sea Beggars" in *Taohairen* (1996:196–208), gives a vivid description of the unique sailors' cant and the importance for novice seamen to quickly master it. See also the insightful discussions on the language of sixteenth-century Spanish sailors in Pérez-Mallaína (1998:225) and of eighteenth-century Atlantic sailors in Rediker (1987:166–168).

[11] Glasspoole 1831:105; also see Ward 1985:12; and E. Anderson 1970:255.

[12] Gutzlaff 1834:61, 141–142. E. Anderson (1970:83) has also pointed out much the same thing about fishermen in modern Hong Kong.

Figure 20. Crowds Enjoying an Opera at a Religious Festival.
Source: *China, Pictorial, Descriptive, and Historical* (1853).

entertainment with street processions, theatrical performances, puppet shows, gambling, singing, and dancing. They also gave opportunity for individuals to get together to meet old acquaintances and make new friends, as well as to get into brawls, another favorite pastime of mariners worldwide.[13]

Violence and Vice

The culture of seafarers was as much as anything else one of violence and vice. The oppressive working and living conditions on ships fostered aggressiveness toward both outsiders and

---

[13] Kani 1967:73; Ward 1985:28–29; and Chen Zhonglie 1994:114.

shipmates. Because tensions easily flared up on overcrowded ships, quarrelling was a daily occurrence.[14] People living along the southern littoral had a reputation, somewhat deserved, for being contentious and bellicose.[15] Children growing up in seafaring families had to harden themselves just to reach adulthood. In port towns such as Jiaotang and Shawan in the Canton delta, parents and other adults encouraged children from an early age to compete in street fights as a regular play activity.[16] In a number of coastal villages in southern Fujian and Taiwan, intravillage rock fights were popular sports.[17] It was unusual if temple fairs, attended by drunken sailors and local residents, did not degenerate into bloody frays.[18] The knocking out of teeth and splitting of skulls was to be expected: fighting was an important mechanism for releasing tension and anger. Seamen lived and worked in a rough and brutal environment where fighting was a requisite skill for survival.

Gambling was also a favorite amusement. In South China during the eighteenth century there were hundreds of popular wagering games played by men, women, and even small children. In the ports of Amoy and Fuzhou there were several well-known streets and markets where nearly every house was a gambling establishment.[19] Near Canton it was said that there was not even a single village in Panyu county that did not have a fantan parlor.[20] Sailors would spend days and all their earnings on betting games such as fantan, mahjongg, and quail fighting. Gambling was not only a way of passing time, but also a means of possibly increasing meager earnings or spending the spoils of a theft. Losers would often pawn their clothes and go into debt so that they could continue to play.[21] A boatwoman's ditty lamented the unavoidable evils of gambling:

> Oh Heaven! Why I am a gambler's wife I simply cannot see,
> For a gambler is a man of very low degree;

---

[14] Gutzlaff 1834:141.

[15] SYD, JQ 12.10.26; *FQXZ* 40; and *Chinese Repository* 1834:2/527.

[16] *PYXZ* 6/12b; also see *CHXZ* 6/2a–b.

[17] YXTZ 3/11b; and DeGlopper 1995:141–142.

[18] *LJXZ* 19/21b, 23a.

[19] *XMZ* 653; and Doolittle 1865:1/347.

[20] *PYXZ:*6/11b–12a. Fantan was (and still is) a popular gambling game in which players bet on the number of coins, beans, or other objects that would be left from the pile after it had been counted off in fours.

[21] YXTZ 3/13a–b; *Chinese Repository* 1832:1/58–61; and Gutzlaff 1834:141.

Other people are happy and gay,
But he roams in the gambling den all day;
He goes and leaves me many a lonely night,
When I wake up he is out of sight;
Three girls are sold into slavery by thee,
Your patrimony is wasted I clearly foresee.[22]

For losers at the gambling tables who were unable to pay off their debts, fleeing to sea and becoming pirates proved attractive.[23] No wonder that officials scorned gamblers as loafers and idlers and blamed gambling for causing affrays, thievery, and debauchery. The laws against gambling, however, were impossible to enforce and often tolerated by the very officials and underlings who were supposed to enforce them. Although frowned upon and prohibited, gambling remained a vexatious vice throughout the Qing era.[24]

Gambling and brawling were inseparable from intoxication. For sailors and pirates, drinking to excess was not unusual both aboard ship and ashore. They enjoyed themselves with a variety of drinking games in which the participants normally ended up drunk. On at least one occasion a gang of pirates got so drunk they passed out and were overpowered by their captives.[25] Sailors and pirates were fond of drinking a blue liquor called "bee-chew," which was served warm in small cups. Edward Brown said it tasted like a mixture of "bilge-water, vitriol, turpentine, copal varnish, tar, fire, and castor oil!"[26] Alcohol was also important as a complement to food aboard ship, providing essential calories to a generally poor diet.[27] Besides drinking strong liquor, seamen amused themselves by smoking opium and chewing betel nut. Brown said that the pirates chewed betel all day long, "and only take it out of their mouths while they are eating."[28] Both opium and betel nut were readily available to seafarers as cargo and to pirates as plunder.

---

[22] Wu Yuey Len 1937:853.

[23] *XMZ* 653; and T. Chang 1983:213.

[24] SYD, JQ 12.10.26; also see Peter Ng's translation of the Yongzheng emperor's decree of 1729 condemning gambling (1983:76).

[25] GZD (1763) JQ 1.12.29.

[26] Brown 1861:49.

[27] Pérez-Mallaína 1998:141.

[28] Brown 1861:49, 117; also see Glasspoole 1831:105. Southern Chinese believe that chewing betel nut is good for the teeth, and on Hainan Island today one pharmaceutical company even manufactures a popular "Bing Lang Healthful Toothpaste" that purports to be pleasant tasting and effective in "cleaning the teeth, killing bacteria, and preventing odontosphacelism [*sic*]."

Intoxication and staying high actually occupied a central place in seafaring culture, offering momentary escapes from the harsh and inexorable conditions of the seaman's life. As men on the margins of respectable society, mariners were daily reminded of their subordinate status, and the heavy consumption of alcohol or opium provided a realm of sociability whereby they could be themselves and set their own rules. Like sailors everywhere they were mostly young and restless, and they lived for the now.[29]

Lecherous Men and Lewd Women

When viewed against the Confucian standards of the day, the sexual habits of seafarers, particularly pirates, were unconventional and nonconformist. They self-consciously defied the sexual mores and family values of the day. In many ways what Qing officials and dominant society considered illicit sex, namely sexual relations outside the bonds of marriage or concubinage, was the norm for sailors, who had reputations for licentious, rakish behavior. For Cantonese "water people," premarital sexual experimentation among teenage boys and girls was taken for granted and even encouraged, and infidelity among married couples was not unusual.[30] Prostitution among boating women and girls, though prohibited by Qing law, was almost endemic. Dan boat people were well known for their lusty, erotic saltwater songs (*xianshui ge*), sung by courting couples and prostitutes alike.[31]

The sexual practices aboard pirate vessels were anything but orthodox. Pirates acted without restraint; they were not bound by any sexual conventions other than their own. As we have already seen, violence and sex went hand in hand with piracy. The pirate chieftain Zhang Bao broke all the rules: he had had a homosexual relationship with his adopted father Zheng Yi, and then after the latter's death (and perhaps even while he was still alive) an incestuous relationship with Zheng Yi's wife, his adopted mother, who had been a prostitute. Only after they surrendered in 1810 were they formally married.[32] Cai Qian's "wife" had been the town slut and had been married several times, and even after settling down

---

[29] See *FQXZ* 488; Gutzlaff 1834:141–142; and Katsuta 1967:32; for interesting comparisons with Atlantic seamen in this period, see Rediker 1987:191–193.

[30] E. Anderson 1970:106.

[31] Qu Dajun [1700] 1985:2/485–486.

[32] Ye Linfeng 1970:68–70.

with her new mate she openly continued her promiscuity with male captives.[33] It was common for pirates to have multiple sexual partners, both female and male.

Ming and Qing erotic literature portrayed a "southern custom" (*nanfeng*) of male homosexuality, particularly strong in the coastal cities of Fujian.[34] That province even had a sodomitical subculture centering on the cult of Hu Tianbao.[35] Sodomy was common among South China's mariners, and perhaps some men became sailors because life at sea was more tolerant of such unorthodox behavior.[36] In any case, in late imperial China, where males always outnumbered females, finding a wife was difficult, especially among the lower social orders.[37] Poverty affected sexual practices; same-sex unions played important roles in the survival strategies of poor, marginalized sailors, whose meager wages could little afford them the luxury of conventional heterosexual marriages. For many seafarers such male sexual bonding also helped fulfill basic human emotional and material needs. As Matthew Sommer has explained, "in such relationships, sex coincides with different forms of resource pooling, coresidence, and fictive kinship (sworn brotherhood, master-novice ties, and the like)."[38]

In 1799, in Zhangzhou, there was the case of a thirty-four-year-old trawler captain named Lin Rong who had strangled his male lover, Zhang Acong, in a drunken rage of passion. Although Lin had a wife and son back home in port, he confessed that because he was away from them for long periods, he became infatuated with Acong, a young crewman who had "feminine features." They maintained a homosexual relationship intermittently over a four-year period. However, when Acong reached the age of nineteen, he took a wife and a job as a shop clerk in the port town of Zhenhai, and thereafter he refused all sexual contact with Lin. Sometime later an intoxicated Captain Lin visited Acong, who again rejected his former lover's advances. A scuffle

---

[33] *MXTZ* addendum 1/57a.

[34] Hinsch 1990:124–133, 153; Vitiello 1992:362–363. The term *nanfeng* is a pun on the homophone meaning "male custom" or homosexuality.

[35] Szonyi 1998.

[36] See, for example, the discussion on seventeenth-century Caribbean pirates in Burg 1984.

[37] Lee and Wang 1999:64–71.

[38] Sommer 2000:155–156.

broke out, and Acong was killed while resisting the older and stronger man.[39]

The above case was typical of others involving sodomy found in the Qing archives. For one thing, age and social status tended to reinforce the hierarchy of sexual roles in homosexual (as in heterosexual) affairs. Lin was not only older but also enjoyed superior status as the ship's captain; he naturally assumed the dominant, active role as penetrant in anal intercourse. Acong, as an adolescent and a subordinate, took the passive, "female" role of being sexually penetrated. Similarly, on pirate vessels, sodomy, whether consensual or coerced, was always initiated by the chiefs or deck officers on younger pirates or captives. Such "trans-generational homosexuality," as Bret Hinsch has called it, tended to occur in ritual contexts as part of "coming-of-age cere-monies."[40] At sea, aboard fishing, merchant, and pirate junks, young crewmen were especially vulnerable to the demands of their older, more experienced mates, and sodomy had long been an important rite of passage for novice sailors. The act of sodomy itself also served as a form of "male bonding," helping to solidify the loyalty of subordinates to their superiors aboard ship.[41]

Such homosexual liaisons appear to have been a phase in the sexual life cycles of some males.[42] According to Sommer, once a young man married, and thereby became a fully socialized adult, he would normally reject the sexual advances of his former lover because he felt himself too mature for such behavior. This did not mean, however, that he would necessarily end his homosexual affairs, but rather that he would attempt to alter his role in such relationships: a mature married adult was expected to be penetrant and was not to be penetrated.[43] Thus although Captain Lin was married he still continued to enjoy his sexual relationship with the younger Acong, as long as Lin acted as penetrant. This scenario also closely matched the pattern of numerous pirate cases I have studied in the Qing archives. What emerges is a complex interplay of homosexual and heterosexual relations, in which some men, especially older men, maintained heterosexual as well as

---

[39] XKTB(H) (43) JQ 4.3.21; for other examples of sodomy cases involving Fujian and Guangdong seamen, see XKTB(H) (113) QL 57.5.19; (71) JQ 8.9.2; and (69) JQ 9.3.18.

[40] Hinsch 1990:11; also see Vitiello 1992:353–354.

[41] Murray 1992:125; and Hinsch 1990:131.

[42] Hinsch 1990:136; and Sommer 2000:145.

[43] Sommer 2000:145–148.

homosexual relationships. There was no apparent loss of face or even masculinity for men to engage in homosexual acts as long as they were the penetrants.[44]

Homosexual activities aboard ship did not preclude heterosexual activities both on and off ship. One Western observer, who had been abducted, reported that pirate vessels often kept anywhere from eight to ten women on board just to serve the pleasures of the crew.[45] In a number of places, as in Chenghai harbor, prostitutes also serviced sailors aboard ship. Fathers, brothers, and husbands would sail out in small boats to pimp their daughters, sisters, and wives to sailors on incoming junks as well as to provide them with opium and liquor. Around Canton there were numerous floating brothels known locally as "flower boats." In 1770 one official estimated that there were as many as eight thousand Dan boats in the Canton estuary that were used in prostitution. Once on shore sailors indulged themselves in fornication with prostitutes. All port towns, even the smallest ones, had whorehouses that catered especially to seamen.[46]

Mastering the Natural Environment

Mariners were necessarily sensitive to the natural environment. Their careful and precise readings of nature were essential not simply for navigation, but also for their survival at sea. They therefore studied and interpreted the movements and characteristics of the oceans and heavenly bodies. The ability to predict atmospheric changes by the color of the sea or the shape of clouds, to smell approaching storms, or to learn how the winds and currents flowed to create highways in the ocean were part of the common wisdom that seafarers possessed. It was knowledge gained from long years of experience of living and working at sea as well as from listening carefully to older sailors. While much of this accumulated knowledge was credible, it was also mixed with a profusion of unscientific folk beliefs. Because life at sea was dangerous and erratic, seamen sought to master their world through both natural observations and through omens, magic, and rituals.[47]

---

[44] Hinsch 1990:123; Szonyi 1998:10; and Sommer 2000:149, 152, 162.

[45] Murray 1987:78; also see GZD (3347) JQ 2.11.12.

[46] Gutzlaff 1834:88.

[47] *LJXZ* 2/33a–36a; also see discussions in Rediker 1987:179–182; and Pérez-Mallaína 1998:229.

Local gazetteers, almanacs, and mariners' handbooks recorded useful information on shipping routes, tides and currents, and weather forecasting. The Lianjiang county gazetteer, for example, included monthly forecasts of weather conditions as well as a detailed compendium for predicting wind conditions and various climatic disturbances. For easy recollection, long-term forecasts were also based on festivals and the birthdays of popular deities. One forecast, for instance, related that the time of Mazu's birthday, the twenty-third day of the third lunar month, was a time of strong winds, which seamen called "Mazu gales."[48] Illiterate sailors could easily remember predictions and forecasts when put into rhyme. One popular handbook, the *Book of Sea Routes* (*Haidaojing*), included a series of jingles describing natural phenomena to help sailors predict changes in weather. One forecast was based on observing lightning:

> If lightning appears in the southwest,
>   tomorrow will be clear.
> If lightning appears in the northwest,
>   it will rain for several days....
> If lightning appears everywhere,
>   there will be no wind and rain;
>   it will be a fair day.[49]

The vastness of the sea and sky made for an abundance of portents. A ring around the moon meant a storm was brewing. Sighting a shooting star or comet presaged bad luck, such as a typhoon, illness, or death. A broken rainbow was a harbinger of bad weather, as was the cawing of a crow. Cirrocumulus clouds, or what sailors called a "fish-scale sky," meant unstable weather that was certain to bring rain. A goose feather floating on the water alerted sailors to an approaching storm, and a mole-cricket detected on the sea meant a gale was coming in two or three days. Schools of porpoises jumping in and out of the water were a sure sign that the wind would blow without ceasing.[50]

Sailors believed that certain sea creatures, such as sturgeon, sawfish, whales, and sea turtles, were sacred and should not be caught. To avoid calamity, if a sacred fish was caught and killed it was taken to a temple and offered as sacrifice. "Failure to treat the fish properly," explained E. N. Anderson, "results in

---

[48] *LJXZ* 2/34a–b; also see *MXTZ* 7/11b.
[49] *Haidaojing* 17b.
[50] Ibid., 14b–19a; *MXTZ* 7/9a; *XMZ* 128–135; and *LJXZ* 2/36a.

extremely bad luck—shipwreck, deaths in the family, loss of livelihood. Consecrating the fish at the temple reverses this and may
even lead to good luck."[51] Fishermen, as Norma Diamond
discovered in the village of Kunshen in Taiwan, took pains not to
offend sacred sea creatures and held elaborate ceremonies and
sacrifices to assure themselves safety at sea and abundant
catches.[52] At the Dragon God Temple on Fujian's Fuqing coast, villagers refused to cast their nets into the ocean, though the fish
were plentiful, for fear of disturbing the dragon that lived beneath
the water's surface.[53]

Worshipping Deities of the Sea

The mariner's view of religion and the supernatural was
shaped by his concern for and confrontation with the sea and
nature. The sea was both bountiful and cruel. While it was a life-
giving force it was also, at times, a merciless agent of havoc and
death. Interestingly, what Marcus Rediker discovered about the
religious beliefs of eighteenth-century Western seamen applied
equally well to their Chinese counterparts: "The uncontrollable
vicissitudes of nature, the extreme vulnerability of seamen, and
the frequency of death at sea gave a special power to superstition,
omens, personal rituals, and belief in luck."[54] For Chinese seafarers fate and good luck, in fact, seemed more important than virtue
and frugality. Beliefs and ritual practices, therefore, were mostly
pragmatic and concerned with practical everyday matters rather
than salvation and the afterlife. Because seafarers made no firm
distinctions between the natural and supernatural worlds, they
envisioned a cosmos in which both realms were intermingled and
inseparable. They had constantly to adjust their lives and
thoughts to the presence of the unseen world of the supernatural.
Ritual and sacrifice were the conduits through which worshippers
could reach the sacred realm and influence the myriad gods,
ghosts, and demons.[55]

Whereas Guandi (God of War) was arguably the most popular
deity among inland peasant communities, Tianhou (Empress of

---

[51] E. Anderson 1972:34.
[52] Diamond 1969:14–15, 26.
[53] *FQXZ* 488–489.
[54] Rediker 1987:186.
[55] Ward 1985:12–13; and Chen Yande 1997:70.

Heaven, or Mazu [Venerable Mother]) was the most popular deity among maritime communities. What began in the tenth century as a minor local deity among fishermen and sailors in Putian county, Fujian, some eight centuries later had become a major cult all along China's seaboard. In recognition of her growing popularity the state appropriated Mazu into the official pantheon, and in 1683 the Kangxi emperor awarded her the title Tianhou as a gesture of gratitude for aiding in the Qing conquest of Taiwan.[56] Considered the patron deity of seafarers, Mazu was but one among a pantheon of gods of the sea. These included such other widespread cults as Beidi (God of the North), Longwang (Dragon King), Longmu (Dragon Mother), Jinghaishen (God Who Quells the Sea), Shuishu Huangdi (Emperor of the Waters), and Fengbo (Wind Uncle), as well as more localized ones such as Hongsheng (Sage Hong) and Tangong (Lord Tan) in the Canton area, Sanshanshen (God of the Three Mountains) in Chaozhou, and Jumu (Gale Mother) on Hainan Island and the Leizhou peninsula.[57] Two of these popular deities are depicted in Figures 21 and 22.

The eighteenth and early nineteenth centuries were an era of general prosperity and commercial growth all along South China's littoral; they were correspondingly times of intensive temple construction and renovation. Most of these temples were in busy commercial and fishing ports or on islands near entrances to harbors. Temple building reflected the wealth that local communities had acquired either directly through trade or indirectly from the economic benefits obtained from trade. Prosperous merchants and gentry became the chief patrons of sea-deity cults, and as the chief benefactors of these temples they were able to use their influence to dominate many temple organizations, festivals, and processions.[58]

---

[56] Ng Chin-keong 1983:91. James Watson (1985:255), however, gives the date of 1737 for awarding the title Tianhou.

[57] For Guangdong, see Qu Dajun [1700] 1985:200–213; and Burkhardt 1966:1/19, 101–107; and for a general overview of the geographic distribution of officially sanctioned temples throughout the province see *GDTZ* [1822] 1934:2/2700–2772. For Fujian, see *XMZ* 63–68. While several of these deities, such as Beidi and Longmu, were not specifically gods of the sea and were represented differently in other areas, at least along the South China coast they were treated as sea deities.

[58] Faure, Luk, and Ng 1984:47–48; Chen Zhonglie 1994:115–117; and Chen Zaizheng 1999:75.

Figure 21. Paper Effigy of the Empress of Heaven with her Attendants. Source: Tianhou Temple, Anping, Taiwan (author's collection).

Figure 22. Paper Effigy of the Dragon
King of the Four Seas with his Attendants. Source: Henry Doré, *Researches
into Chinese Superstitions* (1914–1938).

By the late Qianlong reign nearly every town and village along
the South China coast had an Empress of Heaven temple. A large
number of communities also had more than one temple honoring
deities of the sea. In the early nineteenth century, Amoy had
more than twenty-six temples dedicated to Tianhou, as well as
numerous other temples honoring various sea gods. In Shunde
county, Guangdong, there were more than fifty Tianhou temples
by the 1850s, most of which had been built over the previous century. Many ports and market towns were known locally only by

their temples; thus people called Jizhou "Tianhou market."[59] Besides these officially recognized temples, innumerable unregistered, illegal temples and shrines, labeled by the state as licentious temples (*yinci*), dotted the coastline.[60]

Though not always the case, many seafarers built their own temples and organized their festivals separately from those of landed society. In Hong Kong, for instance, the boat people of Datandu (Tai Tam Tuk) had their own family and group celebrations and did not join with villagers to worship at the local Tianhou temple. Instead, they customarily worshipped at two nearby shrines on the coast, and for major celebrations they went to the Hongsheng temple on Hong Kong Island. Even when villagers and fishermen worshipped at the same temple, their rituals and festivals could be disassociated. On tiny Pingzhou (Peng Chau) Island, where Dan, Hoklo, Hakka, and Punti ethnic groups all worshipped at the same Tianhou temple, there were two separate festivals honoring the deity: one for the land people in the third lunar month and another for the boat people in the fifth lunar month.[61]

Not only did legitimate maritime communities support the temple cults mentioned above, but so did pirates. In fact, they too had a long history of temple building along the coast. According to a recently discovered stone inscription, in 1753 Zheng Lianchang, the father of Zheng Yi, erected a Tianhou temple on Devil's Mountain (Emoshan) at Liyumen near Hong Kong, which was to "remain in the hands of [his] descendants in perpetuity." He also founded another temple on the coast at Chaguoling. Zhang Bao reportedly built two Tianhou temples about 1808 on Hong Kong Island at Jishuimen and Mawan, as well as another on the island of Changzhou. These temples were situated in the vicinity of pirate strongholds. Local tradition has it that Zhang Bao was also an extravagant contributor to Tianhou cults all around the Canton delta.[62] Although there is no information on how the pirates consecrated their temples, we do know that they sometimes stole statues of propitious deities from other temples to put in their own temples or in shrines on their junks.[63]

---

[59] *XMZ* 63–68; Liang Tingnan 1838:5/24b–25a, 6/11b–12a, 25b–26a; Chen Zhonglie 1994:114.

[60] Ng Chin-keong 1983:93; Chen Zhonglie 1994:114; and Szonyi 1998:1–8.

[61] Hayes 1983:46, 68; see also J. Watson 1985:313, 321.

[62] Xiao Guojian 1978:19; also see Burkhardt 1966:1/103.

[63] *DGXZ* 19/8b; Neumann 1831:15–16; and Brown 1861:66.

Besides the temples on shore, aboard every fishing boat, merchant junk, and pirate craft was a shrine in which the sailors put their icons, adorned with tinsel, and before which they kept oil lamps burning day and night. Sailors also often brought with them a few embers or ashes obtained from the censer of a Tianhou temple; they placed the ashes in small red bags, suspended from some convenient place aboard their junk or in the ship's censer, which was placed before their icon.[64] Zhang Bao even had a floating "pagoda" accompany his fleet so that he could better consult its oracles. Sailors adorned the ship's compass with red cloth, and twice daily, at dawn and in the evening, they would burn incense and votive gilt paper. Most boats employed a religious specialist, the "incense burners," specifically to care for the icons and ceremonial needs of the crew. Pirate junks also had their "incense burners," who were frequently captives forced to serve the pirates in that capacity.[65]

The sea-deity cults appealed to diverse groups of people of different statuses and social backgrounds on both land and water. As James Watson reminds us, Tianhou and other Chinese deities "symbolized different things to different people."[66] To the state and landed local elites the Empress of Heaven was a civilizing agent who stood for orthodox values and social stability. In written accounts she was depicted as an aggressive goddess who suppressed disorders, especially piracy, by creating destructive storms, as we have already noted elsewhere in this book. Other sea deities were similarly commemorated, as was the case in 1810 when the Jiaqing emperor bestowed honorific titles on Jinghaishen for helping to quell Zhang Bao.[67] Maritime merchants and shopkeepers worshipped these deities not only to protect their ships and stores from pirates, but also more specifically to beseech good

---

[64] Gutzlaff 1834:55, 58; and Doolittle 1865:1/263–264; also see E. Anderson 1970:48. Naval junks also had altars to Tianhou aboard ship (*JMZ* 97).

[65] GZD (1092) JQ 1.8.30; also see Gutzlaff 1834:55, 59; Brown 1861:47; and Ch'en Kuo-tung 1994:210.

[66] J. Watson 1985:302. Another good example relates to the worship of the Venerable Dipper (Dou Lao), mentioned in chapter 2, in which her cultic followers were inspired to rebel against the Ming dynasty, officials and soldiers prayed to her to destroy pirates, and village women made offerings to her for the protection of their children (*QZFZ* 73/11b; Qu Dajun [1700] 1985:1/213; Doolittle 1865: 2/68–69; and Diamond 1969:98).

[67] *DGXZ* 19/8b, 33/25b–26a; for other accounts of divine intervention that reportedly saved villagers from pirates, see GZD (5520) JQ 5.7.6; XHXZ 4/24b–25a; and *LJXZ* 21/50a. See other examples in Chen Zaizheng 1999:77.

fortune and profit. By the mid-Qing era in maritime South China, Tianhou had replaced Guandi as the leading patron deity of merchant associations.[68]

The above views, however, were not stressed in the oral traditions of fishermen and sailors. They had different values and expectations, and therefore different representations of their deities. They worshipped sea gods chiefly for mastery over the oceans, fruitful voyages, and protection from storms.[69] According to James Watson's fishermen informants, the worship of Tianhou "had nothing to do with social stability or coastal pacification. Their stories dealt primarily with T'ien Hou's [Tianhou's] divine intervention on behalf of people who make their living at sea." She was a powerful deity who, on the one hand, could be entreated to raise storms to destroy pirates, yet on the other hand, could be called on to calm the seas to save sailors and, paradoxically, even pirates. Obviously, boat people and land people had quite different characterizations of deities they worshipped in common; in a word, they were not part of the same "moral community." As Watson's study shows, different individuals or groups could preserve their own representations of a deity in spite of official or elite attempts at hegemony and standardization.[70]

Religious practices reflected the unique environment and special needs of the watery world of seafarers, who spent much of their time in countless ritual activities.[71] Before beginning any undertaking, pirates and mariners always first consulted their gods with prayers, offerings, and incense. Seamen placed great importance on the manipulation of supernatural forces not only at the start and conclusion of their voyages, but during the voyages as well. An auspicious day had to be chosen to set sail, and on that day the entire crew would parade the ship's joss or icon on a palanquin through the streets of the port to the mother temple to ask for blessings. Often too the ceremony would be accompanied by a theatrical performance.[72]

---

[68] Doolittle 1865:1/262; J. Watson 1985:298–304, 308; Chen Zhonglie 1994: 115–118; Jiang Weitan 1995; and Chen Shangsheng 1997.

[69] Chen Yande 1997:71; and Chen Zaizheng 1999:77–78.

[70] J. Watson 1985:322.

[71] According to Hiroaki Kani (1967:70), modern fishermen around Hong Kong spend only 120 to 150 days each year in actual fishing; they spend most of the rest of the time in the observance of religious ceremonies, festivals, and annual events.

[72] Gutzlaff 1834:58–59.

John Gray described a ceremony to the goddess Longmu, which he witnessed in 1861:

> Previous to weighing anchor the master took his place in the bow....and proceeded to propitiate the Dragon's Mother. On a small temporary altar, which had been erected for the occasion, stood three cups containing Chinese wine. Taking in his hands a live fowl, which he continued to hold until he killed it as a sacrifice, the master proceeded in the first place to perform the Kowtow. He then took the cups from the table, one at a time, and raising each above his head, poured its contents on the deck as a libation. He next cut the throat of the fowl with a sharp knife, taking care to sprinkle that portion of the deck on which he was standing with the blood of the sacrifice. At this stage of the ceremony several pieces of silver paper were presented to him by the crew. These were sprinkled with the blood, and then fastened to the door-posts and lintels of the cabin.[73]

The bloody sacrifice, according to Hiroaki Kani, was supposed to exorcise all evil spirits, cleanse away ill fortune, and bring good luck to the crew.[74]

Sometimes offerings were simpler, consisting of a few cakes, boiled chickens, or pork fat. Afterward the crew would partake collectively of the food that had been offered. Another common practice was to burn offerings of paper boats to the sea gods before casting off. Offerings were usually followed by setting off firecrackers and burning a talisman, like the one in Figure 23, for warding off evil spirits or for beseeching the gods for a safe voyage. Sometimes sailors digested the ashes of the talisman. Seafarers also carried ashes, taken either from temple incense burners or from charms, in small pouches on their person for protection and for curing illnesses while at sea.[75] Pirates and smugglers, too, observed the same ritual practices as other seafarers: they burned incense, set off firecrackers, carried pouches of ashes, and sacrificed chickens and pigs.[76]

Throughout the voyage sailors made offerings to the gods of the wind and sea, as well as to the sacred promontories they passed. When they sailed past well-known temples, the crew would make offerings aboard ship or even anchor and go ashore

---

[73] Gray 1878:2/271–272.

[74] Kani 1967:77.

[75] Audemard 1957–1971:3/50–55; and Kani 1967:76.

[76] Glasspoole 1831:113; *Chinese Repository* 1834:3/81; and Brown 1861:46–47. On smugglers see Downing 1838:3/233.

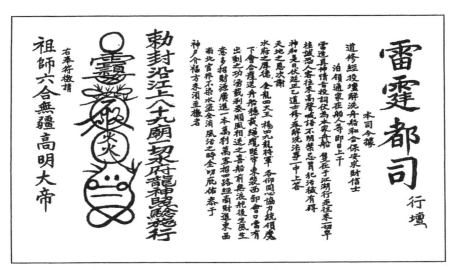

Figure 23. Talisman Burned by Sailors Seeking Protection at Sea.
Source: Henry Doré, *Researches into Chinese Superstitions* (1914–1938).

to worship at the temple.[77] On an island at the entrance to Dianbai harbor there was a famous shrine, and all vessels setting out to sea customarily paid tribute to the deity by releasing a cock on the island. Rather than slaughtering an animal for sacrifice, this was a Buddhist practice of freeing life (*fangsheng*) to obtain merit. As a result the island became known as Releasing Cocks Mountain (Fangjishan).[78] Similar rituals were performed at a Tianhou temple on another Fangjishan Island off the Chenghai coast in Chaozhou prefecture.[79] According to Yuan Yonglun, both seafarers and pirates would always visit a popular temple dedicated to the three female deities known as Sanpo to make offerings and burn incense.[80] Fishermen and pirates both regularly worshipped Mazu at her home temple on Meizhou Island.[81] Both Cai Qian and Zhu Fen made regular pilgrimages to Putuoshan Temple to seek

---

[77] Blussé 1988:110–111; also see Ward 1985:13.

[78] *DBXZ* 6/3b–4a. This refers to the island that became known as the Greater Releasing Cocks Island; there was also another nearby island called Lesser Releasing Cocks Island (see Figure 1).

[79] Ye Xianen 1989:160.

[80] Neumann 1831:15.

[81] Chen Zaizheng 1999:75–76.

blessings for their endeavors.[82] Upon returning to Macao, as they passed the Empress of Heaven Temple, the crews of fishing boats would always burn paper money and set off firecrackers to salute and thank the goddess for a safe return and successful catch.[83]

Although seafarers and pirates were similar in their beliefs and practices, there were certain differences. Both groups prayed for protection at sea and for successful cruises; the difference, of course, was that for pirates a successful cruise meant one from which they returned unscathed in battle and with bountiful booty.[84] When storms arose pirates entreated the gods to blow them out of harm's way. In 1809, for instance, naval forces off Dayushan surrounded Zhang Bao's fleet. According to Yuan Yonglun's account, the pirates prayed to their gods for advice. The oracles, however, predicted defeat in battle and instead suggested breaking through the naval blockade. When a strong southerly wind arose suddenly the next day, they were able to escape out to sea.[85] Pirates took omens very seriously. On one occasion, when Zhang Bao was posed to attack the area around Lianwan village in Xinhui county, he suddenly saw an apparition of thousands of military banners and soldiers in the sky. He decided to withdraw.[86] Glasspoole related how on another occasion the pirates anchored quietly for three days before a town with a mud wall and then withdrew without attacking because "the idols had not promised them success."[87]

Pirates and Human Sacrifice

With the practices of cannibalism and human sacrifice, pirates went far beyond the unconventional to the grotesque and perverse. Pirates, however, were not the first or only ones to engage

---

[82] SYD, JQ 11.5.13; and GZD (9721) JQ 13.1.14.

[83] Chen Yande 1997:71.

[84] See *Chinese Repository* 1834:3/81; and Brown 1861:46–47.

[85] Cited in Murray 1987:74. The Dongguan gazetteer gives a completely different account of this story. Being surrounded at Lantao, Zhang Bao burned incense before his deity; suddenly flames several feet high shot up from the idol's head. The frightened pirate fell prostrate before the statue, and taking this as an inauspicious sign, at that moment vowed to surrender to the authorities. Thus the omen, instead of foretelling Zhang Bao's escape, in this rendition actually persuaded him to surrender early the following year (*DGXZ* 19/8b).

[86] XHXZ 4/25a.

[87] *Chinese Repository* 1834:3/81.

in these bloody rituals. Such practices were as old as China, and even China's most famous cultural hero, the Yellow Emperor, was said to have killed and made a stew out of the flesh and bones of his enemy, Chi You, which he then shared with his followers in a victory feast.[88] Although such blood offerings had been condemned since at least the Han dynasty as licentious (*yin*) and heterodoxical (*xie*), the practice has continued into modern times.[89] Those individuals who practiced cannibalism and human sacrifice not only rejected the conventions of respectable society, but also directly challenged the state's prerogatives to control and define orthodox religious practices. It was, after all, this monopoly over religion that gave the dynasty legitimacy. Therefore, any challenge to that legitimacy was a grave concern to the state.[90]

Cannibalism was the ultimate act of ritualized violence. In ancient China, a time when warfare and sacrifice were closely linked, victors in battle would present prisoners, sometimes killing and devouring them, as offerings to the gods and ancestors.[91] Ancient Chinese rebels, bandits, and pirates (such as the fifth-century pirate Sun En mentioned in chapter 2) also consumed their victims' flesh and blood in magicoreligious rites. Indeed, the killing, offering, and consumption of animals or humans were the central features of any sacrifice. The bloody sacrifice and shared feasting on the meat at the end of battle was a ritual climax whereby both gods and men shared in the spoils of victory. The sharing in the sacrificial feast also bonded the participants and solemnly sanctified the loyalty of subordinates to their leaders. Because the offerings were thought to be sanctified, they were imbued with magical powers that conferred health, fortune, and power on those making the sacrifice. Making sacrificial offerings and then ingesting those offerings were the chief means by which men and gods interacted and reciprocated. The gods depended on men for sustenance and in return granted them material benefits.

---

[88] Lewis 1990:148.

[89] See, for example, Sutton 1995 on cannibalism during the Great Proletarian Cultural Revolution.

[90] According to the Qing Code, anyone murdering and mutilating their victims for magical purposes was punished with death-by-slicing, and their family members, although innocent of the crime, were sentenced to perpetual banishment of two thousand *li*. Even in cases where the crime had only been contrived but not carried out, the principal was sentenced to beheading and his family members to perpetual banishment as above (Staunton 1810:309).

[91] Lewis 1990:23–27.

"The very ability of the gods to bestow blessings," as Terry Klee-man has written, "was dependent upon the sacrificial offerings of men."[92]

The pirates who killed and ate their enemies were perpetuating an ancient heterodoxical tradition. They did so not only out of extreme hatred and revenge against their opponents, but also to gain considerable magical powers as well as certain medicinal benefits. Ritual cannibalism was a frightening act of empower-ment by which the life essence of victims was incorporated into those partaking of the sacrifice. When pirates drank the blood of their victims, they consumed life's vital force; and when they ate the hearts and livers of their enemies certain desirable qualities, namely courage and longevity, were transferred from the dead to the living. When pirates joined together in their bloodthirsty sacrifices, they called upon the gods to witness and consecrate their actions and to solemnly bind everyone together as blood brothers in crime. The human sacrifice underlined the seriousness of purpose and strengthened their resolve, loyalty, and solidarity as a group. It also gave pirates an awesome power that was beyond the state's control and therefore very dangerous.

---

[92] See Kleeman 1994:189–191.

EIGHT

Conclusion: Maritime History from the Bottom Up

This book set out to explore South China's maritime history from the bottom up, to reconstruct the world of ordinary seafarers and pirates through their own eyes in the context of the social and economic transformations of the late imperial period. The story of maritime South China is not simply that of gentry, merchants, and ship owners who engaged in seaborne trade and reaped most of its profits. It is equally the story of those men and women who sailed their ships and endured untold hardships and dangers for barely enough wages to live. Pirates, in particular, played important roles in shaping seafaring culture and society. Only by going beyond the Confucian-dominated stereotypes to examine the poor, marginalized, and criminalized elements in society can we understand more fully and accurately the social history of late imperial China. The underside of history puts everything else in proper perspective.

Let us conclude by addressing several questions. What can we learn about South China's maritime history by looking at it from the bottom up? How, indeed, did pirates and seafarers help shape the maritime economy, society, and culture? Did Chinese pirates attempt to radically remake the world in which they lived? In answering these questions we will draw upon comparisons with Western maritime history to highlight the salient features of Chinese seafaring and piracy and to put this study in a larger historical context.

In China the golden age of piracy lasted from 1520 to 1810, and for no less than half of those 290 years pirates dominated the seas around South China. Never before in world history had piracy been so strong and enduring. In the West the heyday of piracy began to decline by the early eighteenth century, and even at its peak the pirate population had never exceeded fifty-five hundred men at any one time. In South China the number of pirates was no fewer than seventy thousand at its height.

Beginning in the sixteenth century, piracy became increasingly embroiled in world politics and in the burgeoning global economy. During the sixteenth and seventeenth centuries, European monarchs, statesmen, and merchants all backed piratical ventures as important to both state building and commercial growth, and as a result Western piracy greatly expanded and became global in scope.[1] At the same time, during the Ming and early Qing, Chinese rulers adopted anticommercial policies banning maritime trade, thereby driving merchants into piracy. In China piracy was never supported by state policy. Although for different reasons, merchants came to play dominant roles in both Western and Chinese piracy before 1700; commerce and piracy were barely distinguishable.

After 1700, however, the nature of piracy dramatically changed at both ends of the Eurasian continent. In the West, as the power of states and the profits from legitimate trade steadily grew, merchants put pressure on their political leaders to repress freebooting, and governments responded by passing stiff new laws and by building navies to protect their merchant vessels on the high seas.[2] In China, once the Manchus had consolidated their authority over all of China by 1684, the imperial court dramatically rescinded the sea bans, promoted seaborne trade, and, after 1720, began enacting a series of laws to protect private property, including harsh new laws against piracy.[3] With trade open, most merchants ceased being pirates and, as in the West, became partners with the state in the suppression of piracy. Although Western piracy began to decline after 1700, and all but disappeared in Asian waters by the end of the eighteenth century, Chinese piracy crested in new form between 1780 and 1810. The profound social and economic changes of the eighteenth century that produced tensions and contradictions in South China's maritime world pushed tens of thousands of poor, marginalized seafarers into piracy as a means of survival.

The last great wave of piracy, between 1780 and 1810, paradoxically corresponded with an age of prosperity in China. The

---

[1] Thomson 1994.

[2] Ritchie 1986:138–159.

[3] On property laws see Buoye 2000:220; and on the antipiracy laws see Antony 1994.

population boom, rather than producing a Malthusian crisis, stimulated economic growth, which resulted in increased productivity and generally higher standards of living. The conditions in China actually compared favorably to those in Western Europe at about the same time. As a whole, the Chinese people were eating better and living longer.[4] Yet the material benefits were unevenly distributed. Despite the flourishing economy, for China's laboring poor—and seafarers in particular—population pressure intensified competition for jobs and kept wages low. For them the rising standards of living meant higher costs of living. When they looked around they saw a world of plenty, but it was a world not open to them. "From the standpoint of an eighteenth-century commoner," Philip Kuhn has posited, "commercial growth may have meant, not the prospect of riches or security, but a scant margin of survival in a competitive and crowded society."[5] Not surprisingly, therefore, those areas along the southern coast with the highest population densities and highest levels of commercialization—namely around Canton, Chaozhou, and Amoy—also had the highest incidents of piracy.

The vast majority of Chinese pirates came from this discontented underclass of laboring poor. Seafarers, who could count on neither year-round employment nor wages sufficient to keep them out of debt, did not make the same sharp distinctions, as did officials, between legitimate and illegitimate occupations and incomes. Few among poor sailors and fishermen could accept the dictum of Confucianism that it was better to go hungry than to steal. They simply could not afford the same values as their more affluent contemporaries. Seamen were a highly mobile workforce, moving around from port to port and taking whatever jobs were available whenever they were available. When times were hard and jobs were scarce, many seamen took work aboard pirate ships as they would aboard any other ship. Piracy was a rational and viable alternative or supplement to inadequate employment and low wages. As such it had an important function of providing work, even on a part-time basis, for countless numbers of mariners who could not be fully absorbed into the prevailing labor market.

Whenever piracy flourished so too did the clandestine economy, providing tens of thousands of additional jobs to coastal residents. Not only did the growth of legitimate commerce

---

[4] See Wong 1997; Lee and Wang 1999; and Pomeranz 2000.
[5] Kuhn 1990:36.

promote the development of new ports, but so too did the illicit trade. Numerous ports and black markets sprang up in Guangdong, Fujian, and Taiwan just to handle the trade in stolen goods and to service pirate ships and their crews. Black markets operated as a shadow economy alongside and in competition with legitimate trade centers. Pirates and their collaborators became economic pioneers who fostered the opening up of new commercial facilities and opportunities in areas not easily reached by the established trading networks. Like the pirates themselves, most of the individuals who traded with them were ordinary fishermen and sailors, as well as petty entrepreneurs, who engaged in both licit and illicit enterprises as vital for their survival. In many instances the extra money gained from clandestine activities provided an important, even major, part of their overall incomes. Large amounts of money and goods flowed in and out of black markets, all of which were outside the control of the state and normal trading networks.

At the height of their power during the first decade of the nineteenth century, huge pirate leagues gained a firm hold over many coastal villages and port towns, as well as over most of the shipping and fishing enterprises, through the systematic use of terror, bribery, and extortion. Their power in the region overshadowed that of the Qing state and local elites. What is more, pirates increasingly built strongholds not only on remote islands, but, more important, they built them in and around such commercial and political hubs as Canton, Macao, Chaozhou, and Amoy. There they defiantly set up their "tax bureaus" to collect tribute and ransom payments and to conspire with soldiers, yamen underlings, and officials who were on their payrolls. The close proximity of pirate lairs to economic and political centers was clear indication of just how deeply piracy had penetrated South China's maritime society.

Pirates, and seafarers in general, existed uneasily on the fringes of respectable society. They were "social and cultural transgressors," to borrow the words of Hans Turley, who stood in marked defiance of orthodox values and standards of behavior.[6] Many scholars agree with Evelyn Rawski that China's late imperial age was characterized by the "growing integration" between elite and popular cultures, whereby commoners internalized the values and moral principles of Confucian elites. China was becoming more

---

[6] Turley 1999.

homogeneous.[7] This homogeneity, however, was not universally the case—at least not among some segments of the laboring poor, whose culture was in many respects the antithesis of Confucian orthodoxy. Out of hardship, prejudice, and poverty, seafarers created a culture of survival based on violence and vice and characterized by excessive profanity, intoxication, gambling, brawling, and sexual promiscuity. The same sorts of mechanisms—expanding commercialization, market integration, and population mobility—that had helped to spread orthodox culture downward throughout society also helped to spread the not-so-orthodox culture of seafarers among their peers. Mobile seamen carried their ideas and mores from port to port and between ships. The fluidity of crews helped to ensure social uniformity and a common consciousness among mariners. Their sociocultural world was important precisely because it existed outside the mainstream Confucian model.

But did all the tension, alienation, poverty, and prejudice make Chinese seafarer-pirates radical in ways similar to contemporary Western pirates? In the West during the seventeenth and early eighteenth centuries, as a number of scholars have argued, pirates were important because they put into action the aspirations of ordinary sailors. Marcus Rediker has forcefully argued that pirates created "a culture of masterless men."[8] They were outlaws who lived by no one's rules but their own; they owed loyalty to no state. Outside the bounds of law and society, pirates were at liberty to adopt any form of organization they wished. They opted for a democratic and egalitarian social order that stood in "defiant contradistinction to the ways of the world they left behind."[9] Pirates bonded themselves together in "social compacts," normally through formal written articles agreed upon and signed by all crewmen at the outset of voyages. These agreements, which defined gangs as cohesive, self-governing bodies, detailed the allocation of authority, enforcement of discipline, and distribution of booty.[10] The pirate ship was "democratic in an undemocratic age"; it created "a world turned upside down."[11]

---

[7] Rawski 1985.

[8] Rediker 1987:286.

[9] Ibid., 267.

[10] See ibid., 261–262; Hill 1986 and 1996; Casey 1992; Thomson 1994:45–46; and Turley 1999.

[11] Linebaugh and Rediker 2000:162.

For many poor commoners the pirate ship represented liberty and justice not found on shore. Piracy was a way of life voluntarily chosen, for the most part, by people seeking escape from oppression and injustice. Pirates had a "rough, improvised, but effective egalitarianism" and a "distinctive sense of popular justice."[12] According to Robert Ritchie, they created "a democratic system that gave the men a voice in their affairs."[13] The majority ruled. Captains were elected and were answerable to their crews, who also voted on all important matters. "Discipline among pirates always depended on a collective sense of transgression."[14] The crew agreed to hold property in common and to dole it out in shares among all crewmen, thereby leveling the social distance between officers and men and creating a more equitable distribution of profits than was the practice aboard merchant vessels. Besides limiting the power and authority of their captains, pirates meted out just revenge on brutal, tyrannical merchant captains. Generally, those captains who treated their men fairly were released after capture, but those who mistreated their crew were tortured and killed. "To pirates revenge was justice."[15]

Pirate egalitarianism and freedom also extended to gender relations. Women occasionally made their way aboard pirate vessels, though usually when they did it was dressed as men. Anne Bonny and Mary Read, the two most celebrated female pirates, sailed with Jack Rackam's gang. They swore and cursed the same as other sailors, and they worked and fought as hard as the rest of the crew. They were genuine pirates in every sense of the word. "Operating beyond the reach of the traditional powers of family, state, and capitalism, and sharing in the rough solidarity of life among maritime outlaws," Peter Linebaugh and Marcus Rediker have suggested, "they added another dimension altogether to the subversive appeal of piracy by seizing the liberties usually reserved for men, at a time when the sphere of social action for women was narrowing."[16]

Although Chinese pirates were outlaws living by their own rules, they did not exhibit the same sorts of democratic and

---

[12] Rediker 1987:261, 270.
[13] Ritchie 1986:123.
[14] Rediker 1987:265.
[15] Ibid., 273; see also Ritchie 1986:118–124; Hill 1986:175, and 1996:115–119.
[16] Linebaugh and Rediker 2000:167; also see Rediker 1996.

egalitarian ideals found among Western pirates. The ocean bandits of Guangdong and Fujian did not place "authority in the collective hands of the crew" nor did they have a "democratic selection of officers."[17] Aboard Chinese pirate junks there was no
majority rule; captains and officers were not "elected" by their
crews. Instead, among the large fleets, chieftains such as Cai
Qian, Zhu Fen, Wushi Er, and Zhang Bao personally chose their
subordinate commanders on the basis of ability, kinship, and loyalty; among smaller petty gangs normally the owners of boats
assumed leadership roles. Pirate captains were literally bosses
(*laoban*), ruling their ships with iron fists and absolute power of
life and death. They made the rules and all decisions on board
ship. They composed pirate codes not to guarantee the liberty of
gang members but to establish order and discipline. Pirate bosses
relied on traditional methods of authority rooted in seniority, filial
obedience, and loyalty to ensure cohesion and unity within the
gang.

Liberty and egalitarianism aboard Chinese pirate junks were
limited in other ways. Scholars have claimed that among Western
pirates no unwilling person was forced to become a pirate and
that all property was equitably shared among the entire crew.[18]
However, in China pirates routinely coerced and tricked people
into joining with them. Between 1796 and 1810, at the height of
the pirate disturbances in Guangdong and Fujian, there were actually more captives who had been forced into service than actual
pirates aboard vessels. Like their Western counterparts, Chinese
pirates also practiced a "communal sharing of loot" based on the
concept of partnership that was more equitable than the wage system aboard merchant and fishing junks. But the loot was shared
only among the actual pirates. Captives, who were unwilling
pirates, were excluded from any share of the spoils. If liberty and
equality were the foundations of Western piracy in the eighteenth
century, it was just the opposite with Chinese piracy in the mid-
Qing: slave labor was its foundation. The institutionalization of
forced labor was crucial to the growth of large-scale Chinese
piracy and the basis of its longevity.

Among the Chinese pirates, women represented the most radical departure. They represented a threatening "otherness" that
defied accepted notions of womanhood, breaking with established

---

[17] Rediker 1987:261, 262.
[18] Ibid., 264, 266; and Hill 1996:120.

codes of female propriety, virtue, and passivity. Unlike their counterparts on Western ships, Chinese women pirates did not have to disguise themselves as men. They lived and worked openly as women aboard ships. From the perspective of the Qing state, such women who behaved like men perverted the social order and normal gender relationships, turning Confucian orthodoxy on its head. Indeed, they challenged the patriarchal hierarchy upon which both the state and society rested. But for seafaring women, piracy presented opportunities to escape from poverty and the rigid restraints placed on females. It gave them the chance for adventure and freedom unheard of for most women on land.

The mariner's life was filled with violence and brutality not only against dominant society but also against one another. Chinese pirates were not Hobsbawmian "social bandits" robbing the rich to give to the poor or displaying some sort of primitive class-consciousness. In this sense they were significantly different from Western pirates.[19] Chinese pirates used force neither to right wrongs nor to protect the weak. Instead, they robbed, kidnapped, and murdered anyone who got in their way. They indiscriminately victimized not only sea captains and rich merchants but also poor fishermen and sailors. And what just cause was there in abducting, raping, and killing innocent women and children? When they tortured and brutally murdered victims and soldiers, it was not for just revenge; their actions were a psychological tactic to discourage resistance. Both the state and the pirates exercised their power and authority through terror. For most pirates the chief difference between rich and poor was that the former were more attractive targets. We can agree with Barbara Hanawalt that "protest against the wealthy and powerful in society is certainly present in some of the acts of outlaw bands, but more often than not the gang was more interested in profit or personal revenge."[20] There is little to suggest that pirates plundered the wealthy or attacked officials and soldiers because they had been inspired by class hostility or injustice. They never translated such attacks into more refined forms of protest. Men were more likely to turn to

---

[19] The classic formulation of the theory of social banditry is Hobsbawm 1981. As the theory has been applied to Western pirates see Rediker 1987:269; and as it has been used in Chinese history see Perry 1983 and Antony 1989.

[20] Hanawalt 1979:206.

piracy because of hard economic realities than because of vague notions of righting wrongs or championing the poor.

Among Chinese seafarers, piracy was the most radical form of protest against poverty, prejudice, and injustice. Yet pirates did not try to remake the world. What they wanted was to better their lot in the existing one. From their experiences and struggles we can learn how people on the fringes of respectable society adapted themselves to a world that they found increasingly hostile.

Glossary

aogui 澳規

bafeng 把風
baidichuan 白底船
Bai Ling 白齡
bang 幫
baoshui 報水
Beidi 北帝
beilu ruhuo 被擄入夥
beilu zhe 被擄者
beixie fuyi 被脅服役

Cai Qian 蔡牽
Cai Qian Ma 蔡牽媽
caifu 財副
caochuan 艚船
choufen 抽分
chuanzhang 船長
chuanzhu 船主
chuhai 出海

da bang 大幫
da hengyang chuan 大橫洋船
dage 大哥
dangce 檔冊
dao'an 盜案
daofan 盜犯
dashi 大事
dasima 大司馬
diaochuanbang 釣船幫
Donghai Ba 東海八

Donghai wang 東海王
dou 斗
Dou Lao 斗老 (姥)
Dou Mu 斗母
duogong 舵工

ermu 耳目

falü 法律
fan 犯
fangsheng 放生
Fengbo 風伯
fengsu 風俗

ganggui 港規
Guandi 關帝
guanggun 光棍
guanxi 關係
Guo Podai 郭婆帶
gupeng 罟朋

haidao 海盜
haifeng 海俸
haijin 海禁
haikou 海寇
Hainan wang 海南王
haizei 海賊
haizhan 海戰
Hong Dizhen 洪迪珍
Hongsheng 洪聖
Hou Han 候漢

huifei 會匪
huiguan 會館
hunyin jianqing 婚姻姦情
huo 夥
huozhang 夥長

jiangui 姦宄
jianmin 奸民
jiansheng 監生
jiansu 姦宿
jiaofu 剿撫
jiedi zangwu 接遞贓物
jijian 雞姦
jin 斤
Jinghai dajianjun 靖海大將軍
Jinghaishen 靖海神
judao 巨盜
Jumu 颶母

kailangchuan 開浪船

lanzai 爛仔
laoban 老板
li 里
Li Chongyu 李崇玉
Li Xiangqing 李相清
liang 兩
Liang Bao 梁保
liangmin 良民
lijue 立決
Lin Daoqian 林道乾
Lin Ban 林伴
Lin Wu 林五
lingchi 凌遲
lisou 利籔
Liu Xiang 劉香
Longmu 龍母
Longwang 龍王
Lu Xun 盧循

Mazu 媽祖
mianjie piao 免劫票

Mo Guanfu 莫官扶

nanfeng 南風/男風
Nanyang 南洋
Nayancheng 那顏成
niangzijun 娘子軍
niaochuan 鳥船
nizei 逆賊
nongmin yundong 農民運動

piaodan 票單
pin bushoufen 貧不守分
pinku nandu 貧苦難度

Sanpo 三婆
Sanshanshen 三山神
shangyu 上諭
shengfeng 聖風
shi 石
shijie 失節
shuijing 水經 (鏡)
shuishangren 水上人
shuishou 水手
Shuishu Huangdi 水屬皇帝
Su Cheng 蘇成
Su Li 蘇利
sui 歲
Sun En 孫恩

Tangong 譚公
Tiandihui 天地會
Tianhou 天后
tiben 題本
tingfei 艇匪
tongdao jifei 通盜濟匪
toucheng 投誠
touruhuo 投入夥
tudao 土盜
tuofengchuan 拖風船

Wang Guili 王貴利
Wang Zhi 王直

wangming xianxing zhengfa 王命先行正法

wen 文

wokou/wako 倭寇

Wu Ping 吳平

Wu Zhiqing 吳知青

wuji feitu 無籍匪徒

wusheng 武生

Wushi Er 烏石二

xianggong 香工

xianshui ge 鹹水歌

Xiaozihui 孝子會

xie 邪

Xu Chaoguang 許朝光

Xu Dong 許棟

yaban 押班

yagong 押工

yajin cangdi 押禁艙底

yangchuan 洋船

yangdao 洋盜

yangfei 洋匪

yihai weitian 以海為田

yin 淫

yinci 淫祠

yizi 義子

yuan 圓

yue 約

yugui 漁規

zei'ao 賊澳

zeku 擇庫

Zeng Yiben 曾一本

zhan lijue xiaoshi 斬立決梟示

Zhang Bao 張保

Zhang Bolu 張伯路

Zheng Chenggong 鄭成功

Zheng Liutang 鄭流唐

Zheng Qi 鄭七

Zheng Yi 鄭一

Zheng Yi Sao 鄭一嫂

Zheng Zilong 鄭芝龍

zhengdao 正盜

Zhenhai weiwu wang 鎮海威武王

Zhu Cong 朱聰

Zhu Fen 朱濆

Zongbing Bao 總兵寶

zonghan 總捍

zongpu 總鋪

zouzhe 奏摺

Bibliography

Anderson, Eugene N. 1970. *The Floating World of Castle Peak Bay.* Washington, D.C.: American Anthropological Association.

————. 1972. *Essays on South China's Boat People.* Taibei: The Orient Culture Service.

Anderson, John L. 1995. "Piracy and World History: An Economic Perspective on Maritime Predation." *Journal of World History* 6.2:175–199.

Antony, Robert J. 1988. "Pirates, Bandits, and Brotherhoods: A Study of Crime and Law in Kwangtung Province, 1796–1839." Ph.D. dissertation, University of Hawai'i.

————. 1989. "Peasants, Heroes, and Brigands: The Problems of Social Banditry in Early Nineteenth-Century South China." *Modern China* 15.2:123–148.

————. 1992. "State, Community, and Pirate Suppression in Guangdong Province, 1809–1810." Paper presented at the Ohio Valley History Conference, Murray State University.

————. 1994. "Pacification of the Seas: Qing Anti-Piracy Policies in Guangdong, 1794–1810." *Journal of Oriental Studies* 32.1: 16–35.

Atwell, William. 1988. "The T'ai-chang, T'ien-ch'i, and Ch'ung-chen Reigns, 1620–1644." In Frederick Mote and Denis Twitchett, eds., *The Cambridge History of China.* Vol. 7: *The Ming Dynasty, 1368–1644,* part 1, pp. 585–640. Cambridge: Cambridge University Press.

————. 1990. "A Seventeenth-Century 'General Crisis' in East Asia?" *Modern Asian Studies* 24.4:661–682.

————. 1998. "Ming China and the Emerging World Economy, c. 1470–1650." In Frederick Mote and Denis Twitchett, eds., *The Cambridge History of China.* Vol. 8: *The Ming Dynasty, 1368–1644,* part 2, pp. 376–416. Cambridge: Cambridge University Press.

Audemard, L. 1957–1971. *Les jonques chinoises.* 10 vols. Rotterdam: Museum voor Landen Volkenkunde en het Maritiem Museum "Prins Hendrik."

Blake, C. Fred. 1981. *Ethnic Groups and Social Change in a Chinese Market Town.* Honolulu: University Press of Hawai'i.

Blussé, Leonard. 1988. *Strange Company: Chinese Settlers, Mestizo Women, and the Dutch in VOC Batavia.* Leiden: KITLV.

Boxer, C. R. 1975. *The Portuguese Seaborne Empire, 1415–1825.* New York: Alfred A. Knopf.

Brook, Timothy. 1998. *The Confusions of Pleasure: Commerce and Culture in Ming China.* Berkeley: University of California Press.

Brown, Edward. 1861. *Cochin-China, and my Experience of it. A Seaman's Narrative of his Adventures and Sufferings during a Captivity among Chinese Pirates, on the Coast of Cochin-China, and Afterwards during a Journey on Foot across that Country, in the Years 1857–8.* London: Charles Westerton.

Buoye, Thomas. 2000. *Manslaughter, Markets, and Moral Economy: Violent Disputes over Property Rights in Eighteenth-Century China.* Cambridge: Cambridge University Press.

Burg, B. R. 1984. *Sodomy and the Pirate Tradition: English Sea Rovers in the 17th-Century Caribbean.* New York: New York University Press.

Burkhardt, V. R. 1966. *Chinese Creeds and Customs.* 3 vols. Hong Kong: South China Morning Post.

Carioti, Patrizia. 1996. "The Zhengs' Maritime Power in the International Context of the 17th Century Far Eastern Seas: The Rise of a 'Centralized Piratical Organization' and Its Gradual Development into an Informal 'State.'" *Ming Qing yanjiu,* pp. 29–67.

Casey, Lee A. 1992. "Pirate Constitutionalism: An Essay in Self-Government." *Journal of Law and Politics* 8.3:477–537.

Chang, Pin-tsun. 1992. "Maritime China in Historical Perspective." *International Journal of Maritime History* 4.2:239–255.

Chang, Thomas C. S. 1983. "'Ts'ai Ch'ien, The Pirate Who Dominates the Seas: A Study of Coastal Piracy in China, 1795–1810." Ph.D. dissertation, University of Arizona.

Chaolian xiangzhi [Gazetteer of Chaolian township]. 1946.

Chaozhou zhi dashiji [Major events from the Chaozhou gazetteer]. N.d.

Chen Chunsheng. 1992. *Shichang jizhi yu shehui bianqian—shiba shiji Guangdong mijia fenxi* [Market mechanisms and social change—an analysis of rice prices in eighteenth-century Guangdong]. Guangzhou: Zhongshan daxue chubanshe.

Chen Guodong. 1991. "Qingdai zhongye Xiamen de haishang maoyi (1727–1833)" [The maritime trade of Amoy in the mid-Qing period (1727–1833)]. In *Zhongguo haiyang fazhan shi lunwen ji*, vol. 4, pp. 61–100. Taibei: Academia Sinica.

———. 1994. "Shipping and Trade of Chinese Junks in Southeast Asia, 1730–1830: A Survey." *Research in Maritime History* 6:203–214.

Ch'en Kuo-tung. *See* Chen Guodong.

Chen Maoheng. 1957. *Mingdai wokou kaolue* [A study of the *wokou* pirates in the Ming period]. Beijing: Renmin chubanshe.

Chen Shangsheng. 1997. "Qingdai de Tianhougong yu huiguan" [Empress of Heaven temples and merchant associations in the Qing period]. *Qingshi yanjiu* 3:49–60.

Chen Wenshi. 1966. *Ming Hongwu Jiajing jian di haijin zhengce* [Sea prohibition policies of the Hongwu and Jiajing reigns in the Ming dynasty]. Taibei: Taiwan daxue wenxue yuan.

Chen Xiyu. 1991. *Zhongguo fanchuan yu haiwai maoyi* [Chinese junks and overseas trade]. Xiamen: Xiamen daxue chubanshe.

Chen Xujing. 1946. *Danjia de yanjiu* [Studies on the Dan boat people]. Shanghai: Shangwu.

Chen Yande. 1997. "Aomen de yuye jingji yu Mazu xinyang" [Belief in Mazu and the fishing economy of Macao]. *Zhongguo shehui jingjishi yanjiu* 1:70–76.

Chen Zaizheng. 1999. "Cai Qian haishang wujiang jituan yu Mazu xinxiang" [The seaborne armed coterie of Cai Qian and the belief in Mazu]. *Taiwan yanjiu jikan* 2:75–79.

Chen Zhonglie. 1994. "Ming Qing yilai Guangdong minjian 'Tianhou' nüshen chongbai yu shehui jingji de fazhan" [Socioeconomic development and the worship of the folk goddess "Empress of Heaven" in Ming and Qing Guangdong]. *Guangdong shehui kexue* 5:113–119.

Cheong, W. E. 1965. "Trade and Finance in China, 1784–1834: A Reappraisal." *Business History* 7:34–56.

China, Pictorial, Descriptive, and Historical with some Account of Java and the Burmese, Siam, and Anam. 1853. London: Henry G. Bohn.

China Famine Relief Fund. 1878. *The Famine in China*. London: C. Kegan Paul.

Chinese Repository. Macao and Canton, 1832–1851.

CHXZ. Chenghai xianzhi [Gazetteer of Chenghai county]. 1815.

Colquhoun, Archibald R. 1883. *Across Chryse, Being the Narrative of a Journey of Exploration through the South China Border Lands from Canton to Mandalay.* 2 vols. 2d ed. London: Sampson Low, Marston, Searle, and Rivington.

Cushman, Jennifer W. 1993. *Fields from the Sea: Chinese Junk Trade with Siam during the Late Eighteenth and Early Nineteenth Centuries.* Studies on Southeast Asia, no. 12. Ithaca, N.Y.: Southeast Asia Program, Cornell University.

CYXZ. Chaoyang xianzhi [Gazetteer of Chaoyang county]. 1884.

CZFZ. Chiongzhou fuzhi [Gazetteer of Chiongzhou prefecture]. 1890.

Dai Baocun. 2000. *Jindai Taiwan haiyun fazhan* [The development of shipping in modern Taiwan]. Taibei: Yu Shan She.

DBXZ. Dianbai xianzhi [Gazetteer of Dianbai county]. 1825.

DeGlopper, Donald. 1995. *Lukang: Commerce and Community in a Chinese City.* Albany: State University of New York Press.

Deng Duanben. 1993. "Guangzhou yu haishang 'sichou zhi lu' de xingqi fazhan" [Canton and the rise and development of the maritime "silk road"]. In Wu Jiahua, ed., *Lun Guangzhou yu haishang sichou zhi lu*, pp. 3–29. Guangzhou: Zhongshan daxue chubanshe.

Deng, Gang. 1997. *Chinese Maritime Activities and Socioeconomic Development, c. 2100 B.C.–1900 A.D.* Westport: Greenwood Press.

DGXZ. Dongguan xianzhi [Gazetteer of Dongguan county]. 1921.

Diamond, Norma. 1969. *K'un Shen: A Taiwan Village.* New York: Holt, Rinehart, and Winston.

Dianshizhai huabao [Illustrated news from the Dianshi studio]. Shanghai, 1884.

Doolittle, Justus. 1865. *Social Life of the Chinese.* 2 vols. New York: Harper and Brothers.

Doré, Henry. 1914–1938. *Researches into Chinese Superstitions.* 12 vols. Shanghai: T'usewei Printing Press.

Downing, C. Toogood. 1838. *The Fan-Qui in China in 1836–1837.* 3 vols. London: Henry Colburn.

DQSL. Da Qing lichao shilu [Veritable records of the Qing dynasty]. Mukden, 1937.

Fan, I-chun. 1993. "Long-Distance Trade and Market Integration in the Ming-Ch'ing Period, 1400–1850," Ph.D. dissertation, Stanford University.

Faure, David, Bernard H. K. Luk, and Alice Ngai-ha Lun Ng. 1984. "The Hong Kong Region according to Historical

Inscriptions." In David Faure et al., *From Village to City: Studies in the Traditional Roots of Hong Kong Society*, pp. 43–54. Hong Kong: Centre of Asian Studies, University of Hong Kong.

Feray, M. 1906. "Les Japonais a Hai-Nan sous la Dynastie des Ming." *T'oung Pao*, n.s. 7:369–379.

Fitzpatrick, Merrilyn. 1979. "Local Interests and the Anti-Pirate Administration in China's South-East, 1555–1565." *Ch'ing-shih wen-t'i* 4.2:1–50.

FJTZ. Fujian tongzhi [Gazetteer of Fujian province]. 1871.

FQXZ. Fuqing xianzhi [Gazetteer of Fuqing county]. 1987. (Originally published in the Qianlong reign.)

Fricke, Peter, ed. 1973. *Seafarers and Community: Towards a Social Understanding of Seafaring.* London: Croom Helm.

Gaozhou fuzhi [Gazetteer of Gaozhou prefecture]. 1889.

Gardella, Robert. 1985. "The Maritime History of Late Imperial China: Observations on Current Concerns and Recent Research." *Late Imperial China* 6.2:48–66.

GDTZ. Guangdong tongzhi [Gazetteer of Guangdong province]. [1822] 1934.

———. *Guangdong tongzhi* [Gazetteer of Guangdong province]. 1864.

Geiss, James. 1988. "The Chia-ching Reign, 1522–1566." In Frederick Mote and Denis Twitchett, eds., *The Cambridge History of China*. Vol. 7: *The Ming Dynasty, 1368–1644*, part 1, pp. 440–510. Cambridge: Cambridge University Press.

Glasspoole, Richard. 1831. "A Brief Narrative of my Captivity and Treatment amongst the Ladrones." In C. Neumann, trans., *History of the Pirates*, pp. 97–128. London: Oriental Translation Fund.

Gosse, Philip. 1932. *The History of Pirates*. New York: Tudor.

Gray, John. 1878. *China: A History of the Laws, Manners, and Customs of the People.* 2 vols. London: Macmillan and Co.

Guan Wenfa. 1994. "Qingdai zhongye Cai Qian haishang wuzhuang jituan xingzhi banxi" [An analysis of the nature of the maritime armed groups of Cai Qian in the mid-Qing period]. *Zhongguo shi yanjiu* 1:93–100.

Guangdong haifang huilan [A conspectus of Guangdong's coastal defense]. Comp. Lu Kun and Chen Hongchi. Canton: N.p., n.d.

Guangdong haitushuo [Explanation of Guangdong's maritime geography]. Comp. Zhang Zhidong. Taibei: Guangwen shuju, 1969. (Originally published in the late nineteenth century.)

Guishan xianzhi [Gazetteer of Guishan county]. 1783.

Gujin tushu jicheng [Encyclopedia of ancient and modern knowledge]. Shanghai, 1884.

Guo Songyi. 1982. "Qingdai guonei de haiyun maoyi" [The domestic sea trade in the Qing period]. *Qingshi luncong* 4:92–110.

Gutzlaff, Charles. 1834. *Journal of Three Voyages along the Coast of China in 1831, 1832, and 1833, with Notices of Siam, Corea, and the Loo-Choo Islands.* London: Frederick Westley and A. H. Davis.

GZD. Gongzhongdang [Unpublished palace memorials]. National Palace Museum, Taibei.

GZDQL. *Gongzhongdang Qianlong chao zouzhe* [Published palace memorials of the Qianlong reign]. 1986. Taibei: National Palace Museum.

GZFZ. *Guangzhou fuzhi* [Gazetteer of Guangzhou prefecture]. 1879.

Haidaojing [Book of sea routes]. In *Haifang jiyao* [Essentials of coastal defense]. 1969. Taibei: Guangwen shuju. (Originally published in the Qing dynasty.)

Hall, D. G. E. 1958. *A History of South-East Asia.* London: Macmillan.

Hanawalt, Barbara. 1979. *Crime and Conflict in English Communities, 1300–1348.* Cambridge: Harvard University Press.

Hayes, James. 1977. *The Hong Kong Region, 1850–1911: Institutions and Leadership in Town and Countryside.* Hamden: Archon Books.

———. 1983. *The Rural Communities of Hong Kong: Studies and Themes.* Hong Kong: Oxford University Press.

HDSL. *Da Qing huidian shili* [Supplement to the collected institutes of the Qing]. 1818. N.p.

He Changling, comp. 1827. *Huangchao jingshi wenbian* [Collected essays on statecraft for the reigning dynasty]. N.p.

HFXZ. *Haifeng xianzhi* [Gazetteer of Haifeng county]. 1931.

Higgins, Roland L. 1980. "Pirates in Gowns and Caps: Gentry Law-Breaking in the Mid-Ming." *Ming Studies* 10:30–37.

Hill, Christopher. 1986. "Radical Pirates?" In *The Collected Essays of Christopher Hill.* Vol. 3: *People and Ideas in Seventeenth Century England*, pp. 161–187. Amherst: University of Massachusetts Press.

———. 1996. *Liberty against the Law: Some Seventeenth-Century Controversies.* London: Penguin Press.

Hinsch, Bret. 1990. *Passions of the Cut Sleeve: The Male Homosexual Tradition in China.* Berkeley: University of California Press.

HLXZ. Huilai xianzhi [Gazetteer of Huilai county]. 1930.

Ho, Ping-ti. 1959. *Studies on the Population of China, 1368–1953.* Cambridge: Harvard University Press.

Hobsbawm, Eric. 1981. *Bandits.* Rev. ed. New York: Pantheon.

Howells, William Dean, and Thomas Perry, comps. 1888. *Library of Universal Adventures by Sea and Land.* New York: Harper and Brothers.

Hsiao, Kung-chuan. 1960. *Rural China: Imperial Control in the Nineteenth Century.* Seattle: University of Washington Press.

Hsieh, Kuo-ching. 1932. "The Removal of the Coastal Population in Early Tsing Period." *Chinese Social and Political Science Review* 13:559–596.

Hu Jieyu. 1959. "Xiyingpan yu Zhang Baozai huoluan zhi pingding" [Xiyingpan and the suppression of the ravages of Zhang Baozai]. In Luo Xianglin, ed., *Yibasi'er nian yiqian Xianggang ji qidui waijiaotong,* pp. 151–170. Hong Kong: Zhongguo xueshe.

Huang Dianquan. 1958. "Cai Qian Zhu Fen haidao zhi yanjiu" [A study of the pirates Cai Qian and Zhu Fen]. *Tainan wenhua* 6.1:74–102.

Huang Guosheng. 2000. *Yapian zhanzheng qian de dongnan sisheng haiguan* [The maritime customs in the four southeastern provinces before the Opium War]. Fuzhou: Fujian renmin chubanshe.

Huang Miantang. 1988. "Qingdai 'gugongren' wenti kaoshi" [Explaining the problems of "hired workers" in the Qing period]. *Shehui kexue zhanxian* 1:136–143.

Huang Qichen. 1986. "Qingdai qianqi haiwai maoyi de fazhan" [The development of overseas trade in the early Qing period]. *Lishi yanjiu* 4:151–170.

Hucker, Charles. 1974. "Hu Tsung-hsien's Campaign against Hsu Hai, 1556." In Frank Kierman, Jr., ed., *Chinese Ways in Warfare,* pp. 273–307. Cambridge: Harvard University Press.

Hunter, William. 1885. *Bits of Old China.* London: K. Paul, Trench, and Co.

HZFZ. Huizhou fuzhi [Gazetteer of Huizhou prefecture]. 1881.

Jiang Weitan, comp. 1990. *Mazu wenxian ziliao* [Source materials on Mazu]. Fuzhou: Fujian renmin chubanshe.

Jiang Weitan. 1995. "Qingdai shangbang huiguan yu Tianhougong" [Empress of Heaven temples and merchant organizations in the Qing period]. *Haijiaoshi yanjiu* 1:45–63.

Jiang Zuyuan and Fang Zhiqin, eds. 1993. *Jianming Guangdong shi* [A brief history of Guangdong]. Guangzhou: Guangdong renmin chubanshe.

JJD. Junjichudang lufuzouzhe [Grand Council copies of palace memorials]. National Palace Museum, Taibei.

JMZ. Jinmen zhi [Gazetteer of Jinmen]. [1882] 1956. Hong Kong: Chi Sheng Book Co.

Kani, Hiroaki. 1967. *A General Survey of the Boat People in Hong Kong.* Hong Kong: Southeast Asia Studies Section, New Asia Research Institute, The Chinese University of Hong Kong.

Katsuta Hiroko. 1967. "Shindai kaiko no kan" [Pirate disturbances in the Qing period]. *Shiron* 19:27–49.

Kleeman, Terry. 1994. "Licentious Cults and Bloody Victuals: Sacrifice, Reciprocity, and Violence in Traditional China." *Asia Major* 7.1:185–211.

Kuhn, Philip A. 1990. *Soulstealers: The Chinese Sorcery Scare of 1768.* Cambridge: Harvard University Press.

Lai, Chi-Kong. 1995. "The Historiography of Maritime China since c. 1975." *Research in Maritime History* 9 (December): 53–79.

Lam, Truong Buu. 1968. "Intervention Versus Tribute in Sino-Vietnamese Relations, 1788–1790." In John Fairbank, ed., *The Chinese World Order,* pp. 165–179. Cambridge: Harvard University Press.

Lamley, Harry. 1977. "*Hsieh-tou:* The Pathology of Violence in Southeastern China." *Ch'ing-shih wen-t'i* 3:1–39.

Lavely, William, and R. Bin Wong. 1998. "Revising the Malthusian Narrative: The Comparative Study of Population Dynamics in Late Imperial China." *Journal of Asian Studies* 57.3: 714–748.

Lee, James Z., and Wang Feng. 1999. *One Quarter of Humanity: Malthusian Mythology and Chinese Realities, 1700–2000.* Cambridge: Harvard University Press.

Lemisch, Jesse. 1968a. "The American Revolution Seen from the Bottom Up." In Barton Bernstein, ed., *Towards a New Past: Dissenting Essays in American History,* pp. 3–45. New York: Pantheon Books.

———. 1968b. "Jack Tar in the Streets: Merchant Seamen in the Politics of Revolutionary America." *William and Mary Quarterly* 25:370–407.

Leonard, Jane Kate. 1984. *Wei Yuan and China's Rediscovery of the Maritime World.* Cambridge: Harvard University Press.

————. 1988. "Geopolitical Reality and the Disappearance of the Maritime Frontier in Qing Times." *American Neptune* 48.1:230–236.

Leung, Man-kam. 1977. "Piracy in South China in the Nineteenth Century." In Leslie Kawamura and Keith Scott, eds., *Buddhist Thought and Asian Civilization: Essays in Honor of Herbert V. Guenther on His Sixtieth Birthday*, pp. 152–166. Emeryville, Calif.: Dharma Press.

Lewis, Mark. 1990. *Sanctioned Violence in Early China*. Albany: State University of New York Press.

LFZZ. Lufu zouzhe [Grand Council copies of palace memorials]. First Historical Archives, Beijing. (All citations are from the peasant uprisings [*nongmin yundong*] category.)

Li Jinming 1990. *Mingdai haiwai maoyi shi* [A history of overseas trade in the Ming period]. Beijing: Zhongguo shehui kexue chubanshe.

Li, Xiaolin. 1995. "Women in the Chinese Military." Ph.D. dissertation, University of Maryland.

Lian Heng. [1921] 1983. *Taiwan tongshi* [Comprehensive history of Taiwan]. 2 vols. Beijing: Shangwu yinshuguan.

Liang Tingnan. 1838. *Yuehai guanzhi* [Gazetteer of Guangdong's maritime customs]. N.p.

Liao Fengde. 1986. "Haidao yu hainan: Qingdai Min-Tai jiaotong wenti chutan" [Sea bandits and sea distress: A preliminary study of the problem of communications between Fujian and Taiwan in the Qing period]. In Zhang Yanxian, ed., *Zhongguo haiyang fazhan shi lunwen ji*, vol. 3, pp. 191–213. Taibei: Academia Sinica.

Liao Hongji. 1996. *Taohairen* [Sea beggars]. Taibei: Chen Xing.

Lin, Man-houng. 1989. "Currency and Society: The Monetary Crisis and Political-Economic Ideology of Early Nineteenth-Century China." Ph.D. dissertation, Harvard University.

Lin Renchuan. 1987. *Ming mo Qing chu siren haishang maoyi* [Private maritime trade in the late Ming and early Qing]. Shanghai: Huadong shifan daxue chubanshe.

Linebaugh, Peter, and Marcus Rediker. 2000. *The Many-Headed Hydra: Sailors, Slaves, Commoners, and the Hidden History of the Revolutionary Atlantic*. Boston: Beacon Press.

Liu Yongcheng. 1982. *Qingdai qianqi nongye ziben zhuyi mengya chutan* [A preliminary exploration of the sprouts of capitalism in agriculture in the early Qing period]. Fuzhou: Fujian renmin chubanshe.

Ljungstedt, Anders. 1835. *An Historical Sketch of the Portuguese Settlement in China.* Boston: J. Munroe.

LJXZ. Lianjiang xianzhi [Gazetteer of Lianjiang county]. 1927.

LZFZ. Lianzhou fuzhi [Gazetteer of Lianzhou prefecture]. 1833.

Marks, Robert. 1984. *Rural Revolution in South China: Peasants and the Making of History in Haifeng County, 1570–1930.* Madison: University of Wisconsin Press.

————. 1998. *Tigers, Rice, Silk, and Silt: Environment and Economy in Late Imperial South China.* Cambridge: Cambridge University Press.

Maspero, Henri. 1981. *Taoism and Chinese Religion.* Trans. Frank Kierman, Jr. Amherst: University of Massachusetts Press.

Matsuura Akira. 1983. "Shindai ni okeru engan boeki ni tsuite—hansen to shohin ryutsu" [On coastal trade during the Qing period—sailing vessels and the circulation of commodities]. In Ono Kazuko, ed., *Minshin jidai no seiji to shakai,* pp. 595–650. Kyoto: Kyoto daigaku jinbun kagaku kenkyujo.

————. 1995. *Chugoku no kaizoku* [Pirates of China]. Tokyo: Toho Shoten.

Mazumdar, Sucheta. 1998. *Sugar and Society in China: Peasants, Technology, and the World Market.* Cambridge: Harvard University Asia Center.

McKnight, Brian. 1992. *Law and Order in Sung China.* Cambridge: Cambridge University Press.

Miller, Harry. 1970. *Pirates of the Far East.* London: Robert Hale.

Ming shi [Ming history]. [1736] 1974. Beijing: Zhonghua shuju.

Montalto de Jesus, C. A. 1926. *Historic Macao: International Traits in China Old and New.* 2d ed. Macao: Salesian Printing Press and Tipografia Mercantil.

Morse, Hosea Ballou. 1926–1929. *The Chronicles of the East India Company Trading to China, 1635–1834.* 5 vols. Cambridge: Harvard University Press.

MQSLWB. Ming–Qing shiliao, wubian [Historical materials of the Ming-Qing periods, fifth series]. 1972. Taibei.

MQSLYB. Ming–Qing shiliao, yibian [Historical materials of the Ming-Qing periods, first series]. 1972. Taibei.

Murray, Dian H. 1981. "One Woman's Rise to Power: Cheng I's Wife and the Pirates." *Historical Reflections* 8.3:147–162.

————. 1987. *Pirates of the South China Coast, 1790–1810.* Stanford, Calif.: Stanford University Press.

————. 1988. "Commerce, Crisis, Coercion: The Role of Piracy in Late Eighteenth and Early Nineteenth Century Sino-Western

Relations." *American Neptune* 48.1:237–242.

_____. 1992. "The Practice of Homosexuality among the Pirates of Late 18th and Early 19th Century China." *International Journal of Maritime History* 4.1:121–130.

_____. 1997. "Living and Working Conditions in Chinese Pirate Communities, 1750–1850." In David Starkey et al., *Pirates and Privateers: New Perspectives on the War on Trade in the Eighteenth and Nineteenth Centuries*, pp. 47–68. Exeter: University of Exeter Press.

MXTZ. *Maxiang tingzhi* [Gazetteer of Maxiang subprefecture]. 1893.

Naquin, Susan. 1976. *Millenarian Rebellion in China: The Eight Trigrams Uprising of 1813*. New Haven, Conn.: Yale University Press.

Neumann, Charles, trans. 1831. *History of the Pirates Who Infested the China Sea from 1807 to 1810, by Yuan Yung-lun*. London: Oriental Translation Fund.

Nevius, John L. 1869. *China and the Chinese: A General Description of the Country and Its Inhabitants, Its Civilization and Form of Government, Its Religious and Social Institutions, Its Intercourse with Other Nations, and Its Present Condition and Prospects*. New York: Harper and Brothers.

Ng, Chin-keong. 1973. "Gentry-Merchants and Peasant-Peddlers: The Response of the South Fukienese to the Offshore Trading Opportunities, 1522–1566." *Nanyang University Journal* 7:161–175.

_____. 1983. *Trade and Society: The Amoy Network on the China Coast, 1683–1735*. Singapore: Singapore University Press.

_____. 1990. "The South Fukienese Junk Trade at Amoy from the Seventeenth to Early Nineteenth Centuries." In Eduard Vermeer, ed., *Development and Decline of Fukien Province in the 17th and 18th Centuries*, pp. 297–316. Leiden: E. J. Brill.

Ng, Peter Y. L. 1983. *New Peace County: A Chinese Gazetteer of the Hong Kong Region*. With additional material by Hugh D. R. Baker. Hong Kong: Hong Kong University Press.

NHXZ. *Nanhai xianzhi* [Gazetteer of Nanhai county]. 1835.

NYC. *Nawenyigong zouyi* [Collected memorials of Nayancheng]. 1834. N.p.

Ownby, David. 1996. *Brotherhoods and Secret Societies in Early and Mid-Qing China: The Formation of a Tradition*. Stanford, Calif.: Stanford University Press.

Ouyang Zongshu. 1998. *Haishang renjia: haiyang yuye jingji yu yumin shehui* [Sea people: Maritime fishing economy and fishermen's society]. Nanchang: Jiangxi gaoxiao chubanshe.

Pérez-Mallaína, Pablo. 1998. *Spain's Men of the Sea: Daily Life on the Indies Fleets in the Sixteenth Century.* Trans. Carla Rahn Phillips. Baltimore: Johns Hopkins University Press.

Pérotin-Dumon, Anne. 1991. "The Pirate and the Emperor: Power and the Law on the Seas, 1450–1850." In James Tracy, ed., *The Political Economy of Merchant Empires,* pp. 196–227. Cambridge: Cambridge University Press.

Perry, Elizabeth. 1980. *Rebels and Revolutionaries in North China, 1845–1945.* Stanford, Calif.: Stanford University Press.

———. 1983. "Social Banditry Revisited: The Case of Bai Lang, a Chinese Brigand." *Modern China* 9.3:355–382.

Pickering, W. A. 1898. *Pioneering in Formosa: Recollections of Adventures among Mandarins, Wreckers, and Head-Hunting Savages.* London: Hurst and Blackett.

Pomeranz, Kenneth. 2000. *The Great Divergence: Europe, China, and the Making of the Modern World Economy.* Princeton, N.J.: Princeton University Press.

PYXZ. Panyu xianzhi [Gazetteer of Panyu county]. 1871.

Qiao Shengxi et al. 1993. *Guangzhou diqu jiuzhi qihou shiliao huibian yu yanjiu* [A study and collection of historical sources on climate from Canton-area gazetters]. Guangzhou: Guangdong renmin chubanshe.

Qu Dajun. [1700] 1985. *Guangdong xinyu* [New discourses on Guangdong]. Beijing: Zhonghua shuju.

QZFZ. Quanzhou fuzhi [Gazetteer of Quanzhou prefecture]. 1870.

Rawski, Evelyn. 1972. *Agricultural Change and the Peasant Economy of South China.* Cambridge: Harvard University Press.

———. 1985. "Economic and Social Foundations of Late Imperial Culture." In David Johnson, Andrew Nathan, and Evelyn Rawski, eds., *Popular Culture in Late Imperial China,* pp. 3–33. Berkeley: University of California Press.

Rediker, Marcus. 1987. *Between the Devil and the Deep Blue Sea: Merchant Seamen, Pirates, and the Anglo-American Maritime World, 1700–1750.* Cambridge: Cambridge University Press.

———. 1996. "Liberty Under the Jolly Roger: The Lives of Anne Bonny and Mary Read, Pirates." In Margaret Creighton and Lisa Norling, eds., *Iron Men, Wooden Women: Gender and Seafaring in the Atlantic World, 1700–1920,* pp. 1–33. Baltimore: Johns Hopkins University Press.

Reid, Ralph W. E. 1938. "Piracy in the China Seas: Some Aspects of Its Influence upon the History of the Far East." M.A. thesis, University of Hawai'i.

Ritchie, Robert. 1986. *Captain Kidd and the War Against the Pirates.* Cambridge: Harvard University Press.

Scammell, G. V. 1992. "European Exiles, Renegades and Outlaws and the Maritime Economy of Asia c. 1500–1750." *Modern Asian Studies* 26.4:641–661.

SCSX. Shichao shengxun [Imperial edicts of the ten (Qing) reigns], Jiaqing reign. N.d.

Shao Tingcai. 1961. *Dongnan shiji* [Record of the southeast]. In *Taiwan wenxian congkan*, no. 96. Taibei: Taiwan yinhang jingji yanjiushe. (Originally published in the Qing dynasty.)

So, Kwan-wai. 1975. *Japanese Piracy in Ming China During the 16th Century.* East Lansing: Michigan State University Press.

Sommer, Matthew. 2000. *Sex, Law, and Society in Late Imperial China.* Stanford, Calif.: Stanford University Press.

SQXZ. Suiqi xianzhi [Gazetteer of Suiqi county]. 1849.

Stark, Rodney. 1987. "Deviant Places: A Theory of the Ecology of Crime." *Criminology* 25:893–909.

Starkey, David. 1994. "Pirates and Markets." *Research in Maritime History* 7:59–80.

Staunton, George, trans. 1810. *Ta Tsing Leu Lee; Being the Fundamental Laws, and a Selection from the Supplementary Statutes, of the Penal Code of China.* London: T. Cadell and W. Davies.

STDSJ. Shantou dashiji [Major events in Shantou]. 1988. 2 vols. Shantou: Shantoushi difangzhi bianzuan weiyuanhui bangongshe.

Struve, Lynn A. 1984. *The Southern Ming, 1644–1662.* New Haven, Conn.: Yale University Press.

Sun Guangzhe. 1989. *Zhongguo gudai hanghai shi* [Maritime history of ancient China]. Beijing: Haiyang chubanshe.

Sutton, Donald. 1995. "Consuming Counterrevolution: The Ritual and Culture of Cannibalism in Wuxuan, Guangxi, China, May to July 1968." *Comparative Studies in Society and History* 37:136–172.

Suzuki Chusei. 1952. *Shincho chukishi kenkyu* [A study of mid-Qing history]. Toyohashi: Aichi University Research Institute on International Problems.

SYD. Shangyudang fangben [Imperial edict record book, square version]. National Palace Museum, Taibei.

Szonyi, Michael. 1998. "The Cult of Hu Tianbao and the Eighteenth-Century Discourse of Homosexuality." *Late Imperial China* 19.1:1–25.

Tanaka Takeo. 1982. *Wako* [The *wokuo* pirates]. Tokyo: Hanbai Kyoikusha Shuppan Sabisu.

Thompson, Laurence. 1968. "The Junk Passage Across the Taiwan Strait: Two Early Chinese Accounts." *Harvard Journal of Asiatic Studies* 28:170–194.

Thomson, Janice E. 1994. *Mercenaries, Pirates, and Sovereigns: State-Building and Extraterritorial Violence in Early Modern Europe.* Princeton, N.J.: Princeton University Press.

Turley, Hans. 1999. *Rum, Sodomy, and the Lash: Piracy, Sexuality, and Masculine Identity.* New York: New York University Press.

Ura Ren'ichi. 1954. "Shinsho no senkairei no kenkyu" [A study of the coastal evacuation in the early Qing]. *Hiroshima daigaku bungakubu jiyo* 5:124–158.

Vagg, Jon. 1993. "Rough Seas: Contemporary Piracy in South-East Asia." Paper presented at the International Congress of Asian and North African Studies, Hong Kong.

Vermeer, Eduard. 1990. "The Decline of Hsing-hua Prefecture in the Early Ch'ing." In Eduard Vermeer, ed., *Development and Decline of Fukien Province in the 17th and 18th Centuries,* pp. 101–161. Leiden: E. J. Brill.

Viraphol, Sarasin. 1977. *Tribute and Profit: Sino-Siamese Trade, 1652–1853.* Cambridge: Council on East Asian Studies, Harvard University.

Vitiello, Giovanni. 1992. "The Dragon's Whim: Ming and Qing Homoerotic Tales from *The Cut Sleeve*." *T'oung Pao* 78:341–372.

Von Glahn, Richard. 1996. *Fountain of Fortune: Money and Monetary Policy in China, 1000–1700.* Berkeley: University of California Press.

Wakeman, Frederic, Jr. 1985. *The Great Enterprise: The Manchu Reconstruction of Imperial Order in Seventeenth-Century China.* 2 vols. Berkeley: University of California Press.

Waley-Cohen, Joanna. 1993. "Politics and the Supernatural in Mid-Qing Legal Culture." *Modern China* 19.3:330–353.

Wang Shiqing. 1958. "Qingdai Taiwan de mijia" [Rice prices in Qing-dynasty Taiwan]. *Taiwan wenxian* 9.4:11–20.

Wang, Yeh-chien. 1986. "Food Supply in Eighteenth-Century Fukien." *Late Imperial China* 7.2:80–117.

Ward, Barbara. 1985. *Through Other Eyes: Essays in Understanding*

"Conscious Models"—Mostly in Hong Kong. Hong Kong: The Chinese University Press.

Warren, James F. 1981. *The Sulu Zone, 1768–1898.* Singapore: Singapore University Press.

Watson, Andrew, trans. 1972. *Transport in Transition: The Evolution of Traditional Shipping in China.* Ann Arbor: University of Michigan Center for Chinese Studies.

Watson, James. 1985. "Standardizing the Gods: The Promotion of T'ien Hou ('Empress of Heaven') Along the South China Coast, 960–1960." In David Johnson, Andrew Nathan, and Evelyn Rawski, eds., *Popular Culture in Late Imperial China,* pp. 292–324. Berkeley: University of California Press.

WCXZ. *Wuchuan xianzhi* [Gazetteer of Wuchuan county]. 1888.

Wei, Peh T'i. 1979. "Internal Security and Coastal Control: Juan Yuan and Pirate Suppression in Chekiang, 1799–1809." *Ch'ing-shih wen-t'i* 4.2:83–112.

Weibust, Knut. 1969. *Deep Sea Sailors: A Study on Maritime Ethnology.* Stockholm: Nordiska museets Handlingar.

Wen Chengzhi. 1842. *Pinghai jilue* [A short record of pacifying the seas].

Whitbeck, Judith. 1980. "The Historical Vision of Kung Tzu-chen (1792–1841)." Ph.D. dissertation, University of California, Berkeley.

Will, Pierre-Etienne. 1990. *Bureaucracy and Famine in Eighteenth-Century China.* Trans. Elborg Forster. Stanford, Calif.: Stanford University Press.

Williams, S. Wells. [1895] 1966. *The Middle Kingdom: A Survey of the Geography, Government, Literature, Social Life, Arts, and History of the Chinese Empire and Its Inhabitants.* 2 vols. Rev. ed. New York: Paragon Book Reprint Corp.

Wills, John E. 1974. *Pepper, Guns, and Parleys: The Dutch East India Company and China, 1662–1681.* Cambridge: Harvard University Press.

———. 1979. "Maritime China from Wang Chih to Shih Lang: Themes in Peripheral History." In Jonathan Spence and John Wills, eds., *From Ming to Ch'ing: Conquest, Region, and Continuity in Seventeenth-Century China,* pp. 201–238. New Haven, Conn.: Yale University Press.

———. 1993. "Maritime Asia, 1500–1800: The Interactive Emergence of European Domination." *American Historical Review* 98.1:83–105.

————. 1998. "Relations with Maritime Europeans, 1514–1662." In Frederick Mote and Denis Twitchett, eds., *The Cambridge History of China.* Vol. 8: *The Ming Dynasty, 1368–1644,* part 2, pp. 333–375. Cambridge: Cambridge University Press.

WJD. Waijidang [Outer court record book]. First Historical Archives, Beijing.

Wong, R. Bin. 1997. *China Transformed: Historical Change and the Limits of European Experience.* Ithaca, N.Y.: Cornell University Press.

Wu Kun, comp. 1871. *Da Qing lüli genyuan* [Roots of the Qing Code]. N.p.

Wu Liangkai. 1983. "Qing qianqi nongye gugong de gongjia" [Wages of hired workers in the early Qing period]. *Zhongguo shehui jingji shi yanjiu* 2:17–30.

Wu, Yuey Len. 1937. "Life and Culture of the Shanam Boat People." *Nankai Social and Economic Quarterly* 9:807–854.

XHXZ. *Xinhui xianzhi* [Gazetteer of Xinhui county]. 1841.

Xiao Guojian. 1978. "Xianggang zaoqi haidao shilue" [A brief history of piracy in Hong Kong's early period]. *Guangdong wenxian jikan* 8:17–20.

————. 1986. *Qing chu qianhai qianhou Xianggang zhi shehui bianqian* [Social change in Hong Kong before and after the early Qing evacuation policy]. Taibei: Taiwan shangwu.

————. 1995. *Xianggang lishi yu shehui* [The history and society of Hong Kong]. Taibei: Taiwan shangwu.

[Xingbu] *Shuotie* [(Board of Punishments) memoranda]. 1811. Fu Sinian Library, Academia Sinica, Taibei.

XKTB. Xingke tiben [Routine memorials in the Punishment Section of the Censorate]. First Historical Archives, Beijing. (All citations are from the bandit cases [*dao'an*] category, except those labeled (H), which come from the marriage and sex offenses [*hunyin jianqing*] category.

XMZ. *Xiamen zhi* [Gazetteer of Xiamen]. [1832] 1961. In *Taiwan wenxian congkan,* no. 95. Taibei: Taiwan yinhang jingji yanjiushe.

XPXZ. *Xiapu xianzhi* [Gazetteer of Xiapu county]. 1929.

XSXZ. *Xinxiu Xiangshan xianzhi* [Newly revised gazetteer of Xiangshan county]. 1827.

————. *Chongxiu Xiangshan xianzhi* [Amended gazetteer of Xiangshan county]. 1879.

Xu Wentang and Xie Qiyi. 2000. *Da Nan shilu Qing-Yue guanxi shiliao hubian* [Material on Sino-Vietnamese relations in the

Veritable Records of Vietnam]. Nangang: Program for Southeast Asian Area Studies, Academia Sinica.

Yang Guozhen. 1998. *Min zai haizhong: zhuixun Fujian haiyang fazhan shi* [The Min at sea: In search of the maritime history of Fujian]. Nanchang: Jiangxi gaoxiao chubanshe.

Yang Guozhen and Chen Zhiping. 1993. *Ming-Qing shidai Fujian de tubao* [Local fortifications in Fujian in the Ming-Qing periods]. Taibei: Guoxue wenjuguan.

Yang Zhenquan. 1988. *Wuchuan xian wenwu zhi* [Gazetteer of cultural artifacts of Wuchuan county]. Guangzhou: Zhongshan daxue chubanshe.

Yano Jin'ichi. 1926. "Kakei jidai no ran ni tsuite" [The disturbance of boat bandits in the Jiaqing period]. *Rikishi to chiri* 18.2:99–105.

Ye Linfeng. 1970. *Zhang Baozai de chuanshuo he zhenxiang* [The legend and truth about Zhang Baozai]. Hong Kong: Shanghai shuju.

Ye Xianen. 1988. "Ming Qing Zhujiang sanjiaozhou renkou wenti" [The population problem in the Pearl River delta in the Ming and Qing eras]. *Qingshi yanjiu ji* 6:141–168.

————, ed. 1989. *Guangdong hangyun shi, gudai bufen* [A history of Guangdong shipping, ancient period]. Beijing: Renmin jiaotong chubanshe.

Ye Zhiru. 1988. "Shilun Cai Qian jituan de chengfen ji qi fan Qing douzheng shizhi" [An analysis of the composition of Cai Qian's organization and the substance of its anti-Qing struggle]. In *Ming-Qing dang'an yu lishi yanjiu*, pp. 829–842. Beijing: Zhonghua shuju.

————. 1989. "Qian-Jia nianjian Guangdong haishang wuzhuang huodong gaishu" [A general narrative of Guangdong's maritime armed movements in the Qianlong and Jiaqing years]. *Lishi dang'an* 2:96–101.

YJZ. *Yangjiang zhi* [Yangjiang gazetteer]. 1925.

YXTZ. *Yunxiao tingzhi* [Gazetteer of Yunxiao subprefecture]. 1816.

YZD. Yuezhedang [Grand Council monthly record book of palace memorials]. First Historical Archives, Beijing.

Zhang Zhendong and Yang Jinsen. 1983. *Zhongguo haiyang yuye jianshi* [A concise history of China's maritime fishing industry]. Beijing: Haiyang chubanshi.

Zheng Guangnan. 1998. *Zhongguo haidao shi* [A history of Chinese pirates]. Shanghai: Huadong ligong daxue chubanshe.

Zhongguo haiyang fazhan shi lunwen ji [Essays in Chinese maritime history]. 8 vols. 1984–2002. Taibei: Sun Yat-sen Institute for Social Sciences and Philosophy, Academia Sinica.

Zhu Delan. 1986. "Qing kai hailing hou de Zhong-Re Changqi maoyi shang yu guonei yanhai maoyi (1684–1722)" [China's trade with Nagasaki and along the coast after the opening of trade, 1684–1722]. In Zhang Yanxian, ed., *Zhongguo haiyang fazhan shi lunwen ji*, vol. 3, pp. 369–415. Taibei: Academia Sinica.

Zhu Jingying. [1772] 1996. *Haidong zhaji* [A record of the eastern sea]. Taibei: Taiwan sheng wenxian weiyuan hui.

Zhu Qingji and Bao Shuyun, comps. 1834. *Xing'an huilan* [Conspectus of penal cases]. N.p.

ZPXZ. *Zhangpu xianzhi* [Gazetteer of Zhangpu county]. [1928] 1968. Taibei: Chengwen chubanshe.

ZPZZ. *Zhupi zouzhe* [Palace memorials]. First Historical Archives, Beijing. (All citations are from the peasant uprisings [*nongmin yundong*] category, except those labeled *falü*, which come from the law category.)

ZZFZ. *Zhangzhou fuzhi* [Gazetteer of Zhangzhou prefecture]. 1877.

Index

INSTITUTE OF EAST ASIAN STUDIES PUBLICATIONS SERIES

CHINA RESEARCH MONOGRAPHS (CRM)

36. Suzanne Pepper. *China's Education Reform in the 1980s: Policies, Issues, and Historical Perspectives*, 1990
sp. Phyllis Wang and Donald A. Gibbs, eds. *Readers' Guide to China's Literary Gazette, 1949–1979*, 1990
38. James C. Shih. *Chinese Rural Society in Transition: A Case Study of the Lake Tai Area, 1368–1800*, 1992
39. Anne Gilks. *The Breakdown of the Sino-Vietnamese Alliance, 1970–1979*, 1992
sp. Theodore Han and John Li. *Tiananmen Square Spring 1989: A Chronology of the Chinese Democracy Movement*, 1992
40. Frederic Wakeman, Jr., and Wen-hsin Yeh, eds. *Shanghai Sojourners*, 1992
41. Michael Schoenhals. *Doing Things with Words in Chinese Politics: Five Studies*, 1992
sp. Kaidi Zhan. *The Strategies of Politeness in the Chinese Language*, 1992
42. Barry C. Keenan. *Imperial China's Last Classical Academies: Social Change in the Lower Yangzi, 1864–1911*, 1994
43. Ole Bruun. *Business and Bureaucracy in a Chinese City: An Ethnography of Private Business Households in Contemporary China*, 1993
44. Wei Li. *The Chinese Staff System: A Mechanism for Bureaucratic Control and Integration*, 1994
45. Ye Wa and Joseph W. Esherick. *Chinese Archives: An Introductory Guide*, 1996
46. Melissa Brown, ed. *Negotiating Ethnicities in China and Taiwan*, 1996
47. David Zweig and Chen Changgui. *China's Brain Drain to the United States: Views of Overseas Chinese Students and Scholars in the 1990s*, 1995
48. Elizabeth J. Perry, ed. *Putting Class in Its Place: Worker Identities in East Asia*, 1996
sp. Phyllis L. Thompson, ed. *Dear Alice: Letters Home from American Teachers Learning to Live in China*, 1998
49. Wen-hsin Yeh, ed. *Landscape, Culture, and Power in Chinese Society*, 1998
50. Gail Hershatter, Emily Honig, Susan Mann, and Lisa Rofel, comps. and eds. *Guide to Women's Studies in China*, 1999
51. Wen-hsin Yeh, ed. *Cross-Cultural Readings of Chineseness: Narratives, Images, and Interpretations of the 1990s*, 2000
52. Marilyn A. Levine and Chen San-ching. *The Guomindang in Europe: A Sourcebook of Documents*, 2000
53. David N. Keightley. *The Ancestral Landscape: Time, Space, and Community in Late Shang China*, 2000
54. Peter M. Worthing. *Occupation and Revolution: China and the Vietnamese August Revolution of 1945*, 2001.
55. Guo Qitao. *Exorcism and Money: The Symbolic World of the Five-Fury Spirits in Late Imperial China*, 2003
56. Robert J. Antony. *Like Froth Floating on the Sea: The World of Pirates and Seafarers in Late Imperial South China*, 2003

KOREA RESEARCH MONOGRAPHS (KRM)

13. Vipan Chandra. *Imperialism, Resistance, and Reform in Late Nineteenth-Century Korea: Enlightenment and the Independence Club*, 1988
14. Seok Choong Song. *Explorations in Korean Syntax and Semantics*, 1988
15. Robert A. Scalapino and Dalchoong Kim, eds. *Asian Communism: Continuity and Transition*, 1988
16. Chong-Sik Lee and Se-Hee Yoo, eds. *North Korea in Transition*, 1991
17. Nicholas Eberstadt and Judith Banister. *The Population of North Korea*, 1992
18. Hong Yung Lee and Chung Chongwook, eds. *Korean Options in a Changing International Order*, 1993
19. Tae Hwan Ok and Hong Yung Lee, eds. *Prospects for Change in North Korea*, 1994
20. Chai-sik Chung. *A Korean Confucian Encounter with the Modern World: Yi Hang-no and the West*, 1995
21. Myung Hun Kang. *The Korean Business Conglomerate: Chaebol Then and Now*, 1996

24. Lewis R. Lancaster and Richard K. Payne, eds. *Religion and Society in Contemporary Korea*, 1998
25. Jeong-Hyun Shin. *The Trap of History: Understanding Korean Short Stories*, 1998
26. Hyung Il Pai and Timothy R. Tangherlini, eds. *Nationalism and the Construction of Korean Identity*, 1999
27. Nathan Hesselink, ed. *Contemporary Directions: Korean Folk Music Engaging the Twentiety Century and Beyond*, 2002
28. Choi Byonghyon, trans. *The Book of Corrections: Reflections on the National Crisis during the Japanese Invasion of Korea, 1592–1598*, by Yu Songnyong, 2002

JAPAN RESEARCH MONOGRAPHS (JRM)
8. Yung H. Park. *Bureaucrats and Ministers in Contemporary Japanese Government*, 1986
9. Victoria V. Vernon. *Daughters of the Moon: Wish, Will, and Social Constraint in Fiction by Modern Japanese Women*, 1988
10. Steve Rabson, trans. *Okinawa: Two Postwar Novellas* by Ōshiro Tatsuhiro and Higashi Mineo. Introduction and afterword by Steve Rabson. 1996 (2d printing, corrected and updated [1989])
12. James W. White. *The Demography of Sociopolitical Conflict in Japan, 1721–1846*, 1992
13. Winston Davis. *The Moral and Political Naturalism of Baron Katō Hiroyuki*, 1996
14. Michael H. Gibbs. *Struggle and Purpose in Postwar Japanese Unionism*, 2000

RESEARCH PAPERS AND POLICY STUDIES (RPPS)
24. Joyce K. Kallgren, Noordin Sopiee, and Soedjati Djiwandono, eds. *ASEAN and China: An Evolving Relationship*, 1988
29. Richard Holton and Wang Xi, eds. *U.S.-China Economic Relations: Present and Future*, 1989
30. Sadako Ogata. *Normalization with China: A Comparative Study of U.S. and Japanese Processes*, 1989
32. Leo E. Rose and Kamal Matinuddin, eds. *Beyond Afghanistan: The Emerging U.S.-Pakistan Relations*, 1990
33. Clark Neher and Wiwat Mungkandi, eds. *U.S.-Thailand Relations in a New International Era*, 1990
34. Robert Sutter and Han Sungjoo, eds. *Korea-U.S. Relations in a Changing World*, 1990
35. Harry H. Kendall and Clara Joewono, eds. *Japan, ASEAN, and the United States*, 1990
36. Robert A. Scalapino and Gennady I. Chufrin, eds. *Asia in the 1990s: American and Soviet Perspectives*, 1990
37. Chong-Sik Lee, ed. *In Search of a New Order in East Asia*, 1991
38. Leo E. Rose and Eric Gonsalves, eds. *Toward a New World Order: Adjusting U.S.-India Relations*, 1992
39. Harumi Befu, ed. *Cultural Nationalism in East Asia: Representation and Identity*, 1993
40. Yufan Hao. *Dilemma and Decision: An Organizational Perspective on American China Policy Making*, 1997
41. Frederic Wakeman Jr. and Wang Xi, eds. *China's Quest for Modernization: A Historical Perspective*, 1997
42. Loraine A. West and Yaohui Zhao, eds. *Rural Labor Flows in China*, 2000
43. Shalendra D. Sharma, ed. *The Asia-Pacific in the New Millennium: Geopolitics, Security, and Foreign Policy*, 2000

INDOCHINA RESEARCH MONOGRAPHS (IRM)
1. William J. Duiker. *China and Vietnam: The Roots of Conflict*, 1986
2. Allan E. Goodman. *The Search for a Negotiated Settlement of the Vietnam War*, 1986
3. Tran Tri Vu. *Lost Years: My 1,632 Days in Vietnamese Reeducation Camps*, 1989
4. Ta Van Tai. *The Vietnamese Tradition of Human Rights*, 1989
5. Douglas Pike, ed. *The Bunker Papers: Reports to the President from Vietnam, 1967–1973*, 3 vols., 1990
6. Judith Banister. *Vietnam Population Dynamics and Prospects*, 1993

These are new and selected publications. Write for a complete list and prices.
E-mail: easia@uclink.berkeley.edu; http://ieas.berkeley.edu/publications

ISBN 1-55729-078-4

5 1 6 0 0

9 781557 290786

INSTITUTE OF EAST ASIAN STUDIES
UNIVERSITY OF CALIFORNIA • BERKELEY
CENTER FOR CHINESE STUDIES